**EDDY JOKOVICH +
DAVID LEWIS**

THE MONDAY ESSAYS

SELECTED WRITINGS FROM THE YEAR IN AUSTRALIAN POLITICS

The Monday Essays: Selected writings from the year in Australian politics
ISBN (paperback): 978-1-7635701-6-0
ISBN (Amazon):   979-8-2784457-8-4

©2025 Eddy Jokovich & David Lewis

All rights reserved. No part of this book may be reproduced in any form or by any electronic or mechanical means, including information storage and retrieval systems, without written permission from the authors, except for the use of brief quotations in book reviews and promotional material.

December 2025.
Published by New Politics, an imprint of ARMEDIA Pty. Ltd.

New Politics
PO Box 1265, Darlinghurst NSW 1300
www.newpolitics.com.au
Email: info@newpolitics.com.au

Production: ARMEDIA

Published and produced on the lands of the Wangal and Gadigal people.

EDITORIAL NOTE ON THE USE OF AI TECHNOLOGY
We employ artificial intelligence tools in the editing process of our articles. These tools assisted with transcriptions of audio recordings, grammar correction, refinement and formatting.

A catalogue record for this work is available from the National Library of Australia

CONTENTS

Introduction 6
Elon Musk, the clear and present danger 9
Setting the scene for a dirty divisive election campaign 16
Ceasefire: Global failures and the uncertain road ahead 25
Unhappy Australia Day and blocking true Reconciliation 33
Chaos, corruption in the American democracy 40
ABC sacking exposes the actions of the Israel lobby 48
Albanese's gamble on American tariffs 56
Manufactured outrage: The media's alliance with Zionists 62
Australia needs to shift away from Trump's instability 70
The cracks in the empire: America's allies drifting away 77
Manufacturing fear: Fake terror as a political weapon 85
How spin, amnesia and outrage skew the Budget debate 94
Labor's momentum and a shaky start for the Coalition 102
The Dutton disaster in waiting 108
A campaign that fell apart 115
The masterclass in political failure 123
A strange, disjointed week in a campaign slipping away 133
A historic Labor victory and a devastating Liberal loss 143
The big collapse: What's next for the Liberal Party? 150
The Liberal challenge: A new era but who's ready to lead? ... 158
Fight for fairness: Reforming superannuation 167
The government's betrayal of the Commonwealth 173
The honours system or a system in dishonour? 179
American fascisti: Is it the end of an empire? 183
The real agenda behind the bombing of Iran 190
A great Australian silence 200
Criminalising protest in NSW 208
The Segal report, free speech and the politics of fear 216
The irrational fear of China and the imaginary crisis 226
Albanese and Wong are on the wrong side of history 234

Killing journalists won't stop Palestinian statehood 242
When journalism becomes public relations 248
Netanyahu's instability as Australia starts to act 256
The sinking credibility of ASIO 264
From Knesset to Council: Think global, influence local 271
Manufacturing the fear of China 279
The cascading danger of climate change 285
Signs of the American empire in decay 292
The National Press Club shoots the messenger 301
Peace mirage: Will Israel fool the world yet again? 307
Labor's fear of its own shadow 316
Journalism, fear and the price of obedience 325
A big betrayal of the environment 333
The people's victory: What Mamdani's win really means 342
Protecting the neo-Nazis of Sydney 350
Blaming the migrant: The Liberal Party's new strategy 358
Running out of patience with Labor's caution 367
Conclusion 376

ABOUT THE AUTHORS

EDDY JOKOVICH is editor of *New Politics*, and co-presenter of the New Politics Australia podcast. He has worked as a journalist, publisher, author, political analyst, campaigner, war correspondent, and lecturer in media studies at the University of Technology, Sydney and the University of Sydney; has a wide range of experience working in editorial and media production work and is Director of ARMEDIA, an independent publishing and communications company specialising in public interest media.

DAVID LEWIS is co-presenter of the New Politics Australia podcast, historian, musicologist, musician and political scientist based in Sydney. His lecturing and research interests include roots music, popular music, Australian, British and American politics, and crime fiction. He has published in *Music Forum Australia*, *Eureka Street*, *Quadrant*, *Crikey* and has edited several books.

NEW POLITICS AUSTRALIA is a weekly podcast, providing analysis and opinions on Australian and international politics.

THE MONDAY ESSAY is published weekly at *New Politics* and is based on the conversations, analysis and discussions from the podcast throughout 2025.

INTRODUCTION

2025 will be remembered as the year when the veneer finally cracked—not just in Australia, but right across the world. The comforting assumptions that once passed for political commonsense have collapsed under the weight of a rapidly shifting global order, and the idea that democratic institutions could simply "hold" without vigilance or reform was exposed as a convenient myth. What emerged throughout the year was a global political architecture that's being redefined by doubt, misinformation and disinformation—as it has been for some time—and the rise of authoritarian movements, just when the world needs to be guarding itself from these movements.

These essays are a witness to this shifting order. Each week, we seemed to confront a new political crisis, a fresh media failure, another manufactured outrage, or an international disaster made possible by the silence, or cowardice, of governments that should have known better. Elon Musk attempted to position himself as a global political puppet master; Donald Trump returned to the White House with the same disdain for democracy he showed during his first term in office; Israel prosecuted a catastrophic and indefensible war on Gaza with impunity; and the international community, including Australia, responded with platitudes and *measures of concern*, instead of leading with principle.

Australia's own political landscape didn't fare much better. The 2025 federal election campaign exposed two major

INTRODUCTION

parties travelling in entirely different directions but trapped in the same tired cycle of slogans, misrepresentations and the politics of the lowest common denominator. Peter Dutton's Liberal Party embraced a strategy of permanent hostility, and ran a campaign built on anger, fear and the endless stream of confected grievances designed to distract the electorate from their absence of policy and meaningful purpose. Under Anthony Albanese, the government offered competence and stability, but was reluctant to offer the great ambition that usually accompanies Labor when they're in office.

Elected in 2022 to end the chaos of the Abbott–Turnbull–Morrison era, instead, Labor acted as though they are terrified of upsetting the same vested interests that have spent decades undermining public trust and stymieing progressive reform.

And then there is the media—one of the most defining characters within this entire political theatre—a landscape dominated by conservative empires, commercial self-interest and the tightening grip of lobby groups to ensure that truth rarely makes it past the gates of the editor's desk. The ABC, once the paragon of media excellence and independence, showed just how vulnerable it has become as it buckled under pressure from the Israel lobby in the Antoinette Lattouf case—a case easily won by Lattouf, and in the process, making the ABC look weak and timid.

Commercial media outlets continued their race to the bottom, amplifying the narratives of the far-right, reducing complex issues into the tired culture-wars debates, and treating misinformation as a worthwhile contribution to public debate.

These essays highlight a country that's caught between an outdated sense of itself and at odds of the reality of a shifting world. If there is one thread that runs through this collection, it's that Australia stands at a crossroads. We can continue along the familiar path of weak leadership, timid media and political parties terrified of their own shadows—and in the case of the Liberal Party, possibly disappearing altogether—or we can choose something *better*. This collection of essays are a clarion call for something *better*, because the stakes will always be too high to accept second best.

***

ELON MUSK, THE CLEAR AND PRESENT DANGER

6 January 2025

Elon Musk, once lauded as a wily entrepreneur and an innovator by many people, has become a controversial and extreme character on the global political stage and his acquisition of Twitter/X has given him the opportunity to shape the public opinion and political processes to a far greater extent. Over the past few months, Musk's actions have become more unacceptable as he uses his wealth and worldwide recognition to support extreme right-wing movements, attack democracy and shake the political systems of America and Europe. The effects of his actions could become catastrophic and have generated important questions on the role of billionaires in determining political outcomes.

In Germany, the support Musk has given to the Alternative für Deutschland has raised many concerns: the AfD, a party that spreads anti-Muslim propaganda and has links with the neo-Nazi movement, poses a threat to Germany's democracy and pluralism, and Musk's recent promotion of the party is a clear interference in politics. Musk's statement that 'Only the AfD can save Germany' puts him in the same category as a party which has been branded as an extreme right-wing organisation by German intelligence services and by backing the AfD, Musk is not only spreading some controversial opinions—he is endorsing a project that aims at eroding the German democracy.

This behaviour is not an isolated incident but part of a broader pattern of Musk's political interventions in many countries, and his endorsement of far-right figures and movements across Europe is a deliberate strategy to erode centrist and leftist political structures. In Britain, Musk has called on King Charles to dissolve parliament, and has offered £80 million to fund the right-wing Reform UK, and this highlights his intent to reshape British politics in favour of far-right populism. Such actions are a flagrant disregard for democratic processes and an alarming concentration of political influence in the hands of a single individual.

Musk's affinity for far-right leaders extends to Hungary's Viktor Orbán and Italy's Prime Minister Giorgia Meloni, leaders who are emblematic of the rise of authoritarianism in Europe, characterised by attacks on judicial independence, press freedom, and minority rights. Musk's alignment with these figures suggests a shared disdain for democratic institutions and a willingness to embrace authoritarian methods under the guise of "saving" nations from perceived decline.

The implications of Musk's political activities are far-reaching: his financial resources and control over a major social media platform give him the tools to manipulate public opinion on a scale that few others can match. Musk's actions in Europe mirror his interference in the United States, where he played a central role in enabling Donald Trump's resurgence and his substantial financial contributions and use of Twitter/X to amplify far-right propaganda have emboldened anti-democratic movements.

The prospect of Musk exporting his influence to other regions, such as Australia, raises many other concerns. Australia's media landscape is already dominated by abnormally influential figures such as Rupert Murdoch and Kerry Stokes, whose conservative agendas shape public discourse and already have a strong influence in domestic politics. While Clive Palmer's attempts to directly enter politics through the United Australia Party have had limited success, Musk's vast resources and control over Twitter/X allows him to bypass traditional barriers and exert significant influence. The question remains whether Australia's democratic institutions have sufficient safeguards to resist such interference.

HOW UNCHECKED INFLUENCE COULD PROMOTE EXTREMISM

While Australia's political and legislative framework includes safeguards against foreign interference, significant vulnerabilities do still exist. These gaps, when combined with Musk's existing and rapid strategies of influence, suggest that Australia is ill-equipped to prevent such interventions without a significant overhaul of its regulatory and legal systems.

Musk's most obvious avenue for influence lies in his control of Twitter/X, by leveraging its algorithms to amplify far-right narratives, conspiracy theories, or anti-establishment rhetoric to shape public opinion and distort electoral debates, as he has done with suppressing pro-Palestine voices and promoting Israeli propaganda since the war and ongoing genocide in Gaza re-commenced in October 2023.

This control provides an unprecedented ability to set agendas, sway perceptions, and boost specific candidates or policies, all while operating outside Australia's existing media ownership regulations. Unlike traditional media outlets, social media platforms such as Twitter/X are not subject to cross-media ownership rules or requirements for balanced reporting (albeit *very low* requirements), and this allows Musk to manipulate public discourse with minimal oversight, a loophole that urgently needs addressing.

Beyond media influence, Musk can also exploit Australia's political funding system. Although the *Commonwealth Electoral Act* prohibits foreign donations to registered political parties, the law's enforcement is riddled with loopholes. Foreign-controlled entities registered in Australia can still funnel money into the system, and donations below the disclosure threshold of $15,200 can escape public scrutiny (and yes, Twitter Australia Holdings Pty Limited is registered in Victoria, with its head office located in the Sydney CBD). This creates fertile ground for indirect funding of far-right groups or political actors sympathetic to Musk's interests, such as Pauline Hanson's One Nation or other Clive Palmer-style campaigns. By channelling funds through subsidiaries, third-party campaigners, or "associated entities", Musk can effectively bypass restrictions while maintaining plausible deniability.

Another avenue of influence lies in the symbiotic relationship between social media platforms and far-right ideology. Social media tends to prioritise inflammatory and divisive content, which aligns with the strategies from far-right movements. Musk could leverage this dynamic to amplify voices that support his preferred political agendas, further legitimising these movements, creating a feedback loop of amplification and normalisation.

Corporate leverage adds another dimension to the potential threat. Musk, with his many business ventures such as Tesla and SpaceX, could pressure Australian politicians into adopting policies favourable not only to these interests but also his broader ideological goals.

To address these vulnerabilities, Australia should adopt a comprehensive approach to safeguarding its democratic processes. The first step is to close the loopholes in political funding laws—while there were some minor reforms that were belatedly adopted by the Albanese government towards the end of 2024 (with the support of the Liberal Party), these are still inadequate—all donations, regardless of size, should be disclosed, and foreign-controlled entities operating in Australia must be prohibited from contributing to political campaigns, directly or indirectly.

Media regulation must also evolve to meet the challenges posed by global platforms such as Twitter/X. Cross-media ownership rules should be extended to include social media companies, ensuring accountability for their role in shaping public discourse. The Australian Communications and Media Authority should be empowered with stronger enforcement capabilities to hold these platforms accountable for amplifying harmful content or engaging in political interference.

The federal government must also recognise the broader implications of unregulated social media and corporate influence on its democracy. While these essential legislative reforms can't be, or won't be implemented before the next federal election—there just isn't enough parliamentary time available for this—empowering citizens to critically evaluate information and resist manipulation is vital.

Without decisive action to strengthen its democratic processes, Australia risks becoming the next target of Musk's or other foreign billionaires' influence campaigns—Musk isn't the first, and he won't be the last—political power needs to remain in the hands of the Australian electorate, not external actors with extremist agendas.

A THREAT TO AUSTRALIAN DEMOCRACY AND GLOBAL STABILITY

Musk's rapid radicalisation toward far-right extremism demonstrates an unsettling trend: the deliberate exploitation of economic power and media influence to amplify dangerous ideologies, align with extremist groups, and destabilise democratic institutions.

The comparison to Nazi Germany, while provocative, is apt. Critics suggesting that such comparisons are a cliché or just a simple invocation of Godwin's law miss the point: if the historical parallels exist and reflect the failures from the 1930s, these comparisons must be made, otherwise, the mistakes of the past will be repeated.

The alliances between German industrialists and business entities with the Nazi regime at that time were instrumental in facilitating fascism's rise to power. Musk's approach reverses this dynamic—he is the initiator, actively courting far-right extremists in the United States and Europe, providing them with legitimacy, financial support, and a platform to propagate their ideologies. This dynamic is not confined: Australia must recognise that it, too, is vulnerable to such interference.

The Australian political landscape, particularly under the increasingly reactionary leadership of figures such as Peter Dutton, is mirroring the trends seen in far-right movements abroad. The Victorian branch of the Liberal Party, with its flirtations with pro-Nazi and far-right elements, shows a party playing with the allure of extremism, and this drift creates fertile ground for individuals such as Musk to exert influence, either overtly or covertly.

Australia has invested heavily in developing its democratic culture and while it's nowhere near perfect, it needs to be protected and fortified. Elon Musk represents a dangerous nexus of wealth, power, and extremist ideology and his interventions in global politics are not anomalies but part of a broader trend of billionaires leveraging their resources to reshape societies in their image.

Recently, mining magnate Gina Rinehart—heavily invested in Trump's election campaign in the United States and urging the Coalition to adopt his *make our bank accounts great again* ethos, an inane and hedonistic ethos that suggests the sole purpose of humanity is to *make money*—was spotted in Thailand hosting a lunch with Pauline Hanson, reportedly *deep in conversation* (!). While Rinehart is not a foreign agent, her ability and desire to influence Australian politics appears to be growing, as evidenced by her Bush Summit programs and persistent calls for Australia to emulate the right-wing MAGA movement in the United States.

Both of these individuals are inadequate and polarising figures but wield significant clout: Rinehart, with her obscene net worth of $40 billion, amassed primarily through favourable legislation and mineral assets that were inadequately taxed by successive state and federal governments; and Hanson, who has manipulated the Australian media and political landscape since 1996, ultimately securing a Senate seat in 2016 after Malcolm Turnbull's decision to call a double-dissolution election backfired.

Certainly, everyone has the right to participate in Australia's democracy, but no one has the right to manipulate the electoral system or distort the results to serve their own vested interests—whether it be Rinehart, Rupert Murdoch, Kerry Stokes, Gerry Harvey, or, especially, a foreign actor as depressingly inadequate as Elon Musk, whose primary intention is to disrupt existing democratic structures for self-gain. While there is an argument that democratic systems *do* need disruption and renovation, it should not come at the behest of a handful of radical, wealthy, and powerful individuals seeking to dismantle the system for their own gain and profit from the resulting chaos.

If Australia fails to recognise and address this threat, it risks becoming the next battleground in Musk's campaign—or that of any other actor—to erode democratic institutions and promote far-right agendas. This is the time to act, before the fabric of Australian democracy is irreparably torn.

***

SETTING THE SCENE FOR A DIRTY DIVISIVE ELECTION CAMPAIGN

13 January 2025

The political year has barely begun, yet the sounds of a federal election can already be loudly heard. Despite January being a month that is usually reserved for rest and reflection, both major political parties have started positioning themselves for the inevitable contest that must result in an election before 17 May. As the stakes rise, so too does the rhetoric, with Leader of the Opposition Peter Dutton charging into the fray—as he usually does—leveraging a mix of typical conservative Liberal Party talking points and calculated distortions to rally his base.

Dutton's recent soft-launch in Melbourne under the slogan "Let's get Australia back on track" provides an early glimpse into the Coalition's strategy. While it's better than John Howard's "Incentivation" slogan from the 1987 Liberal Party campaign, what is the track that Dutton wants Australia to get back to? The long list of incompetence and corruption between 2013 to 2022, when the Coalition was last in office? An economy that was careering towards recession in late 2019 before the Coalition's undeserved economic reputation was rescued by the onset of COVID? Austerity budgets that undermine social cohesion? Record deficits? Daily division and pitting communities against each other? *That track?*

SETTING THE SCENE FOR A DIRTY DIVISIVE ELECTION CAMPAIGN

The choice of Melbourne—a battleground where the Liberals lost heartland seats to the community independents in 2022—was no accident, and it highlights their attempts to regain urban and suburban electorates disillusioned with the party's leadership and policies in the past. Yet, the messaging from Dutton reveals very little that is new and is likely to result in the same disillusionment: his attacks on renewable energy, unsubstantiated claims about government complicity in rising anti-Semitism, and promises of lower taxes that history repeatedly disproves, shows a strategy steeped in the politics of fear and division.

Dutton's most inflammatory remark came in the context of anti-Semitism, an issue he pushes with little regard for accuracy or responsibility. He claimed a staggering 700 per cent surge in anti-Semitism and placed the blame squarely on the Prime Minister's supposed "dereliction of leadership" following protests at the Sydney Opera House after Israel's actions genocide and ethnic cleansing commenced in Gaza in October 2023. Such rhetoric is as audacious as it is baseless—the exploitation of deeply sensitive issues for political gain is a tactic as old as politics itself—but its overuse risks alienating an electorate weary of hyperbole and does result in harmful social division.

Dutton attempt to resurrect that perennial promise of lower taxes, a pledge that has rarely materialised under previous Coalition governments, also fails: economic data shows that the Howard and Morrison administrations presided over higher tax-to-GDP ratios than many of their predecessors, and taxing levels under Labor governments are consistently lower, undermining the credibility of Dutton's claims. When pressed for specifics, he reverted to that nebulous mantra of "cutting government waste," a trope designed to appeal to fiscal conservatives without committing to meaningful or achievable policy reform.

Dutton's targeting of the public service as "inefficient" is both predictable and disingenuous, ignoring the essential services they provide to the community and the economic stability they support.

Energy policy is another example of the Coalition's empty rhetoric, with Dutton now doubling down on his claim that the government's focus on renewables is undermining Australia's energy security.

His assertion that a "renewables-only policy" has caused market uncertainty is a serious oversimplification and a deliberate misrepresentation. Gas will continue to play a transitional role in Australia's energy mix—whether we like it or not—as highlighted by the government's *Future Gas Strategy*, and Dutton's comments ignores the approach outlined in that very document, an approach that has its antecedents in Coalition policy from when they were last in government. Dutton's framing of renewables as "part-time power" ignores technological advancements in storage and grid stability, pushing a false choice between economic growth and environmental responsibility.

Beneath the surface of Dutton's rhetoric lies a broader strategy: stoke fears of instability and economic decline under Labor's time in government, while offering no alternatives. This is not just political positioning; it is a calculated attempt to shift the narrative, leveraging misinformation to undermine public confidence in the government's ability to manage complex challenges.

However, the contemporary electorate is different to electorates from the past. Australians are more politically engaged, environmentally conscious, and discerning in their assessment of political commentary and claims. The question for Dutton and the Coalition is whether their reliance on old tropes and half-truths will resonate in a landscape where voters are increasingly demanding transparency, accountability, and forward-thinking solutions.

CHOICES IN THE LEADERSHIP FOR AUSTRALIA'S FUTURE

Prime Minister Anthony Albanese's response to Dutton's campaign rhetoric has been quick, countering the opposition leader's divisive strategies with an alternative vision of unity and progress. The Labor government's slogan, "Building Australia's Future," is a rebuke to Dutton's fear-driven narrative and this response perhaps reflects a broader frustration with this reliance on negative politics and empty promises.

Albanese's response to Dutton's inflammatory claims about anti-Semitism also shows the difference between the two leaders—Dutton's attempt to politicise the deeply sensitive issue of anti-Semitism was met with a measured yet forceful response, in which Albanese detailed the numerous ways he has supported the Jewish community and Israel. While Albanese's support for Palestine has been weak, inadequate, and pathetic, his support for Israel has been unwavering and undeniable—much to the dismay of Palestine's advocates—and aside from Dutton and Zionist lobby groups, who would prefer Albanese to adopt a stance calling for the complete destruction of Palestine, no one can deny this.

The broader response to Dutton's campaign launch has been equally damning, where his launch was characterised as "38 minutes of empty rhetoric" by members of the Labor government, with offered no tangible policies to alleviate cost-of-living pressures—for a leader attempting to frame himself as a saviour for struggling households, Dutton's failure to present substantive solutions undermines his credibility.

It is easy to critique; it is far harder to constructively contribute, and Dutton's campaign so far reveals an opposition that remains mired in the politics of negativity. And in an attempt to replicate Donald Trump's proposed Department of Government Efficiency in the U.S., Dutton is proposing $368 billion in spending cuts would inevitably target essential services such as pensions, Medicare, and energy bill relief, and this highlights the dangerous implications of his rhetoric.

Dutton's vagueness on fiscal policy—deliberately avoiding specifics while gesturing at "government waste", a meaningless mantra if there ever was one—shows a reluctance to confront the real impact of austerity measures. Austerity will fail—as it always does (and more recently in Argentina and New Zealand)—and this lack of transparency leaves voters questioning what, if anything, the Coalition genuinely stands for beyond opposition to the government of the day.

Albanese, in contrast, has sought to frame his government as a "builder"—focused on creating a future that balances economic growth with social equity. His emphasis on providing support as something more meaningful than a "sugar hit" reveals a philosophy grounded in long-term nation-building rather than short-term political gains. This perspective, combined with his focus on *uniting* rather than *dividing*, directly challenges Dutton's political instincts, which rely heavily on energising a hard-right base rather than appealing to a broader, more inclusive electorate.

Dutton's campaign, at this early stage, appears to be an exercise in recycling tired conservative talking points: meanwhile, Albanese and his ministers have not only called out the emptiness of these talking points but have also drawn attention to the risks they pose to essential public services and social safety nets. This clear differentiation between the parties—one focused on division and disinformation, the other on unity and pragmatism—will likely become a defining theme as the election approaches.

THE ALBANESE–DUTTON CONTEST BETWEEN UNITY AND DIVISION

While it's clear that the next election campaign has essentially already begun, it's also clear that it will be defined by personal attacks, manipulative narratives, hollow slogans, and relentless mudslinging, and these conditions are ripe for what promises to be one of the most bitterly fought and dirtiest federal election campaigns in Australia's history,

Dutton, lacking substantive policies or ideas, is likely to drag the discourse down to his level, resulting in a campaign mired in obfuscation, sludge, and grinding negativity. This strategy will create a fog of dirt and confusion, where he will be hoping to emerge from this chaos with some kind of victory and, no doubt, he will be supported by the mainstream media. It is a disappointing inevitability, but perhaps the greatest tragedy is that it didn't have to be this way.

Albanese entered office with a clear mandate to lead, bolstered by a public eager for stability and progress after nearly a decade of stagnation under successive Coalition governments. In many ways, his government has been competent and steady, yet Albanese's determination to seek bipartisanship—particularly from a Liberal Party led by Dutton—has diluted his authority and squandered political capital that could have been used to push through transformative policies.

The Voice to Parliament referendum is probably the most obvious example, where Albanese's insistence on securing bipartisan support for what should have been a nation-defining moment of reconciliation and progress allowed Dutton to derail the process, exploiting the opportunity to stoke fear and division. By courting a leader who thrives on wrecking rather than building, Albanese not only weakened his government's position but also deepened the national divide. The referendum's failure is a wound that will linger for some time to come, and it also serves as a cautionary tale of the perils of accommodating an opposition that has no interest in genuine collaboration.

On other fronts, Albanese has similarly undermined his potential for bold leadership. His government's adherence to the unpopular Stage 3 tax cuts for so long—a relic of a bygone era of Coalition economic policy—baffled both critics and supporters, and when the federal government finally came around to amending this legislation, they received no political benefit.

Why, after nine years in opposition, would a government finally in power sacrifice so much fiscal capacity to uphold a policy that overwhelmingly benefits the wealthy and undermines its broader social agenda? Again, the answer lies in a misguided attempt to avoid alienating right-wing interests and the Coalition, even as Dutton has offered nothing in return but contempt and obstruction.

Meanwhile, Dutton has capitalised on every misstep and every opportunity given to him, not with vision or policy but with *relentless negativity*. Like Tony Abbott before him, Dutton is a politician who thrives in opposition, a master of saying "no" but bereft of ideas for governing. His reliance on firebrand rhetoric about "woke" culture, baseless claims about the government's role in societal ills, and constant appeals to conservative fears highlight his lack of intellectual depth and policy substance. If Abbott's tenure as Prime Minister demonstrated the perils of electing a leader driven by destruction rather than creation, Dutton's would likely prove even worse. His ambition is not to *build a better Australia* but to seize power for its own sake.

For Albanese, the upcoming campaign will be a critical test. His government has much to campaign on—stability and policy achievements—but these successes are overshadowed by a perception that he has failed to rise to the moment. The spectre of bold, transformative leadership has given way to slow-moving incrementalism that frustrates progressives and emboldens conservatives. Albanese's inability to effectively counter these corrosive tactics from Dutton, and his reluctance to use the crossbench to bypass the Coalition on most occasions, has created a contest far closer than it needed to be.

Unless something dramatic happens over the next few months, the electorate will be left with a dilemma: choosing a government that has been competent but timid, or an opposition that is reckless and vacuous. The facile "Let's get Australia back on track" and "Building Australia's future" will dominate the campaign trail, but neither slogan captures the disillusionment many Australians feel. In truth, the campaign could be summed up with a sentiment both sobering and aspirational: *Surely Australia Deserves Better.*

A better political discourse. A better class of leadership. A better vision for the future. This is what the nation should demand from its leaders, yet the unfolding reality suggests it is unlikely to be delivered. Instead, Australians will have to put up with a campaign that is likely to be characterised by personal attacks, empty promises, and a sense of frustration with a political system that fails to rise up to the challenges of the modern era. Australia does deserve better, but only if is it prepared to not only ask for it, but *to demand it*—and it's up to us, as a community to make these demands.

Political leadership is not just about winning power; it is about using that power to make a difference and so far, that hasn't been the case. Certainly, political leadership is difficult and the political rewards are rarely presented easily on a platter—but Albanese was provided with an opportunity to wield power effectively and decided to prioritise bipartisanship with an opposition committed to division, and now risks squandering not only his legacy but also the trust and hope of the Australian people.

For Dutton, the path is simpler but far darker—a campaign of negativity and fear designed to secure power without purpose, much like Tony Abbott's approach in 2013. Ultimately, Australia deserves better than either of these strategies. However, if the early weeks of 2025 are any indication, it seems unlikely that anything will change.

***

CEASEFIRE: GLOBAL FAILURES AND THE UNCERTAIN ROAD AHEAD

20 January 2025

The ceasefire in Palestine has offered a reprieve from the violence and destruction that has been inflicted upon Gaza since October 2023 but a deeper historical and political analysis shows a continuing pattern of oppression, resistance, and repeated failures by the international community to address the main issues.

These hostilities are not isolated recent events but are deeply entrenched in the history of occupation, and it is important to remember how we have arrived at this point. The roots of this occupation go back to the Nakba in 1948, where hundreds of thousands of Palestinians were forcibly displaced from their homes to make way for the creation of the state of Israel, a state that was forced through by the British government, under the arrangements of the Balfour Agreement. This initial act of dispossession and the ongoing illegal military occupation of Palestinian territories has defined the relationship between Israelis and Palestinians for decades.

Palestinians living in the occupied territories have faced land confiscations, home demolitions, restricted movement, and the blockade of Gaza. In Gaza, 2.2 million people have lived under severe restrictions, unable to rebuild their lives or access basic resources and this cycle of blockade, violence, and destruction has perpetuated conditions of extreme poverty and despair.

The Hamas-led attack on October 7, 2023, marked a turning point in the ongoing struggle. While Hamas justified the operation as a response to the years of occupation and another attempt to bring global attention to Palestinian suffering, the attack and the subsequent retaliation by Israel unleashed a level of devastation not seen in many years. The Netanyahu government subsequently declared war, aiming to dismantle Hamas and recover Israeli hostages: however, the scale of Israel's military response—targeting civilian infrastructure, refugee camps, and essential services in Gaza—has highlighted the highly disproportionate nature of the conflict.

Statements such as former Defense Minister Yoav Gallant's declaration of a "complete siege" and the depiction of Palestinians as "human animals" also revealed the Israeli government's broader objectives, which targeted not just Hamas but the Palestinian population as a whole. The death toll, now estimated at over 46,000 Palestinians—according to the medical journal *Lancet*, it could be over 186,000—including thousands of children, and the mass displacement of civilians, have shown the consequences of these policies.

International efforts to end the conflict have been woefully inadequate. The paralysis of the UN Security Council, mainly due to the repeated use of U.S. vetoes to shield Israel from condemnation, has shown how limited international diplomacy has been. World leaders' tepid condemnations of violence have often failed to translate into meaningful action, leaving Palestinians to endure unimaginable suffering while the underlying causes of the conflict have remained unaddressed.

Of course, as the ceasefire takes effect, it should bring a moment of hope, but it also raises questions about what lies ahead. The international community has done little to acknowledge what has been happening to Palestinians, not just since October 2023 but going back all the way to 1948, and has done everything to support the actions of Israel; why would post-ceasefire arrangements be any different?

Palestinians are now returning to destroyed homes, schools and hospitals, and face an uncertain future—the international community's repeated failures to hold Israel accountable or to enforce resolutions that could lead to a just and lasting peace will also raise significant questions about progress after Stage 3 of the ceasefire is completed. For Palestinians, a return to pre-October 2023 conditions—systemic apartheid, an illegal occupation of their lands, and brutal dispossession—is totally unacceptable.

This fragile ceasefire is compounded by historical precedents where ceasefires have been frequently broken by Israel or exploited as opportunities for them to regroup militarily. The question of accountability also remains: what mechanisms, if any, exist to prevent a return to violence? Without addressing the structural inequalities and injustices that have been a feature of this deliberately intractable conflict, any pause in hostilities at this stage will just be a temporary measure, and not a long-term solution.

SELECTIVE JUSTICE AND THE EROSION OF INTERNATIONAL LAW

Israel's actions in Gaza and the broader lack of international support for Palestine highlights the selective application of justice and international law. The assassination of senior Hamas negotiators by Israel in 2024 amid discussions of a possible ceasefire are examples of the deliberate sabotage of diplomatic efforts, and far from being isolated incidents, this reflects a broader Israeli strategy of prioritising military action over meaningful conflict resolution.

Despite the clarity of international law and conventions outlining the protection of civilian populations and the prohibition of collective punishment, Israel has defied these principles with impunity. The starvation, mass killings, and forced displacement of Palestinians constitute acts that experts and international bodies have increasingly identified as genocidal, yet the response from the international community, particularly from powerful states such as the United States and Germany, has been characterised by double standards, inaction and hypocrisy.

The United States, Israel's staunchest ally, has consistently shielded it from accountability. By vetoing critical United Nations Security Council resolutions, the U.S. has ensured that Israel faces no meaningful consequences for its actions. At the same time, billions of dollars in military aid and weaponry have flowed into Israel, facilitating its military campaigns against Gaza. This unquestioning support has emboldened Israel to escalate its actions, knowing that it will face no significant repercussions—and, so far, it hasn't.

Germany has also maintained arms trade agreements with Israel while publicly condemning violence in abstract or weak terms. These actions undermine Germany's professed commitment to human rights and international law, exposing a willingness to prioritise political alliances over the lives of vulnerable populations.

In contrast, a small number of Western nations have sought to challenge this: Spain, Ireland, and Norway have demonstrated political courage by recognising Palestine and ceasing arms sales to Israel. South Africa's decision to bring a case against Israel to the International Court of Justice was a significant step toward holding Israel accountable for its actions. The Court's findings, which recognised the likelihood of genocide and called for an immediate cessation of such acts, reflect the severity of the situation.

The International Criminal Court also took decisive action by issuing arrest warrants for Israeli leaders, including Netanyahu and Gallant, and these developments signal an increasing willingness among *some* players within the international system—not all—to confront the Israeli government. However, these efforts have been met with fierce resistance, particularly from the United States, including threats of sanctions by U.S. Senators against nations that attempt to enforce the Court's arrest warrants.

This pattern of selective enforcement of international law not only perpetuates the suffering of Palestinians but also undermines the credibility of global institutions, and the message sent to oppressed populations worldwide is that justice is contingent upon geopolitical considerations rather than universal principles.

ISRAEL HAS LOST THIS WAR AMID GLOBAL MORAL FAILURES

While there will be arguments about the role of Hamas and its actions on October 7, 2023, there is no question that this war was initiated by Israel and is mainly a continuation of its actions since 1948. Conflicts should never be a comparative contest but the comparisons will be made: 1,139 Israelis died on October 7—including many killed by the Israel Defense Forces under the "Hannibal Directive"—and at least 46,000 in Palestine and 3,000 in Lebanon have been killed by Israel since that time. But by any measure at all, this has been a disproportionate response by Israel, even more disproportionate than any of its actions against Palestinian people since 1948.

However, despite the massive destruction inflicted by Israel, its ambitions have been mainly unfulfilled: Israel instigated this war, and it has lost. It targeted Hamas for total annihilation, yet the movement remains intact, and in some respects, is stronger today, at least numerically. Hamas retains its operational capacity, and its symbolic significance as a resistance movement has only grown, particularly as the devastation in Gaza has highlighted to the world the profound suffering of Palestinians caused by Israel. Tensions between Hamas and the Palestinian Authority may emerge, but the broader narrative is one of resilience amid destruction.

In addition to this, Israel's international standing has suffered catastrophic damage. Its status as a pariah state has been cemented by its actions, which have gone far beyond the constraints of international law. Once criticised as an apartheid state and brutal occupier—as if that wasn't bad enough—Israel's recent actions have added accusations of genocide, ethnic cleansing, and ecocide to its record. While its allies in the West have provided diplomatic cover, public sentiment globally has shifted significantly and the massive protests in capitals worldwide and growing condemnation of Israel's actions reveal a rising awareness of the atrocities committed.

The economic fallout for Israel is equally damaging. The war has cost the economy tens of billions of dollars, with long-term projections painting an even worse outcome—over $400 billion in lost revenues over the next decade. Declining investment, shrinking consumer confidence, and disrupted labor markets reflect the broader instability resulting from its militarised messianic policies. Even with its superior military and economic power, Israel emerges as the conflict's biggest loser, particularly as these events have only deepened internal political divisions and societal fractures.

The reconstruction of Gaza, however, presents its own challenges. With an estimated $80 billion required to rebuild, the question is who will bear the cost of this. While nations such as Qatar and Saudi Arabia have stepped forward in the past, the scale of destruction requires an unprecedented global effort. Yet, this reconstruction must come with guarantees that the rebuilt infrastructure and lives will not be destroyed again by Israel in future conflicts inflicted at the whim of Netanyahu, or whomever replaces him. Without accountability for Israel and strong international mechanisms to enforce peace, the cycle of destruction and rebuilding risks becoming endless.

The reputations of Western nations have also been seriously tarnished. The unwavering support for Israel from leaders such as Joe Biden, Anthony Blinken, Keir Starmer, and others has rightfully drawn criticism. Their refusal to hold Israel accountable, the continued sale of arms, and their rhetoric about Israel's "right to defend itself" have shown a deep hypocrisy. Biden could have demanded an end to hostilities in October 2023: why did he wait until his final days in office before engaging in any form of meaningful action? The rights of Palestinians have been consistently ignored, as have their pleas for justice and the indifference shown by these leaders during Gaza's livestreamed genocide will become a moral indictment that history will not forgive, or forget. And nor should it.

In the future, political leaders will be haunted by these questions: where were you when Gaza was subjected to genocide? Why did you enable mass suffering rather than working to end it? The complicity of Western governments in this tragedy will be a stain on their legacies, as will events such as the standing ovation for Netanyahu in the U.S. Congress—a moment that epitomised the moral failure of the global political establishment: Gaza was being destroyed, yet the man who inflicted this reign of terror upon the peoples of Palestine was applauded and encouraged to go even further. How can this ever be forgiven?

Palestine faces a long road to recovery, but there is no doubt that it will recover, as it always does and irrespective of how long it takes. But the moral and reputational damage to the West and its many leaders who supported Israel is this way, is unrepairable. The conflict has exposed not only the brutality of Israeli policies but also the structural failures of an international community unwilling or unable to uphold its own standards. And it may never recover from these failures.

***

UNHAPPY AUSTRALIA DAY AND BLOCKING TRUE RECONCILIATION

27 January 2025

January 26 has, yet again, become the annual circus of cultural and political conflict, and the intent for it to be a "day of national unity" becomes more distant every year. Instead of collective reflection, the day has evolved into social divisions, mainly created by conservative politicians, media outlets, and their supporting institutions, and this has transformed January 26 into a conflict zone in the broader culture wars—a social conflict not searching for resolution but constant agitation.

For many in the Indigenous community, January 26 is not a day of celebration but of mourning, a day that signifies colonial dispossession, violence, and the erasure of cultural heritage—Invasion Day is a more suitable name, as it serves as a reminder of the enduring inequalities and injustices faced by First Nations people, even if no federal government will ever officially recognise the day in this way.

However, for many other Australians, the day's historical and cultural significance remains nebulous: some associate it with Captain James Cook's landing in 1770; others with the federation of Australia in 1901, and many others still view it as nothing more than an opportunity for a public holiday. These different perceptions suggest a deeper historical amnesia and lack of consensus about what, if anything, Australia Day is supposed to signify.

The official recognition of January 26 as a national holiday is a relatively recent development, formalised in 1994. Before this, the day was celebrated on different dates, reflecting the absence of a unified national identity around the occasion and, aside from nationalists, there isn't a universal acceptance or great enthusiasm: here today, gone tomorrow and *forgotten*. Instead, the day has become increasingly polarised, led by conservatives such as Opposition Leader Peter Dutton—surely, a five-star general in the ongoing culture wars—and the Murdoch press, who wield it as a rhetorical weapon in their broader ideological struggle that no one else really cares about.

Dutton's rhetoric about Australia Day as a "day of shame" for those who refuse to celebrate it, despite the millions on the streets across Australia who did just that, reveals no genuine concern for national unity—Dutton actually refused to attend Australia Day events in Canberra—but a calculated attempt to inflame division for political gain. And not to be outdone by the insanity of her leader, Sussan Ley compared the arrival of the First Fleet to Elon Musk's space mission to Mars and claimed that it was "not an invasion", or even an intention to destroy or to pillage, even though that's exactly what the First Fleet did back in 1788.

This weaponised January 26 is part of a larger conservative project to entrench cultural narratives that prioritise uncritical patriotism and historical whitewashing. For Dutton, the day represents an opportunity to rally his base against perceived threats to Australian identity, whether these come in the form of supermarket chains choosing not to stock Australia Day merchandise or vague notions of people being "afraid to celebrate". *Who is actually afraid? Where are these people? What are they afraid of?*

These grievances, often manufactured or exaggerated, serve as distractions from substantial issues facing the nation, and allow conservatives to frame themselves as defenders of "tradition" and "national pride", while avoiding meaningful engagement with the historical and ongoing injustices experienced by Indigenous Australians.

The insistence on treating January 26 only as a joyous occasion, festooned with balloons, streamers, flags, barbecues, and beach parties, reflects a refusal to understand or deal with the complexities of Australia's history. Dutton has a childlike fantasy—a superficial celebration that ignores the deeper wounds and contradictions embedded in the nation's history, an approach that is not only insensitive but counterproductive. By insisting on uncritical celebration, conservatives alienate large segments of the population who want to see the day as an opportunity for reflection, dialogue, and acknowledgment of historical wrongs. In doing so, they perpetuate the very divisions they claim to oppose.

Prime Minister Anthony Albanese's recent framing of Australia Day as an "opportunity to celebrate everything we've built together" and to be "optimistic for the future" provides a more conciliatory tone but still falls short of addressing the underlying tensions, even if Dutton's claims of "a day of shame" are nowhere to be found in Albanese's comments. While optimism and unity are great aspirations, they cannot be achieved without confronting the darker chapters of Australia's history and the structural inequalities that persist today. For many, the gap between the idealised and saccharine vision of Australia Day and the lived realities of the marginalised and the excluded makes the celebration hollow, if not offensive.

The shame and division conservatives claim does not come from public opposition to the day itself but from their own efforts to enforce a singular, exclusionary narrative about its meaning. Their fixation on cultural grievances—whether it be over supermarket shelves or *imagined* fears of celebration—reflects an unwillingness to engage in the difficult but necessary work of national Reconciliation. Until this work is undertaken, January 26 will remain a contested symbol, emblematic not of unity but of the unresolved conflicts at the centre of the Australian identity.

A CONTESTED LEGACY OF DIVISION AND HISTORICAL AMNESIA

For Indigenous Australians, January 26 *is* a devastating part of their history. The arrival of the First Fleet in 1788 saw the imposition of British law, the seizure of land under the doctrine of *terra nullius*—against the specific directions provided to Governor Phillip by King George—and the destruction of Indigenous cultures over time. Resistance, often portrayed by conservatives as a modern phenomenon, is deeply rooted in Australian history: as early as 1938, the Day of Mourning drew attention to the injustices that January 26 represents.

Despite the historically inaccuracy and insensitivity of a reenactment of the First Fleet's landing and British–Indigenous encounters, the choreographed events on that day in 1938 at least recognised that the narrative surrounding Australia Day was incomplete and exclusionary. Also, these protests were not an isolated moment but part of an ongoing resistance: there were further public demonstrations during the Bicentenary events in 1988—37 years ago—where over 40,000 Indigenous and non-Indigenous people marched in Sydney in solidarity, condemning the ongoing injustices faced by Aboriginal communities and demanding recognition of their rights. These protests also marked a significant turning point, embedding the idea of "Invasion Day" into the national consciousness and highlighting the need for a more inclusive and honest appraisal of Australia's chequered history.

Despite the historical flexibility surrounding Australia Day—it has been held in May, June and July—there is now staunch conservative opposition to changing the date. This refusal reflects a broader trend of uncritical nationalism, which, as seen in other countries, is deeply corrosive. Rooted in symbols like the flag and the national anthem, this brand of nationalism thrives on shallow displays of pride, detached from the historical and social complexities of a nation's identity. Australia Day perpetuates this sanitised version of history that ignores the violence and dispossession upon which modern Australia was built upon.

A SYMBOLIC DISTRACTION PUSHED BY CONSERVATIVES

The conservative fixation on Australia Day and their confected outrage over any challenge to its current form reveals a deeper issue—this is not about the date itself or even about national pride: it's about the authoritarian power to define the nation's narrative and resist any acknowledgment of its more uncomfortable truths. For decades, January 26 was a relatively innocuous date for most non-Indigenous Australians, associated more with barbecues and beach trips than with historical reflection, primarily because few people seemed to know what the date was *actually* about. Its transformation into a conservative rallying point is not driven by widespread grassroots sentiment but by a calculated political strategy: to weaponise cultural issues and perpetuate division for electoral advantage.

Dutton thrives on this cycle of outrage. He manufactures a crisis about "woke culture", then accuses his opponent of stoking division, and relies on a compliant media to amplify the narrative: and true to form, this is exactly what happened this year. The 2023 Voice to Parliament referendum is a prime example of this dynamic: a modest proposal to enshrine an Indigenous advisory body in the Constitution—a small, symbolic and practical step toward reconciliation—was met with an avalanche of racist misinformation and scaremongering. The referendum was not defeated because the idea lacked merit but because conservative leaders and media sowed confusion and fear, preying on ignorance and stoking resentment. Albanese's well-intentioned efforts, albeit poorly implemented, to advance Reconciliation were reframed as an "elite" agenda, and he continues to face political fallout as a result.

This relentless cycle is not limited to Australia Day or the Voice referendum. It is part of a broader conservative "Trumpist" playbook that seeks to dominate the public debate by focusing on symbolic battles rather than addressing any policy issues. These tactics are effective because they tap into fear—a fear of change; a fear of losing control; a fear of confronting the past; a fear of everything. For leaders such as Dutton, maintaining this fear is crucial, as it allows them to present themselves as defenders of tradition and stability, even as they undermine genuine efforts to build a more inclusive and just society.

Changing the date of Australia Day would be a symbolic gesture but what Australia does need is a transformation in its attitudes toward Indigenous people and its willingness to confront its colonial history. This is a big task, made more difficult by conservative resistance to any form of acknowledgment or accountability. Their rhetoric, steeped in denial and a child-like view of the world, clings to an idealised version of Australia that erases the voices of Indigenous Australians. It's an ongoing fantasy that prevents the nation from moving forward.

Perhaps it is time to cede Australia Day to the conservatives and allow them to revel in their symbolic victories and expend their energy on the confected outrage and cynical debates that achieve nothing beyond perpetuating division. By stepping away from this performative role-play conflict, progressive leaders and advocates can focus on the more substantial issues that offer real pathways to justice and reconciliation.

A Treaty with Indigenous people, for example, doesn't depend on a referendum or the approval of the conservative Stasi. If the Liberal Party and the people who can be easily swayed by this mindless agitation continue in this way, it's best to leave them out of it, and allow those who have the political will, courage and a commitment to progress, to get on with it. Initiatives such as the First Peoples' Assembly in Victoria and the Noongar Settlement in Western Australia show that meaningful steps can be taken without fanfare or deep polarisation.

The fight over Australia Day is, essentially, a distraction—one that conservatives will never abandon, as it serves their political purposes too well. Progressives must decide whether to remain mired in this conflict or set off on a new strategy, one that bypasses the manufactured outrage and focuses on delivering better outcomes for Indigenous Australians. The road to justice will never be free of obstacles, but it is clear that these obstacles will not be removed by those who benefit from their existence. Maybe it's time to leave the confected outrage of January 26 behind—it's never going to end with the Liberal Party in its current form and it's predictably painful each and every year—and move toward a future that isn't defined by conservatives but defined by the true work of Reconciliation and progressive transformation.

***

CHAOS, CORRUPTION IN THE AMERICAN DEMOCRACY

3 February 2025

Donald Trump is now the president of the United States for a second term, a situation that still requires a double-take and, after the events of 2021 at the Capitol Hill riots—amongst many other incidents during his first term—defies political logic but, as the Americans like to say, *it is what it is*. The echoes of the chaos of 2017 are returning, except this time, the chaos is deliberate, premeditated, and unrestrained by the checks and balances that once tempered Trump's first presidency.

The opening days of his return to power have been filled with the same erratic grandstanding that defined his first term: ridiculous territorial demands, aggressive posturing on the world stage, and a calculated descent into authoritarian theatrics. In just the first week, he has threatened to seize the Panama Canal, issued a demand to annex Greenland from Denmark, and renamed the Gulf of Mexico as the Gulf of America.

But the United States can't just seize the Panama Canal: it's sovereign territory, and any attempt to seize it would be an act of war. Greenland has been under Danish sovereignty for over two centuries: it can't just be handed over to the United States, despite what Trump says.

These demands are ridiculous at face value but that is *precisely* the point. They provoke outrage, confusion, and endless media speculation: *is Trump serious? Can the U.S. military actually be deployed to seize foreign lands at his command? Can he do this?* The moment is reminiscent of the early days of his first presidency when he blustered about NATO, threatened nuclear war with North Korea, and fired cabinet members over Twitter. It is chaos as a strategy, a deliberate means to exhaust opposition, saturate the media cycle, and prevent the public from focusing on his real agenda of extremism.

Trump is making moves that will have profound and lasting consequences for the fabric of American society—behind the smokescreen of his global provocations, he is systematically dismantling civil rights, and his administration has begun its rollback of women's reproductive rights with unprecedented speed.

LGBTQ+ protections, already eroded in his first term, are now being actively dismantled, with federal agencies ordered to purge diversity initiatives and inclusion programs. His government is rapidly moving toward the wholesale disenfranchisement of marginalised communities, curtailing voting rights through gerrymandering, state suppression laws, and judicial manipulation.

He has stacked his administration with loyalists who are not just corrupt but *ideologically extreme*, openly espousing white nationalist rhetoric and religious fundamentalism. The Republican Party, having purged itself of dissenters in the wake of Trump's return, now acts as a rubber stamp, enabling his most draconian policies without resistance.

This corruption is brazen: positions of authority are handed out to unqualified loyalists, many of whom have open criminal records (including Trump) or ties to extremist groups. Government agencies are stripped of career professionals and replaced with sycophants whose only qualification is their unwavering sycophancy to Trump.

Regulations are slashed, environmental protections are removed, corporate oligarchs are given free rein to exploit the economy—America, already teetering on the edge of political and economic instability, is now heading into an era of unrestricted corruption. But despite this, even more alarming is the escalation of Trump's authoritarian ambitions and fascist tendencies.

He has begun floating plans to round up undocumented immigrants and place them in mass detention centres, with Guantanamo Bay openly discussed as a primary holding facility. The administration's rhetoric has shifted from coded language to open calls for mass deportations and state-sanctioned crackdowns. The imagery is familiar, in a historical parallel too obvious to ignore. This is not simply about enforcement—it is about intimidation, fear, and the normalisation of state-sponsored persecution. And we shouldn't worry about revisiting historical cliches or invoking Godwin's law of Nazi analogies: this is brutal fascism, and we shouldn't be afraid to call it out, from wherever we are.

Trump's legal battles, which once seemed like they might prevent his return to power, now appear almost as a footnote of history. The Supreme Court, packed with his handpicked judges, provides legal cover for his most extreme policies. The Constitution, once an obstacle to his ambitions, is now little more than a *suggestion*. Executive orders and legal loopholes are exploited to strip citizenship from those deemed politically undesirable. And, as usual, there are many contradictions—many of Trump's closest allies, including his new head of Department of Government Efficiency, Elon Musk, and even his own wife, Melania Trump, benefited from the very immigration policies he now seeks to dismantle.

Double standards are no longer a liability in Trump's America; it is a feature of the system he is building.

However, despite this unprecedented power grab, there are pockets of resistance: Trump's hold on the federal government is strong, but states with Democratic leadership have begun to fight back. Legal challenges are mounting, with governors refusing to comply with federal directives, and sanctuary cities dig in their heels against mass deportation efforts. The battle lines have been seemingly drawn, and the coming months will determine whether the United States remains a functioning democracy or fully descends into authoritarian rule. The question is no longer whether Trump will push America toward decline; it is whether anyone can stop him before it is too late.

AN OPPORTUNITY TO BREAK FREE FROM AMERICA'S DECLINE

The farcical nature of United States politics has long been a source of derision—for outsiders—even when the Democrats hold power, but under Trump's second presidency, it has escalated from dysfunction to something far more dangerous. *And it is dangerous*, there's no question about this.

The U.S. is still, for now, the world's most powerful and influential nation, but it is slipping, not only because of Trump, but because of a long-term decline brought on by political instability, economic stagnation, and strategic miscalculations, concurrent with the rise of China, which will soon overtake the U.S, militarily and economically. While most of the world watches in despair as Trump takes the sledgehammer and angle grinder to democratic norms, Australia is faced with an unavoidable question: does it continue tying its fortunes to a crumbling and increasingly dysfunctional superpower, or does it grab the opportunity to establish itself as an independent, strategically autonomous nation with new and diversified alliances?

The spectacle of Trump's leadership—an erratic and bombastic return to authoritarian populism, as well as behaving like America's *arsehole-in-chief*—may seem like a uniquely American phenomenon, but there are serious implications for Australia. His first term was a warning sign; his second term is where the results of his reckless ideology will come to fruition. The "idiot king" model of politics, the elevation of incompetence as a virtue, the aggressive use of chaos to mask deeper, more insidious policy shifts—these are not just the problems of the United States, but are symptoms of a political virus that has infected democracies worldwide.

History has seen this before: Mussolini in Italy, Hitler's weaponisation of grievance politics in Germany—leaders who turned democracy into a circus before transforming it into something far more sinister and disastrous. We are seeing this repeated now, and no country that considers itself an ally of the United States can afford to ignore what this shift means for the future.

Australia has long been tethered to American strategic interests, often at the expense of its own. The ANZUS alliance, the AUKUS agreement, the constant diplomatic and military alignment—these have been framed as necessities, but in truth, they have left Australia vulnerable to the chaos of the American decline. Trump's second term is an opportunity, maybe even a final warning, that Australia must reassess its place in the world. Blind loyalty to the United States, especially through AUKUS, no longer serves Australian interests. Instead, Australia must forge new and better relationships—ones that reflect its geographic reality and its economic priorities, rather than outdated Cold War allegiances that are now liabilities.

China, despite the diplomatic strain of recent years, remains Australia's largest trading partner by a significant margin. Under the Albanese government, tensions have eased, but the deeper question remains: why should Australia continue preparing for military confrontation with a nation it is so economically dependent on?

The AUKUS agreement, sold to the public as a necessary counter to Chinese influence, serves British and American interests far more than it serves Australia's. The nuclear submarines promised under AUKUS are unlikely to arrive in any meaningful capacity for decades, and even if they do, they will serve more as an extension of U.S. military power in the Pacific than as an asset to Australian defences. The cost—both financial and geopolitical—is enormous, and it locks Australia into an American strategic framework that assumes perpetual hostility with China. But what if that assumption is wrong? What if Australia's best path forward is not through military escalation but through deeper economic and diplomatic integration with its regional neighbours?

Indonesia, India, and the broader south-east Asian region represent an alternative vision for Australian foreign policy— one based on pragmatism rather than ideological servitude to Washington. Indonesia, a rapidly growing economic power with deep historical trade ties to Australia, should be a priority partner, yet it has often been treated as an afterthought in Australian diplomacy, as though our nearest neighbour with a population of over 270 million, simply doesn't exist.

India, now the world's most populous democracy and a rising global power, offers another key strategic relationship that could be cultivated independently of American influence. The Keating-era view of Asia as Australia's "near north" remains just as true today as it was in the 1990s. A future-oriented Australian foreign policy would recognise that its long-term security does not lie in being America's proxy in an imaginary Pacific Cold War, but in fostering strong, independent partnerships with the nations that will define the region's economic and political future.

This doesn't mean severing ties with the United States entirely: Australia's relationship with the U.S. is deep, and there are areas of mutual benefit that should not be abandoned. But the blind allegiance, the kind that drags Australia into unnecessary military conflicts, the kind that forces it to take economic hits due to American-led trade disputes, the kind that undermines its own regional credibility—that needs to end. Australia does not need to choose between America and China, or between old alliances and new ones, in the same way it didn't need to end the relationship with Britain when it veered towards the U.S. after World War II. It needs to assert its own national interests, something it has failed to do for decades due to the sphere of American influence.

History shows that global power shifts move at a glacial pace and don't happen overnight, but they *are* happening right now. America's decline will not be immediate, nor will China's rise be without complications. But Australia can't afford to wait: it needs to act now to establish itself as a nation with independent strategic capabilities and diversified alliances. The U.S under Trump is a reminder that tying Australia's fate too closely to a declining empire is a dangerous gamble: its future is in the Indo–Pacific region, not in the ashes of American exceptionalism.

It's no longer a question of whether Australia should begin this transition—it's a question whether it has the political will to do this before it's too late. The Albanese government could have dumped the AUKUS deal when it first came to office in 2022 but decided not to. It has taken some steps to repair relations with China and deepen engagement with south-east Asia, but the broader shift required is one that will take a lot more political courage.

It means questioning deeply entrenched assumptions about Australia's place in the world and resisting the pressure from Washington to remain in lockstep with American military priorities. It also means acknowledging the fact that the world is changing and Australia needs to take the crucial steps to change with it.

Trump's second term will be a test for American democracy but it's also a test to see if Australia can finally break free from the outdated mindset that has kept it languishing in America's shadow for far too long. Australia needs to decide whether it will move in synch with a changing world or be left behind, clinging to alliances that no longer serve its interests.

***

ABC SACKING EXPOSES THE ACTIONS OF THE ISRAEL LOBBY

10 February 2025

How far will the ABC go to protect the interests of the Israel lobby? That's the key question in a legal case that exposes all the elements of political influence, media independence, and corporate misconduct. The case centres on the journalist Antoinette Lattouf and her unfair dismissal from the ABC—the catalyst for this case was a social media repost concerning allegations made by Human Rights Watch that the Israeli government was using starvation as a method of warfare in Gaza and in her repost, Lattouf referenced the organisation's work, adding the words "HRW reporting starvation as a tool of war".

Human Rights Watch is a globally recognised organisation that employs researchers, legal experts, journalists, and investigators across seventy nationalities, and received the Nobel Peace Prize in 1997 for its role in the banning of land mines. Despite its reputation as a credible source, the ABC chose to respond to pressure from the Israel lobby by terminating Lattouf's employment—which was a short five-day contract anyway—rather than addressing the substance of what she had shared.

The manner in which Lattouf was dismissed has become the focus of her unlawful termination lawsuit against the

ABC, raising key issues about editorial freedom, legal ethics, and the power applied by interest groups—in this case, the Israel lobby—over national broadcasters and other media enterprises. And, in this case, if the ABC had resisted external pressure and supported its journalist for reposting a fact-based statement from a credible human rights organisation, there wouldn't have been any controversy. None. Instead, the abrupt dismissal drew even more attention to Lattouf's work and questions about how the ABC handles its responsibility to maintain independent reporting.

In its haste to remove Lattouf, the ABC also contended that sacking her could not have been racially motivated because they refused to acknowledge that the Lebanese race exists. These details, which are surfacing as part of the ongoing legal case, reflect both confusion within the ABC's internal processes and flawed legal justifications for the dismissal, as well as confirming the position of the ABC as a white-bread organisation that, instead of stamping out racism, simply applies more of it to appease certain interest groups.

In addition, the *Lattouf v ABC* case has highlighted the double standards in how the ABC applies its own policies over the use of social media. Several high-profile ABC personalities regularly repost seemingly controversial material without being asked to offer a "counterbalancing" piece or present competing perspectives. Lattouf's single repost has triggered a disproportionate reaction.

This discrepancy shows an environment where editorial guidelines are inconsistently applied or easily influenced by powerful interests, such as the Israel lobby. This case could have far-reaching implications, not just for Lattouf's professional future but also for how the ABC, as a public broadcaster, shows its commitment to journalistic independence and freedom. ABC management has allowed interference to come in from one lobbying group and, because of this, the impartiality and integrity that the public should expect from a publicly funded broadcaster has been severely compromised.

THE EROSION OF DEMOCRATIC DEBATE IN AUSTRALIA

The capacity of Israel lobby groups to extract swift and unquestioning compliance from media outlets and political figures shows weaknesses in how power is wielded in Australia. It is not uncommon for influential individuals tied to the Israel lobby to make direct calls to editors and senior executives at mainstream media organisations, including the ABC and major newspapers, calling for particular actions to be taken that serve their interests.

The urgency and success of these demands brings about a culture of fear in which journalists, producers and board members find themselves scrambling to avoid a backlash. This leads to abrupt dismissals and retractions that ironically amplify the very issues these lobbyists seek to bury—the disproportionate response around the *keffiyeh* controversy at the Sydney Theatre Company in 2023 is a clear example of this. Rather than allowing a minor element after the end of the performance to pass unnoticed—the cast wearing *keffiyehs* on stage to show their support for the people of Gaza—the loud objections and funding threats turned a small, local matter into national news over several months.

The influence that flows from such well-connected minority groups is neither universal nor reflective of entire communities; many within the broader Australian Jewish community *do not* support these heavy-handed tactics. Instead, they see this kind of clampdown on discussion and criticism of Israeli government policy as counterproductive and damaging to the community's reputation.

However, the response from these people within the Israel lobby has been to double down, and even attack other members from the Jewish community with whom they disagree with, as shown by the recent commentary from prominent Zionist lobbyist Mark Leibler, where he claimed that "nothing is worse than those Jews who level totally unfounded allegations of genocide and ethnic cleansing against the State of Israel. They are repulsive and revolting human beings... they are vicious antisemites".

The broader outcome is the disastrous effect on journalism, where editors and reporters grow uneasy about even the most factual commentary related to Israel or its policies. In the case of Lattouf, the abrupt manner in which she was removed—before even completing her week-long shift—reflects how immediate and intense the lobbying efforts can be, and how swiftly corporate entities can fold under that pressure.

This environment of excessive sensitivity is made even more complicated by the fact that legitimate criticism of any government—Israeli or otherwise—can be conflated with antisemitism if those protesting the criticism choose to label it as such. Most observers strongly condemn genuine antisemitism, and no one should be singled out or vilified purely for their ethnic or religious background. Yet criticism of policy decisions and human rights records is integral to a functioning democracy. The capacity to examine the actions of governments is considered a core right, and to suppress that right risks eroding the very democratic principles it aims to protect. Exaggerating claims of fear or "being triggered" can also backfire, as it invites skepticism about the genuineness of those concerns, creating a situation where all expressions of genuine alarm risk being dismissed.

The ABC's choice to remove Lattouf immediately—and, it seems, *unlawfully*—has led to costly legal proceedings, and these outcomes cannot be dismissed as inconsequential, as they show a mismanagement of both public trust and public funding. At the same time, this debacle—which could have been easily avoided if senior managers had some backbone and credibility—has chipped away at the ABC's reputation for independence and integrity; when a publicly funded broadcaster caters to one narrow interest group instead of defending staff who are simply relaying credible information, audiences see a loss of editorial courage and it raises the questions about how easily supposed fundamentals of a liberal democracy can be eroded.

Although nearly all mainstream politicians publicly condemn antisemitism, few appear willing to address the merging of legitimate critique with hate speech, avoiding the risk of being targeted themselves. Over time, this removes robust discussion from public debate, replacing it with self-censorship—which is what the Israel lobby wants to achieve. This weakens democracy from within, discouraging the free exchange of ideas and relegating important conflicts—where it's domestic or international—down to whispered conversations, rather than open debate.

The unease reflects a more global phenomenon within the Western world, especially in the United States, where fear, partisanship, and systematic attacks on media outlets have contributed to more fragile institutions. Although the context for Australia is different, these signs are similar to those in other countries where the constant pressure from lobby groups chips away at journalistic independence and the capacity for transparent public dialogue.

SILENCING POLITICAL VIEWS

There is a pattern of incidents involving the dismissal of media figures for views and perspectives that are different to those of specific vested interests: the journalist Mike Carlton was suspended over incidents relating to an article he published about Gaza in 2014, and the cartoonist Glen le Lievre was reprimanded by the *Sydney Morning Herald* after depicting an Israeli man casually observing the bombing of

Gaza from a loungeroom couch. Neither were disseminating hateful material; instead, they were reflecting on events unfolding at that time.

The fact that such commentary could prompt intense pushback from the Israel lobby—enough to cost individuals their jobs—shows the fragility of free expression where certain topics are raised. More recently, the abrupt sacking of the cricket commentator Peter Lalor shows how far-reaching these pressures can be: he posted about Gaza on his personal social media, and before long, objections were voiced to his employer, SEN Radio that, somehow, hearing Lalor's voice over the radio and commentating on test cricket from Sri Lanka was "triggering".

Discomfort or disagreement over someone's views is neither unusual nor inherently dangerous in a pluralistic society. Far more concerning is the perception that a handful of influential figures can force employers, editors, or broadcasters to fire individuals whose opinions stray beyond narrow parameters. Despite the obvious disconnect between Lalor's tweets about Gaza and his capacity to offer cricket commentary, the chain of events suggests that even *minor* social media activity—totally unrelated to the job itself—can lead to immediate action if enough pressure is applied. This approach does not align with values of open debate and diversity of opinion; it instead entrenches a system in which certain ideas can be suppressed with little due process.

It also brings up questions about other journalists who have similarly been "disappeared": the contracts for the ABC's Sarah Macdonald and Simon Marnie were inexplicably not extended in December 2024, even though both had been successful journalists at the ABC for many years and, in the case of Macdonald, a high-rating and popular presenter of the *Morning* program on Sydney radio. Is there anything in their social media accounts or public engagements that was perceived to have been offensive to the Israel lobby—*real or imagined*—and were there any harassing phone calls made to ABC management at the time to remove these journalists? This is an issue that would be worth investigating because nothing else seems to make sense.

Some defenders of these decisions claim that particular forms of speech constitute a genuine threat, invoking antisemitism or other forms of bigotry. While it is critical to condemn actual hatred toward any minority—at *every* occasion—it is also critical to recognise that critique of the actions of a government—in this case, Israel—and calls to end violence do not constitute hate speech or antisemitism. They are part of legitimate, if uncomfortable, public discourse. When the label of antisemitism is overused or misapplied, it loses its potency in confronting real prejudice. And at the same time, the conflation of all criticism of Israel with antisemitism has become a powerful tool to silence journalists, commentators, and others who might otherwise raise credible objections to Israel's policies and actions in the Middle East.

The public expects that journalists, commentators, and political figures can express their perspectives without fear of a sudden, career-ending phone call to their employer and it is vital to recognise the difference between expressing strong positions on international affairs and inciting genuine harm. While genuine incitement requires intervention, routine expression of political or humanitarian concerns should not. By turning so swiftly to sackings and public condemnations, media institutions allow vocal lobbies to skew public discourse in ways that favours secrecy and compliance over truthful, in-depth reporting.

If the numerous dismissals of respected professionals illustrates anything, it is that capitulating to demands premised on "triggered" or offended individuals, without regard for the actual substance or impact of the speech, erodes trust in *all* media platforms. Many Australians—whether they share the same political beliefs or not—recognise that a true exchange of ideas will inevitably feature disagreements, and only in extreme cases should there be calls for someone's removal.

What has happened to these journalists and commentators shows how perilously close newsrooms and broadcasters have become to giving up fundamental freedoms when confronted by small but persistent and secretive voices, such as the Israel lobby. Once it becomes easier to sack commentators than to accept challenging viewpoints, society has lost sight of a key part of democracy—the capacity to engage in dialogue and hold power to account, even when the truth hurts.

***

ALBANESE'S GAMBLE ON AMERICAN TARIFFS

17 February 2025

The imposition of a 25 per cent tariff on steel and aluminium imports into the United States has now become an important political issue, not just for the Australian government, but many governments around the world. The recent phone call made by Prime Minister Anthony Albanese to President Donald Trump was the start of an attempt to secure exemptions from the tariff, and although the volume of steel and aluminium exports that Australia sends to the United States is relatively small, the political ramifications of being denied an exemption are great. In an election year, Albanese can't afford to look ineffective when managing Australia's relationship with the United States, one of its most important strategic and economic partners.

Australia exports around 10 per cent of its overall steel and aluminium to the United States: around $638 million in steel and $275 million in aluminium. While that figure isn't a dominant share of Australian exports in those sectors, there is a symbolic importance of securing an exemption. Trade with the United States has historically been weighted in favour of the U.S., a point Albanese emphasised during the phone call to Trump—a relatively unique position given the current U.S. approach to global trade—and in response, Trump described

Albanese as a *very fine man* and acknowledged that the United States has "one of the few" trade surpluses with Australia, but his promise to give Australia's request "great consideration" remains vague.

The political implications for Albanese are tied to how the Coalition and the mainstream media will interpret a failure to secure an exemption—their responses would be predictably negative—and with a federal election due by May 2025, this is precisely the time when incumbent leaders look to strengthen their standings with policy or diplomatic successes. Failing to secure an agreement would provide fertile ground for his political adversaries, opening the Prime Minister to criticisms that he can't manage the U.S.–Australia relationship.

There is also the broader challenge posed by the unpredictability of President Trump's style of governing, if that's what it can be called. His decisions often appear more *reactive* than *strategic*, and seem to arise from immediate calculations of what might be most politically advantageous to him or to his political MAGA base.

The expectation of results based on rules, longstanding alliances, and careful consultation no longer applies under this president, who is willing to announce or retract sweeping economic policies at whim, and this impulsiveness makes negotiating an exemption fraught with uncertainty: one day, an exemption might be promised or hinted at; the next, a change in the President's mood or priorities could jeopardise that entire arrangement.

TRUMP'S MINDSET AND THE IMPACT ON AUSTRALIA

Trump's unpredictability—and the *purpose* behind this unpredictability—remains the main difficulty for any government attempting to navigate these tariffs, not just Australia. The other consideration is that it is not clear if the stated policy goal of bolstering American steel and aluminium production is achievable in a straightforward way—building new or reviving disused smelters in the United States is a long process that might take twelve months or more, during which time shortages could lead to increased prices for American manufacturers. This outcome would contradict Trump's broader political ambitions for reduced costs and stronger domestic industries, as well as complicating other trade areas, as unpredictability in one policy area could leak into others, potentially prompting more tariffs or retaliatory measures on other products.

From an Australian perspective, the biggest concern is the hit taken by domestic exporters who rely heavily on the United States market. For companies sending the majority of their goods to America, a 25 per cent tariff would make them uncompetitive unless they can quickly find alternative markets. However, as seen in the disrupted trade with China caused by former prime minister Scott Morrison and Peter Dutton in 2020, repositioning to new markets is rarely quick or painless. The complex web of global commerce means exporters need stable, predictable trading environments to manage supply chains and plan for the future. When major partners install sudden barriers, even a moderate drop in export volumes can cascade through entire industries.

Trump's style also highlights how different he is from his predecessors who, even if controversial in their policies—such as George W. Bush—tended to operate within a more defined framework of institutional checks and long-term strategic thinking. For all of his failings, Bush as least listened to a cross-section of quality advisers and recognised the importance of ongoing alliances. In contrast, Trump's style is more theatrical and capricious, leveraging unpredictability in an attempt to extract concessions.

Yet this kind of brinkmanship could also backfire: Mexico and Canada have demonstrated that standing firm does not always result in worse terms. Trump ended up settling for essentially the same deals with these countries, loudly declaring victory in an arrangement that scarcely changed from the previous framework. This pattern suggests that Trump thrives on conflict to project strength, even when the outcomes remain unchanged. In practical terms, that means Australia's best strategy may well be to remain steadfast, continue negotiations, and present a clear-eyed view of the mutual benefits that come from open markets—but also understanding that final decisions could hinge on a whim, an impulse, or a fleeting political calculation by Trump.

All of this makes the current environment precarious for trade partners such as Australia. Just as trade can help maintain positive relationships between countries, it can also become a weapon wielded by leaders who see diplomatic norms as inconveniences that can be easily discarded. While it might be tempting to ignore the theatrics and histrionics of the White House, the potential damage to export industries—and to Prime Minister Albanese's political standing—can't be so easily dismissed.

RETHINKING AUSTRALIA'S SUBSERVIENCE TO THE UNITED STATES

Australia's deep alignment with the United States has long been anchored in shared post-war interests spanning trade, defence, intelligence, and broader geopolitical objectives. Successive governments in Canberra have reinforced these bonds through significant policy commitments and major defence arrangements, sometimes at substantial financial cost with little direct reciprocal benefit beyond broad declarations of "strong" partnerships and media opportunities for political leaders. Decisions such as the recent AUKUS payment of \$US500 million facilitated by Defence Minister Richard Marles show how concessions—and payments—are consistently provided in the hope of preserving good relations and avoiding any appearance of disloyalty. In many ways, this dynamic is reminiscent of the presentation of tributes and gifts to medieval rulers—gold, jewellery or exotic animals—offered more out of obsequious obligation and fear of disfavour than from a balanced negotiation between equals.

The dilemma is not that Australia should seek to jettison its alliance with the United States; the strategic value is clear (somewhat), and there is little appetite to unravel decades of cooperation between the two countries. The question is whether Australian leaders should be more steadfast in articulating national interests, rather than kowtowing to the United States. Time and again, Canberra has matched or even surpassed Washington's requests, whether by allocating funds, supporting military interventions, or echoing foreign policy positions, especially in the Middle East. In return, direct practical benefits have been elusive. This pattern of behaviour suggests that while the alliance's ideological relationship remains strong—rooted in democratic values and a shared history—a default position of unquestioning support places Australia on the back foot whenever disputes arise.

The example of New Zealand in the 1980s is important in this context, when they were suspended from the ANZUS Treaty over visiting rights for nuclear-powered ships and submarines—in 1984, NZ Prime Minister David Lange enacted legislation to keep New Zealand a nuclear-free zone—and this incident has shown that a smaller country can maintain a strong relationship with the United States and its allies, yet still carve out policies that reflect domestic priorities and strategic judgments.

By acting with a measure of independent resolve, New Zealand managed to reinforce its sovereignty—and national dignity—without irreparably damaging trade or relationships with the United States. Australia could adopt a similar stance, promoting the alliance when it aligns with national objectives but drawing clearer lines when pressured to make concessions of dubious benefit, which is what AUKUS essentially is.

The concern, of course, is that Trump—already known for taking perceived slights personally—might retaliate by imposing or refusing to remove tariffs, just because he doesn't like Albanese. Or for comments made by Kevin Rudd. Or Scott Morrison. Or for some other spurious reason. Yet that risk is not a permanent condition, and even within the United States, political support for Trump's combative approach is far from unanimous. Tying national interests too tightly to the impulses of one individual—albeit the President of the United States—can hamper longer-term strategic thinking, especially given the shifting nature of contemporary American politics. A leadership that is consistently ready to meet every whim with acquiescence risks undervaluing its own bargaining position and squandering the chance to negotiate more durable outcomes.

A recalibrated Australian foreign policy doesn't need to reject a longstanding ally. Instead, it would reflect a clear-eyed understanding that large powers act primarily in their own interests, no matter what type of assurances of friendship are provided. If securing an exemption from the steel and aluminium tariffs becomes purely *transactional*—as it undoubtedly will be—Australia should feel entitled to drive a harder bargain and this might even earn greater respect in the long term. The reflexive deference currently on display, however, suggests an unbalanced relationship that will continue to exact a price unless Australia chooses to govern its affairs with the same conviction it has often shown in other facets of its global engagement.

***

MANUFACTURED OUTRAGE: THE MEDIA'S ALLIANCE WITH ZIONISTS

24 February 2025

A recent incident in Sydney's Inner West has raised many questions about the manipulation and creation of anti-Semitic incidents in Australia by right-wing extremists and agitators. Ofir Birenbaum, a prominent member of the controversial Australian Jewish Association and a known Zionist provocateur, attempted to manufacture an incident at the Cairo Takeaway cafe in Newtown where, wearing a Star of David cap, he tried to provoke a hostile or anti-Semitic reaction that could be captured by *Daily Telegraph* reporters waiting outside.

The goal was to create a sensational story about rampant anti-Semitism in Australia, push a narrative of an under-protected Jewish community and, in turn, continue to launch political attacks against the Labor government. Yet in Newtown—a suburb well-known for its diversity and inclusive culture—the provocation didn't succeed: Birenbaum's actions were met with disinterest, and a *best to leave this dickhead alone* approach. No matter what he tried, staff and patrons at the cafe simply went about their day. Consequently, not only did the *Daily Telegraph* fail to get the inflammatory story they were after, it also exposed the larger dynamics between right-wing media outlets and extremist pro-Israel activists who collaborate to manipulate public sentiment.

The issue goes beyond this one incident: Rupert Murdoch's media empire has a long record of backing pro-Israel positions and narratives, with coverage that is often supportive of the Israel's government and policies, leaving no room for more nuanced or critical perspectives. Such one-sided messaging deepens community tensions, stirs up Islamophobia, and delegitimises anyone critical of Israel's policies by painting them as prejudiced or anti-Semitic.

In many cases, it works because they exploit the fear of anti-Semitism—which, of course, is a very real phenomenon—and exaggerate or manufacture incidents to heighten public anxiety. This approach not only fuels prejudice toward other communities, particularly Muslim and Middle Eastern Australians, but it also distracts from legitimate discussions about the Israeli government's controversial policies, such as settlement expansion in the West Bank, the unresolved status of the occupied territories, or the attempts of genocide in Gaza.

Birenbaum's failed attempt to manufacture outrage reveals how much of a miscalculation it can be to try such a stunt in an area like Newtown, where cultural diversity is part of everyday life. Here, anyone is generally free to dress and express themselves as they please, religious symbols included. Ironically, his actions inadvertently shone a light on exactly how certain factions are trying to foment hatred, and strengthened the resolve to reject such divisive tactics in the process.

Beyond this incident, there is a concern about a wider pattern of racially motivated violence and intimidation. Recent incidents, such as two women being assaulted in Epping in Melbourne—one of them pregnant and choked with her own hijab—remind us that hate crimes and racism of all types must be taken seriously. The police response to these cases was relatively slow, which raises other questions about biases in law enforcement.

What emerges from all of this is how particular media operators and ideologically driven individuals can collude to manufacture controversies for political advantage. Broader debates about Israel—whether it pertains to its establishment, the 1948 or 1967 borders, the ongoing violent settlement and policies, or genocide in Gaza—need to occur in an environment where all voices can be heard, without fear of being automatically labeled as hostile to an entire group of people.

ONE-SIDED POLITICAL RESPONSES HAVE AIDED THE OUTRAGE

Australia's political leaders often position themselves as staunch opponents of racial or religious hatred, yet their actions frequently reveal a very different story. In the aftermath of this failed provocation in Newtown, the conspicuous silence from key figures, including the Prime Minister, Anthony Albanese, shows how officials can shrink from manipulative media narratives—especially when they originate from powerful outlets.

The fact that this incident took place in Albanese's own electorate of Grayndler without so much as a public statement of support for the workers at the Cairo Takeaway cafe speaks volumes. Political leaders are busy people, but they often find the time to comment on a range of local matters, and it would not have been unreasonable for the Prime Minister or even the NSW Premier to express concern or, at the very least, check on the concerns of a business drawn into a media stunt. That nothing of the sort happened fuels the double standard, where criticism or scrutiny of certain individuals or groups is all but off-limits and the political class mostly looks away.

It seems that nobody in government wants to risk the wrath of a media apparatus that holds the power to amplify or dampen political fortunes. As a result, the government's message to the public is one of tacit acceptance, suggesting that if powerful media barons or well-connected interest groups orchestrate disinformation, officials will quietly stand aside.

The weakness of political leadership is also apparent when sensational, potentially harmful media stories go unchallenged. An example of this is the *Sydney Morning Herald*'s report about a caravan allegedly loaded with explosives on the outskirts of Sydney and a supposed list of Jewish targets. Their alarmist headlines—which were then magnified in other media outlets—implied Australia was on the verge of a serious terrorist plot, but the follow-up revealed that the explosives were decades old, likely to be inactive, and that the "list" of targets just simply didn't exist. Someone had just made the story up.

Despite the story's debunking, there was no *mea culpa* from either the newspaper or public officials who might have questioned the narrative's origins. Instead, the correction was buried, and the fleeting panic it caused lingered in the public consciousness. Such episodes show how easy it is for the media to manufacture panic that benefits specific agendas, with little pushback from political leaders who ought to defend the public's right to fair and accurate information.

By tolerating these fabrications, or at least failing to challenge them, political leaders are enabling a climate of mounting tension. When false or exaggerated stories about anti-Semitic plots are circulated, it leads to inflated fears within Jewish communities. Meanwhile, some in the broader public grow cynical, feeling that accusations of bigotry and hatred are wielded more like political tools than genuine concerns—which then dilutes the seriousness of real incidents of anti-Semitism.

This same dynamic spills over into other forms of prejudice, including Islamophobia, contributing to an atmosphere where the term "hate crime" can be weaponised for political point-scoring rather than addressing actual offenses. Ultimately, those who face genuine discrimination, whether they be Jewish, Muslim, or any other group—are left in a precarious position, unprotected by political leaders who are more interested in appeasement rather than principled leadership.

The real tragedy here is that such timid political responses harm both majority and minority communities. They allow extremist viewpoints—those that genuinely do advocate racist or hateful ideologies, such as News Corporation—to flourish amid the loud noises of manufactured outrage. By not calling out hoaxes out with the same force used against legitimate cases of discrimination, the government places all of these incidents on the same level, fostering public confusion and weakening the seriousness of legitimate concerns. This environment emboldens individuals who truly harbor anti-Semitic or Islamophobic sentiments, giving them more credibility than they should ever have. It also undermines the possibility of critical debate about foreign and domestic policy related to Israel, Palestine, and other contentious issues.

What is needed is simple yet it remains elusive: principled leadership willing to hold media organisations accountable, regardless of the political risk, combined with a commitment to confronting bigotry in all its forms. When politicians refuse to waver in the face of powerful media proprietors, they send a clear message that weaponising hatred for clicks, sales, or political favour will not be tolerated. Conversely, by not doing anything about these issues, it suggests that these political leaders either condone the behaviour, or are simply too weak and lack the courage to call out these manipulations, regardless of the source.

THE SILENT STRINGS: HOW THE ISRAEL LOBBY MUTES CRITICISM

One of the other parts of the ongoing manipulation in Australia's public debate is the growing list of individuals who find their voices muzzled the moment they challenge or question Israel's policies. From the journalist Antoinette Lattouf to the academic Tim Anderson, and now the artist Khaled Sabsabi, whose commission at the 2026 Venice Biennale was withdrawn by Creative Australia, each example shows a pattern of swift and disproportionate retaliation. Instead of open dialogue or genuine engagement with the substance of their critiques, these people have faced professional setbacks, terminations, and erasure from cultural and academic institutions.

The rationale is almost always vague—somehow "offensive" work or "controversial" statements—while the real story, as many suspect, is that a small, well-connected lobby has exerted influence behind the scenes, usually through threats of withdrawing funding or other retaliations. When art containing images of the Palestinian flag is quietly censored—the National Art Gallery in Canberra censored the tapestry created by the art collective SaVĀge K'lub—or individuals are dropped from high-profile exhibitions without transparent explanations, it's obvious that the criticism of Israel is being relegated to the margins in a supposedly free society.

What makes this trend unacceptable is that it dismantles the very principles that Australian democracy claims to hold dear. The nature of academic inquiry is supposed to be rigorous, involving a contest of ideas tested against facts and peer review. If a professor calls Israel an apartheid state—as

Tim Anderson did in 2018—a proper response should emerge through research and debate rather than abrupt dismissal.

The same principle applies to the arts; creative expression often provokes discomfort or controversy, and that is precisely its job. By punishing artists who reflect on real-world conflicts, cultural institutions abandon their commitment to diverse perspectives. In these acts of censorship or "quiet removals", officials are placating a tiny but influential lobby, stifling conversation on issues that deeply affect Australia's multicultural population. Meanwhile, the broader public is left wondering why certain topics are off-limits and who decides that some viewpoints must vanish without explanation.

This climate is evolving into a modern-day McCarthyism, in which the smallest suspicion of being "too critical" of Israel triggers punitive measures. For those who stand up for Palestinians, it can feel like a precarious balancing act. Rather than fostering a safe environment for legitimate dissent, Australia's institutions are sending a message: *speak out and you will be removed*. The result inhibits not only controversial or provocative voices but also anyone who might support them. Eventually, public debate becomes sterile, absent of the kind of fearless, critical thought that marks a robust and healthy democracy. And this, ultimately, is not good for *any* democracy.

Yet this level of censorship, even if it might be effective in the short term, rarely silences an idea *forever*. The anger it generates often leads to stronger, more unified calls for change. As more people notice the removal of dissenting voices, they begin to question the motives and the power structures behind such decisions. Although censorship on behalf of the state of Israel may not be on the scale of the United States, where media consolidation and lobbying are furiously ridiculous, bordering on fascism, the echoes in Australia are loud enough to raise alarm.

It's unlikely to happen, but this is the moment that demands courage from those who occupy positions of influence, whether in government, media, academia, or the arts. People who promote free speech and the right to critique power must be willing to protect those who offer inconvenient truths or unpopular perspectives. The irony is that open debate would likely strengthen Australia's institutions; it would give communities—Jewish, Muslim, or otherwise—more confidence that concerns and criticisms can be aired without fear of reprisal and the refusal to engage openly simply breeds more mistrust.

No matter how strong the attempt to silence critics, the fundamental issues remain: the complex reality of the Israel–Palestine conflict, the consequences of foreign policy decisions, and the moral questions raised by longstanding military occupations, genocide and human rights abuses. Suppressing discussion about these matters only heightens divisions, disenfranchises the marginalised, and allows genuine extremism to grow in the shadows, such as the extremism that is promoted by News Corporation.

Australia's best defence against imported hatred and internal strife is a forthright commitment to democratic values—ones that do not kotow to pressure from any lobby, no matter how well-funded or influential. It doesn't require additional protection, just application of the laws *as they exist*: protecting those who challenge entrenched power structures, insisting on transparency in decision-making, and standing up for the free flow of ideas—even when doing this poses a risk. Only then can a functional, pluralistic Australia thrive, unburdened by the question of whose voices are being silenced, and why.

***

AUSTRALIA NEEDS TO SHIFT AWAY FROM TRUMP'S INSTABILITY

3 March 2025

The United States, once considered a beacon of international diplomacy and domestic stability—for many people, but not all—is now demonstrating inconsistencies and alarmingly unpredictable behaviour that is becoming unsettling for both its closest allies and the global community at large. Australia's changing perceptions of the AUKUS agreement serves as an example of how Washington's shifting allegiances and perplexing policy decisions are eroding international confidence.

The recent decision by the United States to vote with seventeen other countries against a United Nations resolution calling for a comprehensive, just, and lasting peace in Ukraine has stunned many observers, especially in light of the global support Ukraine has received over the past three years. Suddenly, the United States has aligned itself with a small group of nations characterised by authoritarianism, extremist right-wing behaviour, or other forms of political repression, including apartheid (Israel) and this kind of alignment is a departure from the traditional American positioning, where partnering with or being backed by these kinds of regimes would have been unthinkable. Certainly, the Ukraine–Russia war is complex, based on many historical, economic and political factors, but the swift change by the U.S. has surprised many observers.

Even more troubling is the effort by the United States to negotiate access to rare minerals in Ukrainian territories currently under Russian control while simultaneously trying to court the Ukrainian government for a deal of its own which, based on the events over the weekend in the Oval Office where Donald Trump and Senator J.D. Vance did their best to publicly humiliate Ukrainian President Volodymyr Zelenskyy, is now unlikely to happen.

Far from maintaining a predictable framework of foreign relations, the United States now exhibits the hallmarks of an aggressive fascist state. As these trends accelerate, the ramifications for allied nations like Australia are becoming apparent: the bonds once grounded in shared values and mutual respect may be unravelling under the weight of an unpredictable Washington.

This unpredictability is further magnified by the precarious nature of the current U.S. administration. Past administrations—however flawed—at least possessed a certain degree of organisation and expertise capable of limiting the potential damage of rash decisions. The Trump *Mark II* government lacks sufficient depth in foreign policy knowledge and remains prone to confusing shifts in direction. The dismissal of seasoned advisors, replaced by those short on both practical experience and coherent vision but an unquestioning loyalty to Trump, has produced an environment in which critical decisions are made impulsively, often contingent on the president's audience at any given moment. This type of governance causes allies to question the reliability of American commitments, fuelling concerns that high-stakes international agreements can be undermined by domestic U.S. political pressure or simply cast aside on a whim.

Now, with a government stacked with conspiracy theorists, untested media figures, and individuals seemingly motivated by ever-shifting impulses—even a *podcaster*—the United States appears unable to sustain even the veneer of coherent policy. This chaos magnifies risks for allies who rely on American leadership and consistency and there is now a genuine alarm over how easily joint ventures can dissolve, how fast treaties might be discarded, and how arbitrarily the United States might upend previously secure alliances. For a nation such as Australia, caught in the crosscurrents of international power politics, the situation poses difficult dilemmas about whether continued strategic dependence on Washington remains sensible or even viable in the long run.

A looming question for Australia, and for much of the world, is whether the United States has entered a new stage of internal decline coupled with external belligerence—an inward fracturing coinciding with erratic expansions of power. Allies must decide if they can still consider themselves part of a principled alliance where values and strategy align, or if it is time to re-evaluate the alliance altogether. The uncertainty and instability coming from Washington has the potential to shake the foundations of existing geopolitical structures, and the urgency to reassess engagements and treaties has become more urgent.

AUSTRALIA'S DILEMMA IN A WORLD OF SHAKEN CONFIDENCE

Australia's concerns over whether the United States would genuinely honour its defence commitments in the event of an invasion have resurfaced with renewed intensity. Prime Minister Anthony Albanese's recent assertion that Australia must maintain self-reliance despite the ANZUS security pact illustrates a deepening unease, a realisation that treaty obligations on paper do not necessarily translate into consistent, reliable assistance on the ground. Fortunately, these obligations have never been tested but how certain could Australia be that the United States would offer support in the unlikely event of an invasion?

The Prime Minister has emphasised the critical importance of national sovereignty and pointed out that while the United States is a valued ally, Australia must remain prepared to protect its own interests. Skepticism about Washington's support is understandable; after all, American actions have previously exposed the fragility of "rock-solid" accords. The free trade agreement between the two nations did not stop the U.S. from imposing tariffs on Australian steel and aluminium—an unsettling precedent that raises questions about how other alliances might be disregarded should geopolitical pressures suddenly shift.

Amid these anxieties over security, global power dynamics are evolving at a rapid pace. The continuing conflict between Russia and Ukraine, already marred by territorial disputes, historical grievances, and illegal invasions, has become a contest of competing narratives. Where once Russia was deemed the sole aggressor, figures like Trump now openly accuse Zelenskyy of dictatorship, blaming *him* for a war that was long framed as Russia's doing. One moment, Zelenskyy was depicted as a heroic defender of national sovereignty; the next, he is subjected to the public humiliation—in one instance, *for not wearing a suit*—in the Oval Office by Trump and Senator Vance. The head-turning of these contradictory messages is now symbolic of how American discourse can change abruptly, leaving allies and observers alike to wonder which version of events aligns with underlying reality—or if any of it does at all.

The broader significance of the U.S. adopting volatile stances extends beyond Ukraine. Washington's purported willingness to forge backdoor resource deals in Russian-occupied Ukrainian territory has sown fresh discord in diplomatic circles. Such behaviour, coupled with strident denunciations of long-standing partners one day and conciliatory overtures the next, has contributed to a sense that the United States is not only an active destabiliser but one embracing tendencies historically associated with fascist regimes.

What was once a superpower that championed a particular vision of democracy and international norms seems increasingly driven by inward-facing populism and fractious domestic agendas. This unpredictability—and unhinged inconsistency—shifts the terrain for countries dependent on the U.S. security umbrella, especially Australia, which must now consider whether an America inclined toward fluid realignment can truly be relied upon in a moment of existential crisis.

The spectre of U.S. unreliability plays neatly into the strategic ambitions of adversaries. Figures such as the President of Russia, Vladimir Putin, a former Cold War operative with a long-standing aspiration to erode American influence, must be relishing this chaos. Whether fuelled by Russian interference in U.S. elections, social media misinformation campaigns, or larger machinations behind the scenes, an America consumed by domestic upheaval provides great opportunities for historical geopolitical rivals to advance their own interests. Australian policymakers, looking on from afar, can't afford to ignore these shifts or cling to outdated assumptions rooted in pre-2001 mindsets. The cascading consequences of the 9/11 era still reverberate nearly a quarter-century later, yet today's global environment also presents a distinctly new breed of instability—one that merges Cold War tensions with modern propaganda tools, with the United States both shaped by and shaping the chaos.

Each of these factors converges on the unnerving possibility that if real conflict ever erupted on Australia's shores, the U.S. response might be decided not by any enduring sense of alliance or moral obligation but by the political turbulence of the moment—and inherent American *self-interest*. Nations that once could bank on American leadership face a predicament: *join the chaos*, resist it, or distance themselves altogether. Australia, given its long history of alignment with Washington, may soon be forced to make a choice that was almost unimaginable even just a few months ago, as global fault lines shift and alliances that once seemed monolithic suddenly look far more transient.

WHY CANCELLING AUKUS COULD SECURE AUSTRALIA'S FUTURE

Australia's alliance with the United States, once seen as unbreakable, faces a moment of reckoning. The AUKUS deal was signed in 2021 as a monumental security arrangement promising to transform Australia's naval capabilities and fortify its strategic posture in an unpredictable global landscape. Yet the deal's lack of transparency and the speed at which it was concluded have left the Australian public and many experts questioning whether the project truly serves the national interest. The precedent set by scrapping the French submarine contract—as a result of the AUKUS agreement and resulting in a multi-billion-dollar payout for which Australia received little benefit—shows that foreign-policy decisions can be reversed when they no longer align with core objectives. Daring to reconsider the AUKUS agreement, especially given the unprecedented turbulence coming out of Washington, might be the more prudent path.

Australia should rely more on relationships with nations in its own neighbourhood, ensuring stronger diplomatic ties with regional partners such as Indonesia (and China) while exploring collaborative ventures with countries less entangled in the domestic chaos now gripping the United States. That chaos has raised troubling questions about Washington's ability to deliver on its security obligations: tariffs have demonstrated how swiftly a partnership can be undermined when the U.S. shifts its policy priorities and concerns about the American political climate drifting toward fascist and authoritarian tendencies only magnify the urgency of looking elsewhere for reliable partnerships.

Leaving the AUKUS agreement would neither be easy nor cost-free, but Australia's economic and security frameworks might benefit more from cultivating a pragmatic distance from its traditional ally—at least until the U.S. regains a semblance of stability. The key lies in governments engaging with the electorate honestly: a government bold enough to reconsider AUKUS could present a compelling case that stepping away from an increasingly erratic partner is not an abandonment of security but a redefinition of it.

By reshaping foreign policy, Australia might not just avoid entanglement in conflicts it never sought; it may also discover that a more balanced approach to its regional relationships offers greater long-term stability.

***

THE CRACKS IN THE EMPIRE: AMERICA'S ALLIES DRIFTING AWAY

10 March 2025

Most of the Western world is preparing for a shift in their relationship with the United States, as the once-unshakable alliances that defined global politics in the post-war and Cold War eras are beginning to erode, replaced by a cautious pragmatism among America's closest partners. The assumption that Washington would always be the uncontested leader of the free world is being reconsidered as allies—quietly or openly—recalibrate their strategic positions.

The dynamic between the United States and its allies is changing dramatically, and trade disputes, inconsistent foreign policies, domestic upheaval, and an erratic approach to international commitments have led these partners to reassess their long-standing ties. Canada has also responded with its own economic measures, imposing tariffs in retaliation.

Its Prime Minister (as of last week) Justin Trudeau has gone beyond traditional diplomatic protests, urging Canadians to personally disengage from American economic and cultural products, when he suggested "we're going to choose not to go on vacation in Florida... we're going to choose to try to buy Canadian products and forego American products... and, we're probably going to keep booing the American anthem." These remarks were made not from a fringe activist but from the leader of a G7 nation—a clear sign that even America's closest neighbours are growing weary of Washington's shifting priorities.

The British government is firming up its stance on NATO, evidence of its frustration with the American leadership, and in the post-Brexit landscape, is increasingly seeking to redefine its role within the Western alliance.

Yet, despite these global undercurrents, Australia remains notably silent. Unlike Canada and Britain, where leaders have at least acknowledged changing realities, both the Australian government and the opposition continue to echo the same unwavering rhetoric about the U.S. alliance. The usual platitudes regarding American leadership are repeated with near-religious fervour, while the rest of the world watches and wonders—*why are they doing that?*

For decades, Australia has been a steadfast ally of the United States, but history shows that this loyalty has not always been reciprocated. Australia followed the U.S. into Vietnam under questionable circumstances, joined wars in Iraq—twice, despite widespread skepticism—and committed forces to Afghanistan, a conflict that, in hindsight, offered little strategic benefit to Canberra or, perhaps, even to the United States.

Yet, Canberra's alignment with American interests is like an instinctive reflex action, as if questioning the alliance is taboo and diplomatically unpalatable. This loyalty contrasts with the aggressive approaches of other Western allies, who are reasserting their independence on global security and economic policy.

Despite these realities, the shifting nature of the U.S.–Australia relationship is downplayed at home. This alliance *should be* a major political issue—a topic of national debate and even an election-defining discussion—but it *isn't*. Instead, it remains cloaked in an aura of unbreakable commitment and clichés, ignoring a growing sense that Washington is no longer the reliable partner it once was and that this situation has changed rapidly.

As the world increasingly moves beyond automatic deference to American leadership, Australia is one of the few nations still clinging to the old but changing order. But for how much longer? With U.S. influence in flux, the question isn't whether the alliance will face challenges, but *when*.

WHY A SUBMISSIVE AUSTRALIA WON'T QUESTION THE ALLIANCE

Anthony Albanese's careful approach to foreign policy is nothing new. As a Prime Minister who values caution and steadiness, he has done all he can to keep Australia's alignment with the United States beyond debate. But at what cost? Australia's subservience to Washington has become a self-imposed straightjacket, preventing any meaningful discussion of what the nation actually gains from this long-standing arrangement.

The leader of the opposition, Peter Dutton, meanwhile, would never contemplate opposing U.S. policy, as his instincts and behaviours mirror hardline Trumpian Republican stances. The Coalition opposition, much like Labor, seems intent on avoiding any debate over U.S.–Australia relations, preferring to stick to the grandiose talking points about the "unbreakable" bond between the two nations. Yet this tactic is becoming less tenable. The geopolitical landscape is evolving, and sooner or later, Australia will have to confront an uncomfortable question: beyond serving American strategic interests, what exactly does this alliance achieve for Australia?

Australia's role as Washington's obedient partner is well documented. Pine Gap? Created in 1966 without hesitation, and even led indirectly to the dismissal of prime minister Gough Whitlam, after he had considered closing the base down in 1975 with the completion of the initial nine-year treaty. Troops to Iraq and Afghanistan? No resistance and presented without debate. AUKUS? A staggering $368 billion for nuclear submarines that may never be delivered. The pattern is clear: the U.S. demands, and Australia complies. This is not a partnership in the true sense—it is deference, with Canberra appearing more eager to placate Washington than asserting its own national interests.

Despite this track record, foreign policy is largely absent from Australia's political conversations. It's rarely discussed during election campaigns, partly because neither major party sees any benefit in doing so and the last time foreign affairs took centre stage in an Australian election was in 2001, under the shadow of the 9/11 attacks in New York. Since then, talk of Australia's global position has been side-lined, and political leaders have prioritised domestic concerns which, of course, is understandable—domestic concerns will always trump international issues when it comes to elections in Australia. But that silence can't last forever.

The United States is growing more unpredictable by the day, yet Australia remains unwilling to acknowledge it. While Canada adopts retaliatory economic measures and Britain quietly distances itself from certain American military positions, Australia clings to habit. Even the Labor Party, historically more inclined to question blind loyalty to Washington, avoids breaking ranks, perhaps in the fear is that the Coalition could exploit any deviation on national security grounds.

Still, Australia is not without leverage. Though it may lack Canada's economic might or Britain's global weight, it has options—particularly concerning AUKUS. This was a hastily brokered under the unpopular Scott Morrison government in 2021, and even Donald Trump seemed to be unaware of it when asked about it last week.

If a future U.S. administration deprioritises or cancels it, Australia will have little to show for a massive financial outlay. Even Elbridge Colby, Trump's nominee for undersecretary of defense, recently suggested selling submarines to Australia under AUKUS would be "crazy" if tensions between China and Taiwan arise. Renegotiating—or withdrawing altogether from the AUKUS deal—would not be an act of rebellion but a rational move in the country's own interest.

The British Prime Minister, Keir Starmer, has already shown that challenging U.S. policy need not destroy alliances. His public support for Ukraine, despite America's antagonism towards President Volodymyr Zelenskyy, proves that a nation can maintain strong ties with Washington while exercising its own judgment, and Australia has every right to do likewise. The concern that any challenge to U.S. policy might lead to political backlash ignores the reality that many voters are ambivalent or would actually favour a reassessment: according to the Pew Research Center, 60 per cent of Australians in 2024 had an *unfavourable* view of the United States, a number which would have dropped even further since the inauguration of Trump in early 2025.

The real question is whether anyone in Canberra has the courage to act. Maintaining the status quo—quietly accepting every American directive while pretending there's nothing to discuss—may seem like the easiest option, but it's just an illusion. As global circumstances change, this silence will break—whether through political upheaval, electoral realignment, or pure necessity. The only uncertainty is whether Australia will set its own course or simply react when it can no longer avoid doing so.

AUSTRALIA MUST STAND UP AND RECLAIM ITS NATIONAL INTEREST

For too long, Australia has walked on eggshells with its relationship with the United States, as though any minor step away from a complete alignment would be catastrophic. But standing up to Washington need not be reckless; instead, it would affirm Australia's sovereignty. Far from weakening the alliance, it could bolster it by establishing a more balanced and transparent foundation. Politically, challenging the U.S. might even prove advantageous.

Given this situation, what is the Albanese government so afraid of? The U.S. is a powerful country but it's not invincible. Its leadership grows more chaotic, and its strategic goals shift unpredictably. Blindly adhering to Washington—despite self-destructive or counterproductive policies—is not sound diplomacy; it's *submission*, and no self-respecting country should be placing itself in this position.

Honesty is what the alliance lacks the most. Simon Crean, the then opposition leader in 2003, made that clear when he told U.S. President George W. Bush that true friends can disagree, emphasising that "honesty is the foundation stone of that great Australian value, mateship". That kind of candour has been missing from Australia's foreign policy for years.

No one expects Albanese to confront the United States aggressively, even if he should. No one is suggesting he threatens to close Pine Gap in protest over tariffs or military policy which, as Whitlam discovered in 1975, could be politically dangerous move for him. But acknowledging that the alliance is deeply skewed would be a start. Whether it's AUKUS, the Iraq War, Afghanistan, or trade disputes, Australia often bends to American demands in exchange for little more than vague assurances of security and partnership.

This lack of transparency extends beyond defence matters to the broader political landscape. Politicians, the media, and the political establishment rarely address the reality that the U.S. often treats Australia as a subordinate. When Western Australian Premier Roger Cook candidly called U.S. Vice-President J.D. Vance a "knob" and suggested that Trump represents uncertainty—if not *outright danger*—he gave voice to what many people already believe. The fact that this moment of honesty was so surprising illustrates the deep-seated reluctance to discuss Australia's true status in this alliance.

If a state premier can speak frankly, why can't the Prime Minister? Why can't federal leaders question American policies that don't align with Australian interests? Why must major defence and foreign policy decisions be rubber-stamped by Washington before Canberra can even debate them?

Australia's alleged lack of leverage is often cited as an excuse for inaction, but that rationale doesn't hold water. Britain has shown that even the closest U.S. allies can stand firm when they choose. Canada has levied tariffs in defiance of American economic pressure. Smaller nations across Europe and the Pacific have asserted their independence when dealing with Washington.

There are many things Australia could do. It could rethink its participation in American military ventures and avoid being dragged into conflicts irrelevant to its own security. It could use its influence in the Pacific and Southeast Asia to balance China on Australia's terms, rather than uncritically following U.S. directives, which ultimately damage Australia's diplomatic, economic and political interests.

Stepping away from automatic deference is not disloyalty; it's an act of *self-respect*. It would signal to Washington that Australia is an equal partner, not a subservient ally. Crucially, it could also be politically advantageous—the Australian electorate is far from oblivious to the dysfunction in Washington.

Before long, the U.S. alliance will inevitably become a national issue, as global events are changing too rapidly for America's dominance to continue unchecked. The real question is whether Australia will redefine its global role proactively or wait until circumstances force it to respond. If it waits, it risks missing a critical chance to reshape its position on its own terms. If it acts, Australia may finally gain a more balanced and honest partnership with the United States—one that primarily serves Australian interests.

***

MANUFACTURING FEAR: FAKE TERROR AS A POLITICAL WEAPON

17 March 2025

There was a new development during the week in the widely-reported terrorist caravan plot and threat from January—it didn't actually exist. The fabricated nature of this alleged attack—a caravan was found on the outskirts of Sydney supposedly filled with *live* explosives to be used against synagogues—was clear to those who were willing to scrutinise this incident and ask the right questions. Yet, raising these doubts at the time was met with accusations of antisemitism, which provided a convenient deflection from the larger question: *who* orchestrated fabrication, and *why*?

Who knew that the plot was likely a hoax, and when did they know? It seems that the leader of the opposition, Peter Dutton, *did know* but either deliberately avoided a security briefing in January or has denied receiving a briefing when he actually *did*. The Australian Federal Police were aware at the time that the incident was highly likely to be a hoax but kept this information under wraps to avoid jeopardising their investigation into the origins of the threat which, on face value, seems to be a reasonable proposition. But if Dutton was aware early on that the incident was not real, why did he persist in pushing the narrative of a terror threat for political gain?

Throughout February, Dutton continued to exploit this "attack" to fuel anxiety within the Jewish community and amplify a rising tide of antisemitic behaviour. He repeatedly raised his alarmist rhetoric in Parliament and scored political points by constantly framing the government as *weak on security*, attempting to boost the Liberal Party's 'tough on crime and terror' position while pushing the message that the Albanese government is incompetent in handling national security matters.

Despite the confirmation from the shadow Home Affairs Minister, Senator James Paterson, that the Liberal Party *had* received a security briefing, Dutton continues to deny any personal knowledge of the hoax at the time. It stretches credibility to believe that the party leader would be left out of such a crucial briefing on national security and if Dutton was truly uninformed, it then raises questions about why his own party failed to update him. More likely, he *was* well aware but saw an opportunity for political exploitation.

The complicity in this deception extends beyond federal politics. NSW Premier Chris Minns was also privy to the information that this incident was a hoax, yet his government proceeded to fast-track draconian antisemitism legislation in response. While combating antisemitism is, without question, and issue that needs to be stamped out, Australia already has robust legal frameworks at both state and federal levels to address racism and hate speech. The speed with which these new laws were introduced raises another question: was it forced by political agendas rather than a genuine concern for Jewish communities?

Even more troubling is the sphere of influence held by extremist Zionist organisations and Israel lobby groups in Australia, who have long pushed for increased criminalisation of criticism against the state of Israel. If this legal path continues, even journalists and commentators discussing these developments—let alone questioning them or discussing the issues of concern in an article such as this one—may soon find themselves at risk of prosecution. The effect on free speech is not speculative paranoia; it's a clear direction in which legal frameworks are shifting.

The question of who ultimately benefits from these legislative changes and heightened public fear is critical. If the fabricated plot had instead targeted a mosque, a church, a Hindu temple, or any other religious institution, the political response would have been vastly different—we've seen that happen time and time again. The selective outrage and opportunistic exploitation of this event reflects a broader strategy: the manipulation of public fear for political and ideological gain.

HOW NSW'S REACTIVE LAWS THREATEN CIVIL LIBERTIES

The consequences of knee-jerk legislation extend far beyond the immediate moment of the political environment in which they were introduced. The NSW government's rapid introduction of these new laws not only have troubling implications—they are damaging to the basic principles of democracy, free speech and civil liberties. These laws were passed, even though Minns knew the threat was a fabrication, raising concerns about the motivations behind them and the longer-term ramifications.

Once a government introduces these kinds of security measures, they are *never* rolled back. Even when such measures are later revealed to have been unnecessary or disproportionate, the act of attempting to repeal them would become a political minefield. Any future government that attempts to amend or remove these laws will inevitably face accusations of enabling antisemitism, even if their only goal is to restore civil liberties eroded under false pretences. This is the insidious trap of reactive policymaking: once embedded, these laws become entrenched, unchallengeable, gradually normalised, and weaponised by groups such as the Israel lobby.

The deeper issue here is that laws passed in response to hysteria or political pressure are rarely about protecting the public at large. Instead, they serve as tools of political leverage for interest groups with a vested stake in controlling public discourse. The new NSW laws effectively set a precedent that elevates one particular type of discrimination above all others, making it more difficult to critique specific political movements or international actions—particularly those related to Israel—without the risk of legal repercussions. This is not about addressing genuine hate crimes, which existing laws already cover, but about reshaping the limits of acceptable political discussion.

Once the state grants itself the power to criminalise certain opinions under the broad banner of "antisemitism", it's only a matter of time before these laws are used in ways that go far beyond their original intent. Activists who protest against the Israeli government's policies may soon find themselves legally silenced, as was the case with the unlawful arrest by U.S. Immigration and Customs Enforcement of the permanent resident and Palestinian student activist, Mahmoud Khalil. Academics engaging in legitimate historical analysis may be accused of incitement. Journalists who dare to investigate the political influence of foreign lobbies could be prosecuted under the very laws designed to combat extremism. This is the creeping authoritarianism that masquerades as moral righteousness, and it is precisely how democratic societies slide toward repression under the guise of protection.

The fact that these laws were introduced following a fabricated event makes the situation more unacceptable. It also raises the question: if laws can be passed based on an event that never actually happened, what else can be legislated into existence? If politicians and lobby groups can manufacture a crisis, weaponise it for political gain, and then cement their advantage through law, the danger is not just restricted to one particular issue—it is to the entire framework of democratic governance.

The broader problem with legislating based on fear is that it plays into the hands of those who thrive on division and control. The Israel lobby, like any powerful political entity, understands the value of creating an atmosphere of perpetual crisis. When the perception of threat is constant, the justification for ever-expanding state powers never disappears. Governments, in turn, benefit from having new tools to suppress dissent, regulate speech, and brand opposition as dangerous. This is why the trend of enacting hyper-specific legislation in response to politically sensitive events is so dangerous—it is not about solving a problem, but about shifting the power dynamics of public discourse in a way that is near impossible to reverse.

The NSW government has set a precedent that will be difficult to undo. Today, the laws are framed around antisemitism; tomorrow, they could be expanded to other forms of political speech. Once you establish the principle that certain criticisms are off-limits under threat of legal action, the logical next step is to broaden the scope. Could criticism of U.S. foreign policy be labeled as "anti-Americanism" and subject to the same restrictions? Could protests against military interventions be categorised as "undermining national security" and shut down? The possibilities are endless once the principle is accepted.

The most glaring irony in all of this is that far from preventing hate speech, laws like these often create the conditions for more resentment and division. When the government is seen as selectively protecting one group's interests over the broader community, it fuels the very animosity it claims to be fighting. The public, sensing that they are being manipulated, becomes increasingly distrustful of official narratives and far from reducing tensions, such measures can push discourse underground, creating a breeding ground for genuine extremism that festers outside of public scrutiny.

PLACATING THE ISRAEL LOBBY, NEGLECTING ISLAMIC COMMUNITIES

The political establishment in Australia has made its allegiances clear. When it comes to support, advocacy, and policy decisions, the Israel lobby enjoys unwavering quick and bipartisan backing, while Palestinian and Islamic communities are usually met with silence, neglect, or outright hostility. From funding allocations to legislative changes, there is a massive imbalance in how these communities are treated and this situation exposes a deeper political reality: Australia's ruling class is willing to serve the interests of Israel and its allies, even at the expense of its own social cohesion.

A Home Affairs report from November 2023 confirmed what many in the Palestinian and Islamic communities had already been feeling for years—there is no place for them in mainstream political discourse. That report warned that the one-sided political support for Israel was creating divisions in Australian society yet, instead of attempting to bridge these divides, both the government and the opposition doubled down, choosing to amplify their commitment to Israel rather than acknowledge or mitigate the social exclusion of Palestinian and Muslim Australians.

The clearest evidence of this bias is the financial support directed toward different communities. Following the October 7 attacks and the subsequent Israeli assault on Gaza, the Australian government provided $7 million to SBS and AAP to "combat misinformation" about Islamic and Palestinian communities. But instead of directing any of that funding to the very communities affected—to organisations on the ground, to Muslim or Palestinian advocacy groups, or to civil society organisations that could offer direct assistance—every cent went into government-approved media narratives. In contrast, $25 million was provided directly to the Executive Council of Australian Jewry, an organisation that actively lobbies for pro-Israel policies in Australia. The message from government could not be clearer: one community is entitled to state-backed advocacy, while the other is deemed a public relations problem to be managed.

This isn't just about money; it's about the broader institutional landscape. Jewish community groups have the full weight of government support behind them, from new antisemitism laws to enhanced security measures, even when the threats they claim to face turn out to be fabricated. Meanwhile, documented Islamophobic attacks have doubled since 2023, and yet there has been no comparable response— no task force, no emergency funding, no high-profile government statements condemning these acts in Parliament.

Why is this happening? The Israel lobby is politically well-organised, well-funded and well-connected to both major political parties, enjoying direct ties to influential figures in media, business and government. And it has the *confidence* and the *swagger* to exploit these relationships. In a recent video exchange, David Adler from the reactionary and aggressive Zionist agitator, Australian Jewish Association, bragged to the Liberal MP, Julian Leeser, that he had compiled a dossier of the "hostile acts by the foreign minister [Penny Wong] and Labor" against Israel and the Jewish community and sent it off to the Israeli Knesset.

In contrast, Palestinian and Muslim advocacy groups have nowhere near the same level of institutional influence and their concerns are routinely dismissed as fringe or inconvenient. Even the most basic acts of solidarity—such as calling for a ceasefire in Gaza—have been met with political cowardice from Labor and outright hostility from the Liberal–National Coalition.

Even when Israel launched one of the most brutal military assaults in recent history, killing at least 46,000 Palestinians, including thousands of children, Australia's political class refused to shift its stance. Instead, it issued weak statements about Israel's *right to defend itself* and repeatedly blocked even symbolic measures of support for Palestinian civilians. This unwavering support continued even as international legal bodies began investigating Israel for war crimes. No such hesitation would have existed if the situation were reversed—if an Arab state were inflicting such mass atrocities, Australia would have been at the forefront of diplomatic condemnations and sanctions.

This is not just an issue of fairness; it is an issue of democracy. A society that selectively protects one group while neglecting or demonising another is not a free society. A government that aligns itself with a powerful foreign-backed lobby at the expense of its own citizens is not acting in the national interest. And a political class that criminalises legitimate criticism while allowing real discrimination to go unaddressed is failing in its most basic responsibilities.

The reality is that this dynamic will not change by itself. The entrenched power of the Israel lobby in Australia ensures that political and media institutions will continue to serve its interests unless a serious challenge to this dominance emerges. This challenge will not come from within the political class—it will have to come from the public, from activists, from independent media, and from the communities that have been abandoned by those who claim to represent them.

Until this changes, the message remains clear: in the eyes of Australia's political establishment, some communities are worth protecting, and others are expendable. The growing anger, frustration, and disillusionment among neglected communities will not simply disappear—it will continue to build, and when it reaches a breaking point, the political class will have no one to blame but itself.

***

HOW SPIN, AMNESIA AND OUTRAGE SKEW THE BUDGET DEBATE

24 March 2025

As Australia edges closer to the federal Budget announcement, the political atmosphere feels subdued and unusually calm—too calm for a nation whose media and political class is addicted to economic alarmism every single day of the week. But beneath the surface, the old ideological machinery is grinding into gear, preparing to unleash the same tired narratives: deficits are *disasters*, surpluses are *sacrosanct*, and the only measure of economic competence is whether the Budget is in the black or red. It's as though the Australian media, in lockstep with conservative politicians, is gearing up to recycle the same well-worn clichés—one that barely survives a moment of honest scrutiny.

The prevailing narrative is clear: when Labor runs a deficit—which is expected this week—it is cast as the end of the economic world, if the not the *world itself*, a fiscal apocalypse borne of incompetence, recklessness, and spendthrift ideologies. However, when Labor delivers a surplus, it's brushed off as *dumb luck*, timing, or the favourable result of external forces well beyond their control. Conversely, when a Coalition government runs deficits—and they've run quite a few—it's always attributed to unfortunate circumstances, international headwinds, or inherited problems. And when they scrape together a surplus? It's trumpeted as the product of prudent, responsible, adult economic management, regardless of the reality.

Over the last two years, Treasurer Jim Chalmers has quietly delivered two consecutive budget surpluses—an achievement not seen in almost two decades. He's now signaling a return to deficit in the upcoming budget, but the context matters: it's a manageable deficit, designed to address neglected public services, essential recovery programs, and inflationary pressures without tipping the economy into stagnation. Yet this nuance is lost in the mainstream coverage, which is already gearing up for doomsday headlines, as if Australia were hurtling toward hyperinflation or a debt spiral worthy of a banana republic.

This predictable hysteria is not just economically incoherent, it's journalistically *lazy*. It thrives on the financial illiteracy of much of the media commentariat—many of whom parrot phrases like "back in black" or "budget black hole" with no understanding of how macroeconomics, sovereign currency systems, or public investment work in practice. In this alternative universe, a deficit is treated as a moral failing rather than a fiscal tool, and budget policy is assessed through the lens of household accounting analogies that have no business being applied to national economies. It's economic populism dressed in the language of prudence, and it's designed to serve a political agenda, not the public good.

Chalmers is not above criticism—*far from it*—but compared to his recent predecessors, he appears at least grounded in reality. He's resisted the temptation to turn fiscal policy into a weapon of ideology. Instead, he's focused on stabilising the Budget, reducing the structural deficit left behind by the Coalition, and targeting spending where it's needed: disaster recovery, healthcare, infrastructure, and the education sector, which has been starved of reform and funding for years. He's also juggling the enormous financial weight of the AUKUS submarine deal—a geopolitical indulgence cloaked as somehow a strategic necessity, draining public funds that could otherwise transform domestic policy settings.

But this isn't the conversation the electorate is being offered. Instead, the national discourse is being hijacked by scare campaigns and superficial talking points. Deficits aren't inherently *bad*. In fact, in times of global economic uncertainty, they're often necessary: the Menzies government ran large budget deficits between 1958–59 and 1966–67, much larger than any deficits in the modern era, and very few commentators complained at the time. What matters is what the money is spent on, and whether it improves national capacity, social equity, and long-term prosperity. But these questions rarely get asked on morning TV panels or in tabloid headlines. *It's all about the debt.*

The coming Budget will almost certainly provoke a tidal wave of outrage from conservative commentators and Coalition politicians—claims of reckless spending, irresponsible governance, and impending fiscal catastrophe. But Australians have lived through nearly a decade of Coalition Budgets marked by increasing inequality, underinvestment in essential services, and economic stagnation. They remember the real outcomes, not just the slogans. And for all the criticism Chalmers will receive in the coming days, what he's actually doing is something the political system hasn't seen in a while: using economic policy to try to help people.

It's still nowhere near enough but that, in itself, might be the most radical act in this entire Budget process: putting *people first*, not last.

THE BUDGET AS PURE POLITICAL THEATRE

Budgets in Australia have increasingly become stage-managed political performances designed to control the media cycle for a brief moment before vanishing into the fog of public disinterest. For all the theatre, most Budgets are lucky to command a full day's attention. The Budget reply delivered by the Opposition Leader two nights later is even more marginalised—often broadcast during late-night shopping or up against Thursday night sport, and lost to a nation more interested in starting to think about their weekend than digesting political financial details. This short attention span has only emboldened governments of all stripes to rely on drip-feed announcements in the lead-up, deploying a scatter-gun strategy of selective funding reveals weeks in advance, long before the Budget itself is formally tabled.

This year, we've already seen announcements on boosted Medicare funding—Labor's ideological heartland—a push toward universal access to early education and childcare, support for metal and steel industries, state-targeted infrastructure spending, and funding for public education in NSW. These announcements blur into one another, lacking distinction or memorability, and often appear recycled from earlier press conferences. It becomes difficult to tell whether they are new initiatives, re-packaged promises, or just politically expedient reminders of previous commitments. This confusion isn't a flaw in the strategy—it *is* the strategy, perfected by the previous Morrison government.

The Budget itself won't necessarily introduce bold new policies or radical fiscal directions. Instead, it will act as a giant ledger, pulling together months of disparate funding measures and policy intentions into a coherent framework that can be marketed as proof of responsible governance. The message will be simple: Labor has delivered targeted investments in health, education, infrastructure, and industry without blowing out the Budget or fuelling inflation. There will be a deliberate contrast between these measures and the memory of a chaotic, ad-hoc Coalition era, where announcements were made for political convenience and often left unfunded or unrealised—again, a strategy perfected by Scott Morrison.

In an election year, every line item of the Budget becomes both a signal and a shield—signalling to the public the values and priorities of the government, while shielding it from anticipated attacks on economic management. The Coalition will attempt to revive its tired trope of Labor's fiscal irresponsibility, but it's likely to fall flat in the face of Labor's recent track record—two surpluses, falling interest payments, a shrinking deficit, and visible improvements to essential services. In contrast, the Coalition has not yet presented a convincing economic alternative, beyond slogans and structural opposition to public investment.

But the issue here is that the entire Budget process has become an act of political choreography rather than genuine policymaking. When the budget is treated as a public relations opportunity rather than a serious moment of economic direction-setting, the conversation stays stuck in public image, not impact. This is especially troubling given the underlying issues that continue to plague the nation: a sluggish housing market and unaffordable rents, underemployment, stagnant wages, a still-strained health system, and an education sector—including early education—which is overdue for major structural reform. A few billion dollars here or there won't be enough to reverse decades of systemic neglect, and there remains the lingering concern that even well-intentioned spending can be overtaken by the demands of political pragmatism.

This kind of budgeting is less about vision and more about legacy. The Albanese government isn't aiming for just the headlines; it's aiming for permanence—of course, a government is always going to be interested in getting re-elected and remaining in office, but it has to keep sight of *why* it wants to remain it office and how it can best work towards the public interest.

ECONOMIC GASLIGHTING: THE COALITION'S LIES WON'T BE ENOUGH

Desperate to frame the Albanese government as fiscally irresponsible and economically destructive, the Liberal Party, through its Shadow Treasurer Angus Taylor, has started throwing around the exaggerated tax claims that are designed to provoke rather than to inform. But these claims aren't just politically cynical—they're transparently false, economically incoherent, and increasingly at odds with the lived reality of most Australians.

Taylor's headline-grabbing assertion that every Australian is paying "$3,500 more in tax" since 2021—conveniently, the last year of Coalition government—isn't just misleading; it's untraceable. There's no source, no calculation and no context, just a vague allusion to the Parliamentary Budget Office, without any of the analytical rigour or transparency one would expect from a Shadow Treasurer, and calibrated to sound just plausible enough to enrage the disengaged, while being vague enough to avoid immediate fact-checking by casual listeners.

But in today's media environment, such laziness is reckless. If the figure were somehow based around increased tax receipts, it would reflect rising incomes, stronger employment, and consumer activity—all indicators of a healthier economy. If it's based on the GST, then it's a function of more consumer spending, not government greed. Australians pay more GST when they spend more—and if they're spending more, they're generally earning more. If Taylor's data source was the tax-to-GDP ratio (which has increased), it still doesn't support his narrative. That ratio is well within historical norms, and under Coalition governments, it's often been higher. In other words, whatever metric he's chosen—if any—it's either good economic news or bad analysis, and in this case, *probably both*.

The Coalition's economic messaging has become a case study in political gaslighting. Taylor and his colleagues aren't attempting to engage with policy or macroeconomic reality, they're simply counting on voters to feel financially squeezed and then offering up a scapegoat—taxes—without any honest exploration of cause or context. But unlike the shock-jock era of political messaging, this kind of shallow economics doesn't hold up anymore. Australians are more economically literate than the political class gives them credit for, and while they might not glean through the reams of Budget papers, they certainly know the difference between personal experience and political bluster. If their pay slips haven't changed in the way Taylor claims, they're not going to swallow his talking points just because he yells them out louder.

This is the central political problem the Coalition faces: *the narrative dissonance*. Political leaders can't keep insisting that the economy is on fire when millions of Australians are quietly noticing that—while far from it being perfect—the economic picture is not as dire as the Coalition claims. Households may be feeling the pinch from inflation and interest rates, but they can also see that the government has made serious investments in Medicare, early childhood education, and infrastructure. They've watched as a $78 billion deficit has been reduced, and they understand that patching up a decade of Coalition neglect takes more than slogans and soundbites.

In this climate, trying to scare people into voting against their own experience and their own interests is a political dead-end. It's no longer enough to weaponise deficits or throw around meaningless tax claims. The modern electorate demands specificity, realism, and—above all—honesty, and this is not something Taylor appears capable of delivering.

His faux theatre might play well in press conferences or right-wing radio circles, but for a voter standing at the checkout or opening up their payslip, it's a hollow message.

Politics isn't just about who shouts the loudest: it's about whose version of reality people choose to believe. Right now, the Coalition is offering nothing more than a caricature of economic collapse, held together by dubious statistics and assumptions about voter ignorance. If they want to be taken seriously, they'll have to start offering something real. Until then, their economic critiques will remain exactly what they appear to be: made-up numbers, shouted into the void.

***

LABOR'S MOMENTUM AND A SHAKY START FOR THE COALITION

31 March 2025

The opening days of the federal election campaign have revealed more than just policy announcements and talking points—they've exposed a difference between a government that appears match fit and ready to go, and an opposition still fumbling around and trying to find its balance. While the early parts of any campaign are marked by adjustments and recalibration—it's only day four of a 36-day campaign—one major party has hit the ground running, and it's not the Coalition. Of course, this will change—or, at least, it *should* change—but it should be of concern that the leader of the Liberal–National Party Peter Dutton seemed so unprepared. The prime minister Anthony Albanese didn't call an early or a snap election and the final date that the election could be held was always going to be May 17, so this lack of preparation comes as a surprise.

Albanese seems to have made a confident start to the campaign, with a the populist pitch targeting the supermarket giants—Coles and Woolworths—many in the electorate have become increasingly resentful of. By promising to outlaw price gouging and create mechanisms to penalise excessive profiteering (*after the election*), Labor is trying to boost its cost-of-living credentials and positioning itself as a defender of everyday consumers. Albanese's rhetoric of accusing supermarkets of "taking the piss" wasn't trying to be deliberately crude, but it was politically calculated. At least a sweary Albanese and a willingness to be aggressive, populist and blunt in language, will cut through the abstraction that often grinds federal election campaigns down, where everyone tries to be the most inoffensive and obtuse. And this is one message the prime minister wants to put out: Labor will take on the corporate giants, whereas the Coalition will not. But will it work?

On the other side of the political fence, Dutton's start has been marked by disarray and rhetorical backflips. Over the past few days, he's floated the possibility of two separate referendums—four-year parliamentary terms, and stripping dual nationals of citizenship—only to backflip quickly, and this follows on from the constitutional recognition of Indigenous people that he promised in 2023, only to retract that proposal as well. It's difficult for oppositions to be fully prepared for an election that is always the prerogative of the prime minister to call, but even still, it's a sign that Coalition has not been properly war-gamed or grounded in a unified message.

The confusion has continued into other policy areas, particularly around the Coalition's gas plan. Dutton has made bold claims about reducing gas prices through a form of domestic reservation, forcing Queensland producers to divert up to 100 additional petajoules to the east coast. Aside from the difficulties of trying to announce and debate the esoteric issues of *petajoules* to the electorate (and we're pretty certain that 'petajoule' is probably at the point that an audience is going to start looking away), neither the modelling nor the mechanics of this proposal have been released.

Former ACCC chair Rod Sims has led the criticism, pointing out the flaws and impracticalities in this plan, while the Minister for Climate Change and Energy, Chris Bowen, accused Dutton of "making it up as he goes". The absence of economic detail, industry backing, or a coherent regulatory strategy weakens what could have been a centrepiece cost-of-living pitch for the Coalition. It looks instead like a reactive move: a bid to grab relevance in a news cycle, rather than shape it—it's possible to get away with this type of approach for most parts of a parliamentary term but during an election campaign, it instead puts out the message that they are just not ready to return to office.

It's not just the policy vacuums that are hurting Dutton—it's the tone and posture. For most of this parliamentary term, Dutton has avoided direct scrutiny, seeking media opportunities with right-wing commentators and Coalition-friendly journalists and he now finds himself exposed in the spotlight of a national election campaign. *There is nowhere to hide during an election campaign.*

Albanese, for the first few days at least, appears more comfortable, shaping the campaign narrative early with a confident media presence. Dutton, in contrast, has appeared flat-footed, reactive and unconvincing.

While it's far too early to claim that this election result is clear and it's all over—it's not—the early optics matter and set the tone for the campaign. And right now, the Coalition is presenting itself as unprepared, fractured, and searching for a message. The latest opinion polls are beginning to reflect this sentiment, with little indication that Dutton is making meaningful inroads into Labor's lead.

THE LATEST POLLS SHOW A CHANGE IN THE ELECTORATE

A series of new opinion polls—the Morgan Poll showing 53–47 per cent to Labor in in two-party-preferred voting, YouGov, Newspoll and Resolve all giving Labor a 51–49 per cent lead—continue with a pattern that commenced just over a month ago: the electorate is moving towards the government. While no single poll is definitive, the cumulative picture is one of a campaign drifting away from the opposition at precisely the moment it needed to be gaining traction.

Betting markets are starting to reflect this reality too, with odds shortening in Labor's favour: these markets should be ignored though and are quite often incorrect—betting agencies paid out early on Bill Shorten winning in 2019, only for Scott Morrison to go and win the election—but they do reflect some sentiment within the community, or at least those who are prepared to part with their money in a volatile market. These early trends don't guarantee a Labor victory, but they signal trouble for the Coalition.

For most of this parliamentary term, Albanese has been a cautious, defensive prime minister but, so far, he's embraced a sharper, more confident position on the campaign trail—and perhaps Albanese is a far better campaigner than he is as prime minister and, if the Labor Party does win this election, it's something that they will need to address.

In recent exchanges with the media—asked irrelevant questions by Sky News' Simon Love (about the removal of a Liberal Party sign by the husband of the independent MP, Monique Ryan)—Albanese highlighted the absurdity of the question and the triviality of the media's priorities. In another exchange with the ABC journalist Patricia Karvelas, where she falsely claimed that Infrastructure Australia had deemed Victoria's Suburban Rail Loop project unviable, Albanese called her out and set the record straight. Why has Albanese waited so long to push back against the endless attacks and mistruths spoken to him by the mainstream media? And, perhaps more importantly, why does the media always get things wrong or just make stuff up?

The contrast with Dutton couldn't be more different: increasingly low-energy, jittery, defensive, reactive and arrogant, recently claiming that he will live in Kirribilli if elected, because he would "take Sydney any day over living in Canberra". Perhaps they never had it anyway, but that's the Coalition vote in Canberra gone for good.

His early campaign stumbles so far—the confused messaging around proposed referendums and a half-baked gas plan—have already sown doubt about his preparedness. But it's his tone that stands out: not assertive, not energised, but desperate. In media appearances, Dutton is relying on recycled attacks on Labor's cost-of-living management and when challenged, he goes to old tropes about negative campaigns and media bias—not the behaviour of a leader with a compelling case for change and governing for all people.

And then there's the issue in Dutton's seat: the electorate of Dickson has always been marginal, but this time it's being targeted not just by Labor's Ali France, but by a rising community independent, Ellie Smith, who is gaining traction among voters disillusioned with both major parties. That Dutton might be forced to fight for his political survival and spend more time in his own seat, while trying to sell himself as a future prime minister is a major disadvantage, and he probably knows it. It's rare for an opposition leader or senior minister to be facing a real risk of losing their own seat in an election campaign—he only needs to refer to the difficulties the former Treasurer Josh Frydenberg had in trying to spread a message on the national stage, but holed up in Kooyong during the 2022 election campaign, trying to hold on to the seat which he ultimately lost to Monique Ryan.

Because of his insulation from media scrutiny, three days into this campaign, Dutton is being already tested in ways the past three years have not. For all the assistance offered by the conservative press, from *Sky News* to *The Australian* to sections of the ABC (for all of Sunday on ABC *News 24*, Dutton's appearances and mentions outnumbered Albanese by a ratio of 2:1)—Dutton is still struggling to connect and the more voters see of him, the less convinced they seem to be, which is what the opinion polls are currently suggesting.

In politics, self-belief is critical. Leaders need to exude not just confidence, but purpose. At the moment, Dutton's campaign feels that it's missing both. Where once there may have been a longer-term strategy for the Coalition—lose this election, gain ground, then mount a serious challenge in 2028—there is now visible panic. The spring in his step is gone, replaced with a sense of clinging on, not surging forward. Dutton has always been a front-runner and now that he's struggling and has fallen behind, he's not displaying the energy of a government-in-waiting; it's more the actions of a man on borrowed political time.

Of course, campaigns *can* turn. Momentum *can* shift. Scandals *can* erupt, and established narratives can easily fall apart. In the 1993 federal election, the Coalition was leading by 53 to 47 per cent in the two-party preferred vote on the first day of that campaign—even holding a five-point buffer in the final week—only to lose on election day. And in a reflection of the 1993 election, the Labor Party lost the 2019 election, after leading nearly every opinion poll after the 2016 election. Things can always change, and the opinions polls can sometimes be wrong.

But with each passing day, it becomes harder to see how the Coalition can gain the support it needs to win majority government, or even position itself credibly as a minority government. The idea that this was going to be a 'close-run contest' in the parlance of horse-race journalism, and as many in the media have suggested, is fast evaporating. And while Dutton might still believe in his chances, belief alone doesn't win elections—traction does. And right now, Dutton and the Coalition are just not getting it.

***

THE DUTTON DISASTER IN WAITING

7 April 2025

The first week of the federal election campaign has ended, and what's immediately clear is just how under-prepared, incoherent, and self-destructive the Liberal Party appears to be under Peter Dutton's leadership. What should have been an opportunity to showcase discipline, vision, and a credible alternative to the Labor government has, instead, become a case study in political mismanagement. From tone-deaf gaffes to rhetoric designed to inflame the public, the Coalition's opening week reveals a party that's out of touch, stuck in an echo chamber and *cul-de-sac* of outdated culture wars, and unable to articulate a compelling agenda for the country.

Dutton, who was expected to use this campaign to reframe his public image and project leadership potential—or a chance to "smile and maybe show a different side" and the rest of his character, as he said in his challenge against then Prime Minister, Malcolm Turnbull in 2018—has only reinforced the perception of a figure out of step with the electorate.

His fallback on tired old tropes—China fear-mongering, accusations of 'indoctrination" in school education, the anti-'woke' rhetoric—makes him appear trapped in the past, and not opening up to the future. These tactics might stir up parts of the conservative base, but they appear tone-deaf to a broader electorate searching for optimism and clarity. Leaders who want to win elections need to appeal to a wider audience, not just the conservative rump of their own party who argue the pathway to victory would be assured, if only the Liberal Party could become even more right wing.

This was evident in his response to a Chinese research vessel travelling through international waters near Tasmania and Victoria, as part of a joint China–New Zealand ocean floor project. Prime Minister Anthony Albanese said he would "have preferred the ship wasn't there" but Dutton immediately escalated the matter, accusing Albanese of having "lost control of national security" and falsely claiming the vessel was gathering intelligence. It was a reckless accusation, showing the same combative mindset that once led him to label asylum seekers "illiterate and innumerate", or "African gangs" causing havoc in Melbourne. This sort of inflammatory rhetoric with racist undertones might appeal to the hardliners, but it telegraphs desperation to the broader public. Of course, unreconstructed racists are out there in the community and they do vote—just like everyone else—but there's not enough of them out there to turn this into a winning formula.

Meanwhile, the Coalition bungled its response to the big trade issue of the week: the 10 per cent tariff imposed by the United States on Australian goods. Rather than offering a considered response, Dutton reached for the populist megaphone, insisting that he would have secured an exemption—despite the fact that no country has achieved this under the new U.S. trade measures, not even the Heard and McDonald Islands, Australian territory which is uninhabited by humans, but populated with penguins and many other birds, wildlife and sea creatures. These were empty talking points in place of substance, another example of a campaign more interested in grievance and outrage than governance.

Then came the comments about official residences: Dutton declared he would prefer to live in Kirribilli House in Sydney rather than The Lodge in Canberra if elected Prime Minister, dissing the people of Canberra at the same time. In the midst of a national housing crisis, the optics were terrible. To voters struggling with rising rents and home ownership out of reach, a prospective leader appearing to pick and choose between luxury homes was not just out of touch—it was insulting—as if to suggest that the position of prime minister for Dutton is going to become a procession of holidays in a harbour-side mansion. Certainly, these are just minor issues but it does provide an insight into the lack of discipline within the Coalition's campaign.

Compounding all of this are growing reports of internal disunity. Leaks from the New South Wales division of the Liberal Party suggest that moderates are actively working against the leadership, even supplying information directly to the Labor Party. It's a clear sign of the discontent brewing within the ranks, as the moderate faction of NSW seeks to wrest back control from the conservative Queensland rump.

By the end of the first week, Dutton looked like a man stumbling through a minefield of his own making. The campaign was supposed to be his moment to prove he could lead the nation. Instead, he delivered panic, provocation and, above all, a constant stream of negativity. The Coalition had a chance to reset and offer a real alternative but what it offered instead, was chaos. They've squibbed it.

THE OPINION POLL NUMBERS ARE DROPPING FOR THE COALITION

Across every major opinion poll, the trend is consistent and a pattern is forming: voters are drifting away from the Coalition and speculations and *feelings* about this drift are now being confirmed by numbers. If the current figures are any indication, Dutton and the Liberal Party are heading for a disaster on election day.

Four major polls—Roy Morgan, Essential, Resolve and Freshwater—were released during the week, and while the figures are all slightly different, all point to a clear loss of momentum for the Coalition. Even Freshwater, which has historically leaned toward the Liberals and gave them a narrow 51–49 per cent lead in their recent poll, now shows a softening trend compared to previous results.

The most influential opinion poll, Newspoll, released late on Sunday night, paints an even more difficult picture for the Liberal Party: 52 per cent to Labor and 48 per cent to the Coalition on a two-party-preferred basis, which is similar to the results of the 2022 federal election. While a four-point gap may seem surmountable, in the context of federal elections, it can spell the difference between a marginal loss and a complete rout.

Despite the cliché of *the only poll that matters is the poll on election day*, the hard heads in the respective campaign strategy teams would know that these trends *do* matter. Polls taken in aggregate don't just tell you who's ahead at any given time; they reveal where momentum is building, the messages that are resonating, and where all the vulnerabilities lie. And right now, the data suggests Dutton's campaign is repelling more voters than it's attracting, especially women.

Pollsters have a vested interest in accuracy, especially when it gets much closer to the date of the election. While some may have ideological biases and interpret the results to support political agendas outside of the election period, their business model depends on being taken seriously so close to when the real result—the *actual* election—is revealed. So, when every opinion poll is now showing the same pattern, it becomes impossible to ignore: the Liberal–National Coalition is in serious trouble.

EVEN SKY NEWS IS TURNING AWAY

One of the more telling moments of the week—albeit small—came not from a politician, but from the Coalition's unofficial media wing. On *Sky News*—long regarded as the centre of conservative spin—even the propaganda machine seemed to have enough. In a series of vox pops conducted in Melbourne, voters offered their views on the party leaders, and rather than cherry-picking favourable responses, Sky aired raw, unfiltered public sentiment—and it didn't favour Dutton.

Asked about Albanese, voters described him as "doing a good job" or "okay". When Dutton's name came up, the reactions were quick: "He's not that popular"... "No" ..."I don't think he'll do good." For a network known for its editorial manipulations and fabrications at every opportunity, this was a deviation from the script, and definitely not *on message*. Not that many people watch *Sky News*, but it does have a dedicated hard-core audience, addicted to conservative bias and the politics of outrage, just like its big brother in the U.S., *Fox News*. Whether intentional or accidental, this signalled a rare admission: the public isn't buying what the Coalition is selling.

The bigger question is: why wasn't the Coalition ready for this campaign? Everyone knew the election had to be called by May 17 and even if the actual date—May 3—wasn't known, there would have been an expectation after the summer break in late January, that an election would have to be called soon. Yet the Liberals began the campaign by being caught off guard, unsure of their footing. The messaging lacked cohesion, their agenda appeared thin, and their overall tone reeked of complacency and incompetence.

In contrast, Labor looked disciplined, prepared and confident. Perhaps learning from the Voice to Parliament referendum, where the 'No' side mobilised early and seized the agenda, Albanese's team has struck early and decisively. Of course, they knew exactly when the election was going to be called, but they have framed the campaign even before Dutton knew what was going on.

While Dutton is obviously borrowing from Trump's *chaos campaign* playbook—by projecting disorder and chaos now to conceal strategies that might arrive later in the campaign (or even policies announced *after* the election is over)—it's a tactic that doesn't translate into Australian politics. Although there is a small number of instances of voter fraud, double voting and electoral manipulation in Australia, there is not enough of it to influence election outcomes—our electoral system is too robust, too transparent, and too decentralised to allow chaos to become a campaign strategy. And besides this, Dutton has neither the charisma nor the ability to pull it off. As much as he'd like to try, *he's not Donald Trump*.

With opinion polling numbers becoming more set, internal divisions widening, and the public losing interest, the early warning signs have turned into alarm bells. Even the Coalition's staunchest media allies start to back away—*Sky News* but, interestingly, not the ABC—if only subtly. When the echo chamber starts to crack, it's often a sign of the entire edifice beginning to collapse.

There are still just under four weeks remaining in the 2025 election campaign and anything can still happen: *it always does*. A five-point lead in the opinion polls evaporated for opposition leader John Hewson in the 1993 federal election and he lost that election, even though just the day before the election, the Liberal Party was still highly expected to win. *That* was a surprise victory, as was the 2019 federal election, which was lost by the Labor Party. If the Dutton-led Coalition does win the 2025 election, it will be a surprise election victory, and these types of surprise victories tend to only happen once in a generation.

THE MONDAY ESSAYS

Week one of this campaign was supposed to set the tone. Instead, it exposed fragility, lack of preparation, and a deep disconnect between Dutton and the electorate. And it already has a feeling that, unless things change dramatically, it might already be all over.

***

A CAMPAIGN THAT FELL APART

14 April 2025

The second week of the federal election campaign—a stage when political parties are seeking stability—descended into yet more misfires for the Liberal Party, and it started off with bringing one of the worst deals in recent political history into the campaign: the lease of the Port of Darwin to a Chinese company, the Landbridge Group. Despite having implemented the entire deal, the Coalition sought to reframe the issue as a national security threat in an attempt to reignite anti-China sentiment and regain some control over their campaign.

Peter Dutton was scheduled to announce the cancellation of the lease as part of this scare campaign, but the move backfired *spectacularly*. Labor—tipped off directly by the Liberal Party itself—pre-empted the announcement with Anthony Albanese revealing a near-identical policy the day before. It wasn't just a political embarrassment—it completely nullified the issue. What was meant to be a moment of nationalistic megaphoning for the Coalition became an echo of the government's position, with Dutton left to agree with a plan that had been in the public domain for less than twenty-four hours. Worse still, the very issue the Coalition had tried to weaponise, reminded voters that they were the ones who had signed off on this poor deal in the first place.

The Coalition's attempt to magnify this into yet another chapter from their now-familiar China scare campaign exposed the big contradiction at the heart of their message: how can a nation's largest trading partner also be its greatest security threat? It's not an existential question—if China really is *that* threatening, why sell or lease major infrastructure to Chinese companies in the first place?

This focus on the Port of Darwin wasn't just about national infrastructure or foreign policy. It was about the cynical recycling of fear for political gain—and this time, it didn't work. Labor outflanked them—ironically, with the direct help of a leak from some unhappy people within the Liberal Party—the media saw through the tactic, and voters were reminded once again that the greatest national security threat of all is the political cowardice that always arrives wrapped in a healthy dose of hypocrisy.

THE LIBERAL PARTY'S CIVIL WAR

This party leak to the Labor Party, didn't come from an external source or was accidentally found in a discarded filing cabinet on the outskirts of Canberra. It came directly from *within*, and all signs point to the New South Wales division of the party as the *saboteur*. It's the result of a long-standing power struggle between the more ideologically conservative Liberal-National Party of Queensland—Dutton's base—and the moderates of New South Wales, who would prefer to see their own ascendancy after an election defeat, even if that means handing Labor the win.

It's not a new dynamic in Australian politics, but rarely has it played out so obviously in the middle of a federal campaign. Behind the scenes, the NSW division, hardly a pinnacle of liberal moderation itself, is increasingly preparing the ground for an Angus Taylor leadership in the event of a Coalition loss. For them, losing in 2025 is an acceptable price to pay for retaking control of the party, silencing the Queensland-led hard-right, and charting a new direction that could win in 2028. If Dutton were to lose his own seat of Dickson in the process—which is a strong possibility—that would be an added benefit.

And while it might seem counterintuitive to sabotage your own campaign, political operatives often view factional victory within the party as more important than electoral success—especially when the electoral odds are already looking grim. The Labor Party also has a strong tendency to do this—*the experts!*—although it greatest act of factional bastardry would have to be the period between 2010–13, when it destroyed itself during the Rudd–Gillard–Rudd years, and handed the Liberal Party a nine-year period of government on a plate.

Dutton is clearly aware of this internal bleeding. His recent complaints about "elites within the Liberal Party" weren't random grievances—they were directed at the very people who are undermining him. Yet this public airing of these internal grievances has done little to stop the quiet campaign against him. The NSW division isn't without its problems: its leadership is fragmented, its ideological direction is confused, and while it's not the far-right circus that the Victorian branch has become—now home to Christian nationalists and conspiracy theorists—it still harbours its own internal instability.

A MID-CAMPAIGN POLICY DUMP

To add to his terrible week, Dutton's abrupt abandonment of the Coalition's plan to force public servants back into the office full-time was less a policy correction than a public confession of political incompetence. In a rare display of a campaign apology, Dutton openly admitted the policy was a mistake, and tried to frame it as a case of miscommunication—

blaming Labor for twisting the message, as though the policy hadn't already collapsed under its own contradictions. In reality, this was not a complex or nuanced idea misrepresented by opponents—it was a shambles from the beginning. Announced with great fanfare to appeal to a supposed silent majority of tradies and working-class voters tired of 'lazy' remote workers, it quickly unravelled under the weight of its own impracticality, potential illegality, and hypocrisy.

The sudden backflip didn't just happen because the policy was debated, articulated over time and then found wanting: it happened because voters *hated* it. It alienated not only the public servants it directly targeted, but also their families, colleagues, and entire segments of the electorate who had come to see remote work as an essential part of modern life. The Coalition's attempt to pit 'real workers' against 'keyboard loafers' collapsed when it became clear that many of those 'real workers' were relying on the flexibility of their partners, family members, or housemates working from home.

This flip-flop has confirmed what has been already suspected: the Coalition's policy platform had been hastily put together, poorly vetted, and driven more by political messaging than any real belief in this platform. Dumping the work-from-home policy in the middle of a campaign sends a message to the electorate—not that the party is being responsive to public sentiment, but that it was *unprepared*. And worse still, it gave Labor and independents a line of attack that will endure for the rest of the campaign: if the Coalition is already disowning its own policies, how can voters trust anything else they promise?

Ultimately, this isn't just about one failed idea. It raises a broader question about the Coalition's readiness for government. What other policies haven't been tested? What else might collapse under scrutiny? Nuclear energy? Education reform? Taxation? There's a growing sense that the Coalition, out of government for only three years, hasn't done the hard policy work in opposition and is only relying on outdated ideas and cynical stunts. And that might be the most damning conclusion of all: a party that once could win by simply showing up, now faces a political world that demands a great deal more—and hasn't got much to offer.

LEADERSHIP IN THE AGE OF TALKING POINTS

The first leadership debate of the federal election campaign came and went with barely a ripple, a tightly managed exercise in message control more than any genuine contest of ideas. Albanese and Dutton stood before a studio audience of 100 'undecided' voters and delivered performances that were technically competent but left no lasting impression, with each sticking to their pre-packaged talking points. Albanese rattled off economic achievements, Dutton leaned into cost-of-living anxieties, and the entire event felt like a well-rehearsed dress rehearsal for a show no one particularly wanted to see.

While Albanese won the debate with 44 per cent, to Dutton's 35 per cent—21 per cent were still undecided—there was no real persuasion, no momentum gained. It was just another night in a campaign going through the motions.

But the problem runs deeper than just an uninspiring debate. It's what these debates have become—tightly managed performances with no spontaneity, no improvisation, and no real test of leadership under pressure. They're relics of a past political culture that demanded less but offered more, where decades ago, political leaders faced unruly, unpredictable crowds and had to sink or swim in real time. Today's debates are risk-managed into irrelevance.

It's hard to imagine either Albanese or Dutton confronting a crowd not handpicked by a research firm, let alone dealing with hecklers or winning over a room determined to dislike them. The oratory that once defined great Australian leaders has been replaced by scriptwriters and communications consultants. Politics now happens within the safe walls of subscription media and strategic messaging, not out in the open, where views are tested and leaders either rise or fall on the strength of their character. The electorate deserves to see leaders tested in a way that isn't choreographed within an inch of its life. The current format teaches us nothing and challenges no one.

Two more of these debates are scheduled before election day. They will come and go, and one leader will probably win the polls on the night, but as history shows, it doesn't matter: Labor leaders have won every election debate since the 2010 election—in most cases, comprehensively—but only Albanese has gone on to win government. What really matters is what happens beyond the studio—on doorsteps, in workplaces, and at the polling booths. But still, these debates continue, more out of tradition than necessity.

There is a perception that the leaders who try not to attend these debates are avoiding scrutiny and are running away from the public, but even when they do show up, it still feels like they *are* avoiding scrutiny, even if they are physically present.

And so, we're left with debates that confirm, rather than challenge. They confirm the instinct of many Australians that their leaders don't really say anything anymore. They confirm that politics has become more about *avoiding* damage than *taking* risks. And they confirm that, in a campaign where leadership is supposedly at stake, neither contender wants to be caught off guard. But the real tragedy is that without *risk*, there is no inspiration—and without inspiration, there is no leadership worth following.

A CAMPAIGN THAT FELL APART

FOOTBALLS AND FOSSIL FUELS

Every election campaign has its unscripted moments, and these unexpected incidents reveal more about a leader's temperament and values than any carefully rehearsed debate or media conference. This week, two such moments stood out, small but significant in their symbolism. The first involved Dutton, a *football*, and a *cameraman*; the other saw Albanese confronted by a climate change activist. Neither moment will decide the election, but the respective reactions say a lot about the politics they represent.

At a photo-op on a football field, Dutton managed to kick a ball directly into the head of a cameraman, Ghaith Nadir. Accidents do happen, but Nadir was an Iraqi refugee and asylum seeker, the very type of person Dutton has spent much of his political career vilifying and targeting with punitive policies and rhetoric. That alone gave the incident a clear subtext, but it was Dutton's response that turned a simple mishap into something more sinister.

Instead of showing concern or even mild embarrassment, Dutton shouted out that he "got him!", and then made a joke about the cameraman not catching the ball, laughed it off, and suggested that had it been Albanese, he would have 'lied' about the whole incident. It was an oddly triumphant, almost gleeful reaction to an accident that left a man with a head injury, revealing a man more comfortable deflecting with ridicule than showing empathy.

It's hard to shake the feeling that these moments aren't just gaffes—they're brief insights of the leadership style on offer. Where empathy should appear, we see *sarcasm*. Where humility might have made an impression, we see *bravado*.

On the other side of the campaign trail, Albanese was confronted by a climate change protester, Alexa Stuart, furious about the government's continued approval of new coal and gas projects. She accused the Prime Minister of condemning her generation to a future of climate catastrophe, and she had every right to be angry: despite all the rhetoric about net zero and clean energy, Labor has green-lit 173 new fracking wells in Queensland and continues to approve existing fossil fuel projects under the fiction that they are not 'new' developments, but 'expansions'. But a bigger gas field is still a *bigger* gas field, and a deeper coal mine still burns *more* coal.

Albanese's response was to brush it off. He refused to comment, claiming that engaging would only encourage more protesters. But this isn't a time to be avoiding engagement. Elections are one of the few moments when political pressure has real leverage—when leaders can be held to account by the very people they claim to represent. Protest during a campaign isn't a disruption; it's a democratic *necessity*. These aren't just votes at stake—they're lives, futures, and the shape of the planet to come. The climate crisis isn't going to pause for polling day.

These two incidents—one flippant, one furious—reflect deeper fractures in the political landscape. Dutton's football blunder became a metaphor for his political instinct to punch down and dismiss criticism with derision. Albanese's evasion of a powerful challenge from a young activist highlighter the contradiction between his party's climate narrative and its actions. But at the least, both moments broke through the campaign veneer. And in a race already marked by strategic missteps and clichéd performances, it's these raw flashes of character that voters might remember most.

***

THE MASTERCLASS IN POLITICAL FAILURE

21 April 2025

The third week of the federal election campaign has confirmed what many political observers suspected a couple of weeks ago: the Liberal Party's campaign is not just failing—it's falling apart. And while the previous week was best described as *disastrous*, this week has arguably been even worse. Where most governments benefit from incumbency by running disciplined, focused, and generally positive campaigns—touting achievements, pushing hopeful messaging, and strategically avoiding pitfalls—what we're seeing from Peter Dutton and the Coalition is the opposite: a miserable, mistake-ridden, directionless, and relentlessly negative campaign that appears to lack the energy or coherence required to inspire confidence with the electorate.

It's not just the gloom-laden dystopian talking points about Australia being on the brink of collapse—it's the absence of a compelling alternative vision. The Coalition has placed all its eggs in one basket: trying to convince the electorate that everything—*absolutely everything*—is so bad, and only getting worse, and that the Labor government is to blame for *absolutely* everything. Nothing is good... *it's all so terrible*.

Yet, as comprehensive as this message has been, it's a message that's failing to have the impact that was intended. The supposed dystopia Dutton wants Australians to believe in simply doesn't reflect reality. The sun still rises, people still go about their lives, and while challenges exist—as they always do—Australians don't appear to be buying into the apocalyptic narrative being peddled by the Coalition, if the current opinion polls are to be believed. It's a strategy that feels increasingly out of touch with how most voters actually experience the world.

At the centre of this malaise is Dutton himself—a leader whose performance has been characterised by mistakes and a lack of political groundwork, not just during this campaign, but for this entire parliamentary term. For someone who has had three years to prepare for this campaign, Dutton seems astonishingly unready and underprepared. Compared to previous opposition leaders: Bill Shorten used his six years to criss-cross the country, regularly subjecting himself to hostile town halls, testing policy ideas, and building a campaign machine. Anthony Albanese, while less aggressive and productive during his time as leader of the opposition, still made use of every available moment in opposition to refine his messaging and build credibility.

Dutton, on the other hand, has spent the bulk of his time in the right-wing media bubble—appearing regularly on Sky News and 2GB, ignoring critical outlets such as SBS, denouncing the ABC, and speaking only to a narrow audience already predisposed to support him. This isn't a winning strategy for an opposition leader; it's a regression and the wiser heads within the Liberal Party—if there are any who still exist—should have worked on broadening the experience of Dutton far earlier.

Leadership demands visibility, flexibility, and effort. But Dutton frequently disappeared from public view when the going got tough. He's failed to test ideas in the public arena, avoided uncomfortable questions, and relied instead on ideological comfort zones filled with culture war rhetoric and attacks on 'woke' media and 'indoctrinating' school education across Australia. This hasn't sharpened his message, it's done the opposite: it has dulled his appeal. It has left him unchallenged, untested, and unprepared for the rigours of a national election campaign. What's emerging now is the result of that neglect: a leader lost in the fog of his own negativity, unable to present himself as a credible alternative Prime Minister. Why did nobody within his team prepare Dutton for this election campaign? Why did nobody notice the clearly ringing alarm bells?

And what would a Dutton government even look like? At best, it would be a Morrison government redux—without even the modest veneer of competence, considering the Morrison government left behind a legacy of dysfunction, secrecy, and poor administration. The idea that voters are crying out for a return to that style of governance that they clearly rejected at the 2022 federal election is delusional. For all the Coalition's attempts to stoke fear and division, the one thing it has failed to provide is a coherent sense of purpose—*the raison d'être* behind their bid for power. Once any of Dutton's campaign rhetoric is peeled back, there is no reason in this bid: it appears to *power* for the *sake of power*.

This is what makes this campaign not just ineffective, but potentially one of the worst opposition efforts in recent memory. There's no grand contest of ideas, no bold vision to debate, no clear sense of what the Liberal Party actually *stands for* beyond not being Labor, endlessly criticising the government, and wanting *to be the government*. Even those who might be sympathetic to conservative principles are being left cold by a campaign that seems designed more to inflame than to inspire. And as pre-poll voting opens this week, time is rapidly running out to turn things around.

Australians want a government that functions and works for them—not one that just constantly offers blame. They want *leadership*—not constant complaints about the media or dog-whistling about *woke* culture. We've been here before—through Scott Morrison—and it seems that the Liberal Party picked up all the wrong lessons from the 2022 federal election result, which they comprehensively lost.

And while the Labor Party is not promising any type of revolutionary reform or providing anything outstanding to the electorate, at least it's offering a coherent and largely positive agenda. For the Liberals, this campaign has devolved into an excellent case study about what happens when an opposition fails to do the hard work, refuses to grow beyond its ideological comfort zone, and underestimates the intelligence and optimism of the electorate.

THE WORST OPPOSITION CAMPAIGN IN POLITICAL HISTORY?

It's a question that keeps coming up—among journalists, political analysts, and increasingly from the public itself: *is this the worst election campaign run by an opposition in modern Australian political history?* As the third week of the 2025 campaign draws to a close, it's becoming increasingly clear that the Liberal Party's performance under Dutton is not just uninspiring—it's *historically* bad. And while the final judgment will have to wait until election day, the signs already suggest that we are witnessing a campaign that may well become the new benchmark for political failure.

To fairly assess whether this is *the* worst, it helps to reflect on past campaigns that have gone off the rails. The 2004 Labor campaign under Mark Latham is often cited as one of the most disastrous in living memory—not because it started poorly, but because it collapsed spectacularly in the final week with the announcement of a poorly conceived forestry package in Tasmania, and general perceptions about whether Latham was suitable or ready to become prime minister.

What had been shaping up as a competitive challenge to John Howard ended in humiliation, delivering Labor its worst two-party preferred result since the Great Depression era of 1931. Then there's John Hewson's 1993 campaign—the infamous 'birthday cake' GST interview that blew up what had been a well-structured campaign until that moment. Hewson's honesty in attempting to explain the complexities of his tax policy became the very issue that sunk him, crystallising voter anxiety and ridicule in a single media moment.

But in each of these cases, the narrative of collapse hinged on a *single* major failure—Latham's handshake gaffe, poor forestry policy and erratic late-stage behaviour; Hewson's GST stumble, or even H.V. Evatt's paranoid mismanagement of the Petrov Affair in the 1954 campaign. What sets the current Liberal campaign apart is not one major blunder—it's the sheer, consistency and relentless accumulation of smaller ones. It started badly, it has worsened each week, and there has been no sign of course correction. It's a campaign which seems devoid of strategy, vision, or momentum, led by a figure who appears more comfortable delivering apocalyptic soundbites than facing the public with credible policies.

Even among Liberal Party campaigns that were deemed to be poor, some went on to succeed due to external factors. Tony Abbott's 2010 campaign was scattershot and gaffe-prone, but still nearly toppled a first-term Labor government. Malcolm Turnbull's 2016 campaign was widely criticised for its lack of energy and clarity but ended in a narrow victory.

Scott Morrison's 2019 campaign was less a masterclass in politics than a masterclass in luck, bolstered by Labor's internal missteps and relentless support from News Corporation. What each of these examples share is a degree of chaos—but also a broader media narrative and party apparatus and insiders working overtime to cover for that chaos. Dutton, in contrast, is running a campaign without cohesion nor external cheerleaders. Even the Murdoch press, usually a reliable megaphone for the Coalition, has been lukewarm in its support: there haven't been any *Australia Needs Peter* headlines (as there were for Tony Abbott in 2013); he's not being depicted as the 'man who saves Australia', or that Dutton is 'the answer'.

Dutton also carries baggage that previous Liberal leaders didn't. Persistent rumours about his past behaviours in the police force, his property wealth, and his temperament have followed him into this campaign, even if they've never been substantiated in a way that could stick in a courtroom. But in the court of public opinion, perception always trumps reality. For a political figure to be continually haunted by questions about character—and to never properly address them—is a fatal flaw in any campaign, especially one that hinges so heavily on personal leadership credentials. It's too late in the campaign to have a *real Peter* moment, to replicate the attempts by Julia Gillard with her own *real Julia* moment which she used to resurrect her faltering election campaign in 2010 and, aside from this, the electorate is seeing the *real Peter* anyway. There is no other persona or vaudeville act that he can switch to: *this is it*.

And then there's the issue of *political vision*. Whatever faults previous opposition campaigns may have had, most at least attempted to present a vision of what government under their leadership might look like. Latham pushed a radical education agenda and a forestry policy that had merit but was poorly conceived; Hewson had economic reform; Evatt had the promise of postwar nation-building (however bungled in the delivery). Dutton's campaign, by contrast, has offered little beyond fear and resentment. If there is a policy centrepiece, *it's nowhere to be found*. If there is an optimistic case for change, *it hasn't been made*. The campaign is driven almost entirely by slogans about restoring law and order and fighting 'wokeness'—hardly a compelling electoral message for the millions of Australians focused on housing affordability, wages, climate change, and cost-of-living pressures.

MOMENTUM MATTERS—BUT WHO'S GOT IT?

As this election campaign heads into its final fortnight, one word is beginning to appear more often: *momentum*. It's the intangible force that can carry a party to unexpected victory—or accelerate its descent into a disaster. For the Coalition under Dutton, that force is just not there; the opinion polls are slipping away when they need to be flowing in their favour. After three chaotic and lacklustre weeks, there is no real sense that the Liberal Party has any forward motion at all. And while the Labor Party's campaign hasn't exactly electrified the electorate, it has presented itself as steady, competent, disciplined—and—most importantly, in the context of its previous time in office between 2010–13—not self-destructive.

Momentum in election campaigns is a curious thing: it's possible to have it and still lose. Labor had it in both 2016 and 2019, where Bill Shorten's campaign in 2016 closed the gap significantly and gave Malcolm Turnbull a massive fright, and the 2019 campaign generated genuine optimism and an expected victory among progressives—until it all fell apart on the day of election. But the presence of momentum in both cases signalled a party with energy, belief, and a message that at least part of the electorate found compelling. By contrast, a campaign without momentum—especially one mired in negativity and confusion—has never succeeded in winning office, at least not in modern Australian political history.

Anthony Albanese had this momentum in 2022: there was a mood for change in the electorate and he used it to go past a shaky start and lead the Labor Party to a modest but decisive victory. And while the current Labor campaign isn't bursting with innovation or bold policy reforms, it doesn't need to be: it just needs to avoid major mistakes and let the Coalition implode under the weight of its own contradictions.

That isn't to say this is a landslide in the making. This election is taking place in a new political era—one where minor parties and independents have consolidated their place in the national political scene. Over a third of the electorate is expected to vote outside the traditional two-party structure, and while that makes the national vote share more unpredictable, it also supports the strong belief that the Coalition cannot regain government without significant inroads into seats they have lost in recent elections—many of them lost to independents who were elected precisely *because* of a rejection of Liberal values and behaviour.

While the Liberal and National Coalition was leading in the opinion polls before the election campaign commenced, many observers still believed that it was virtually impossible for the Liberal Party to win a majority in its own right. A pathway to minority government now appears to have been closed off as well. Too many of the electorates the party would need to flip are held by popular independents or are urban progressive seats where the Liberal brand has been damaged—perhaps beyond repair, unless major internal reforms are made. The party hasn't done the work to rebuild relationships with these communities, let alone articulate why they deserve to govern again.

Of course, in politics, nothing is impossible. A major scandal involving a senior Labor figure in the final weeks of this campaign could change the dynamics but there is no indication that such a scandal is looming. The best the opposition dirt units have managed so far are feeble attempts at character assassination—reheated rumours, personal attacks, or strange claims such as Anthony Albanese's failure to publicly kiss and acknowledge Tanya Plibersek at the recent Labor campaign launch is a sign of leadership instability. It's *hardly* Watergate. If the Coalition is banking on an Albanese disaster to rescue their campaign, they're not only clutching at straws—they're showing just how little agency they have left in this race.

It's also worth revisiting that old political adage: *oppositions don't win elections, governments lose them*. And while the Albanese government hasn't dazzled during this campaign, it hasn't self-sabotaged either. There is no strong evidence that suggests the public has an insatiable appetite for change, as they did in 2013 and again in 2022. And even if there was, Dutton hasn't offered any great reasons for the electorate to make a switch over to the Liberal Party.

And that's the deeper problem for the Coalition. They have failed to generate a momentum for change, and a campaign without momentum becomes a campaign of desperation: errors are made, and it breeds paranoia, stunts, contradictions, and a disassociation from what's really happening in the campaign. That's what we've seen over the past three weeks. And while the final two weeks is still enough time for surprises, it's not enough time to reverse the trajectory of a campaign that's been broken from the start.

So, *who* has the momentum? On the surface, no one is racing ahead. But politics isn't just about who's running—it's about who's standing still while others stumble. And right now, Labor is moving forward in all the right ways. The Coalition, meanwhile, is staggering towards the finish line, weighed down by its own inertia. Of course, events can always change, and the unexpected can always arrive quickly from the horizon, when it's least expected.

And leaders can, all of a sudden, change tact. But Dutton doesn't appear to be the crazy–brave maverick who can throw caution to the wind, and exploit the new circumstances that might appear after a disruption. He's just *not that sort of leader*. Unless something extraordinary happens, the next fortnight will simply confirm what this campaign has already revealed: Dutton's Liberal–National Party is out of time, out of touch, out of ideas, and out of momentum.

***

A STRANGE, DISJOINTED WEEK IN A CAMPAIGN SLIPPING AWAY

28 April 2025

The fourth week of the federal election campaign was quite a bit different—a strange, fragmented few days and a disjointed rhythm. With Easter Monday and ANZAC Day to start and end the week, there were just three formal campaigning days in between, and these were overshadowed by the major global event of the death of Pope Francis. While almost 40 per cent of Australians now hold no religious affiliation and only 20 per cent identify as Catholic, the Pope was an international figure of stature, and his death subdued the campaign atmosphere, making an already difficult task for Peter Dutton even more difficult. Campaigning lost its energy, major events were paused, and both Anthony Albanese and Dutton suspended their activities to attend church—a truce in an otherwise relentless campaign.

Early pre-poll voting began on the Tuesday, which signified a major change in the campaign—the election was no longer a *theoretical* exercise; no longer just about changing minds; the election was suddenly *very real* with real votes being lodged. A record 542,000 Australians cast their votes on the first day of pre-polling, with around two million by the end of the week—meaning that by election day on May 3, close to half the electorate will have already made their voted. This change in recent times from an *election day* to an *election period*—voting stretched across two weeks—makes it more difficult for all candidates to sustain momentum, but it does rewards discipline, consistency and energy.

This was always going to be a Coalition campaign running against the tide—a challenger needs a clean path to build their momentum: a routine, a rhythm, a clear run of days to hammer home messages and shift voter sentiment. Instead, the Coalition had to deal with a messy timetable—school holidays, two long weekends, public holidays, and now the death of a global religious leader. A campaign that already stumbled through its first three weeks was thrown further into disarray just at a time when it needed to be coherent.

Of course, such a disjointed timetable also impacted the Labor Party, but as the incumbent and the frontrunners, they didn't need to build a momentum for change: Albanese didn't need to convince an electorate of *change*—he just had to reassure them that *stability* was preferable to *risk*. And while dissatisfaction with Labor has been simmering, there doesn't seem to be a 'change the government' mood in the air. That time may come by 2028 if Albanese becomes even more disliked than he is now, and if the Liberal Party can provide a credible leader, but that point hasn't arrived yet. In contrast, Dutton faces mounting problems not just with voters, but within his own party. Leaks have been flowing directly to Labor strategists, bypassing the media entirely—a clear sign that many in the Liberal ranks have lost faith in their leader.

In a campaign week where building a momentum was absolutely critical, the Coalition found itself stranded by events outside its control and by its own ineptitude. The question now isn't whether Dutton can pull off a miracle comeback in this final week—it's about how the Liberal Party can lessen the expected loss, and whether they can avoid an even more catastrophic result than expected.

COALITION CAMPAIGNS ON DEFENCE, BUT THE MESSAGE MISFIRES

As the Coalition struggled to find footing during this week, it turned to what it believed was one of its few remaining strengths: defence policy. In Perth, Peter Dutton and shadow defence minister Andrew Hastie announced a $21 billion boost to defence spending, framing it as essential to Australia's national security and regional stability, and the "single most important task for the Australian government is to keep the Australian people safe", positioning this as an imperative for maintaining alliances and deterring threats.

Yet while playing to perceived strengths is a textbook campaigning tactic, the Coalition's defence pitch exposed further problems within its election strategy. The announcement lacked depth, offering little detail beyond big-ticket spending figures and a parade of militaristic slogans. There was no discussion about veterans' services, no proposals for reforming the ADF's outdated structures, and no vision for modernising the force to meet the complex, non-traditional threats of the 21st century. Missing too was any reflection on Australia's strained regional relationships—and how careless diplomacy under Dutton's previous time in office as defence minister, including recent inflammatory remarks about Indonesia and Russia, has jeopardised Australia's standing in the region.

Even more baffling is how Dutton proposed to fund this $21 billion spend: reversing Labor's HECS debt reduction policy, scrapping subsidies for electric vehicles, and reversing tax cuts promised by the Labor government—hardly a recipe for electoral success. Few voters, irrespective of income bracket, want to surrender tax relief for the promise of more F-35 fighter jets or military hardware, particularly when trust in defence procurement is low after years of scandals, blowouts, and wastage.

Dutton then went down yet another culture war *cul-de-sac*, pushing for anti-Semitism questions to be added to the Australian citizenship test and suggesting a new round of scrutiny of existing Palestinian visa approvals. These were naked appeals to the Zionist lobby and attempts to wedge Labor on national security, but again, they felt out of step with the current priorities of the electorate: cost-of-living pressures, health, housing, and education dominate voter concerns—not heavy-handed changes to citizenship tests or ethno-political dog-whistling.

It is true that the Liberal Party has historically polled better on defence, economic management, and border security but as the years have rolled on, that reputation has become frayed. The myth of Coalition superiority on economic management has crumbled in the face of Labor's record in office: the evidence suggests that the Liberal Party is *not* the better economic manager, yet the perception persists. On border security and immigration, Dutton's heavy-handedness has alienated moderate voters and reinforced an image of cruelty over competence.

Defence remains as the last symbolic refuge—but even there, the Coalition's approach is intellectually thin and politically tone-deaf. It focuses on spending billions with no accompanying narrative about how Australia can genuinely strengthen itself without alarming neighbours such as Indonesia or inflaming tensions in a volatile world.

Instead, Dutton's defence policy feels trapped in a 20th-century mindset—obsessed with the *boys' toys* and geopolitical sabre-rattling—while Australia's real needs in the Indo–Pacific era demand a far more thoughtful, deft, and forward-looking approach. Hastie's military background might lend credibility to these announcements, but experience in combat does not necessarily translate into strategic wisdom in procurement, diplomacy, or military reform.

Ultimately, this defence announcement revealed more about the Coalition's weaknesses than its strengths. It highlighted a party unable to adapt to modern campaigning realities, unable to read the room, and increasingly speaking to a shrinking, aging base that wants to hear that everything can be solved by spending on fighter jets and tightening immigration controls: it felt less like a bold and enticing move and more like a desperate one.

MORE LEADERS' DEBATES: WHERE'S THE INSPIRATION?

This week has two debates—Nine/Fairfax's *The Great Debate* and Seven West's *The Final Showdown*—and both delivered what was to be expected: tightly controlled, stage-managed events that offered more of the same arguments in slightly different packaging. In more direct formats, both Albanese and Dutton faced a series of timed questions from political commentators and moderators, and forced to answer in a strict window of 60 seconds. These tighter formats did inject some energy, but the substance remained predictable, and the debates quickly descended into the same familiar campaign themes.

Perhaps the most revealing moment of *The Great Debate* came not from the leaders but from moderator Ally Langdon—a theme also picked up by *The Final Showdown*—who asked why neither leader was inspiring the public. Neither Albanese nor Dutton could convincingly answer it, because both major parties—and the media structures that cover them—have long abandoned the idea of *truly inspirational* politics. In today's Australia, political courage is punished, not rewarded; big, community-centred ideas are demolished by corporate media before they can ever take hold.

What would inspirational leadership even look like? Not another round of tax cuts for the wealthy or shallow slogans about *choice* and *opportunity*, but bold systemic changes:

super-profits taxes on mining giants such as Gina Rinehart or Andrew Forrest, free higher education and dental care, massive investment in public housing, demilitarising Australia's foreign policy, rebuilding a genuine sense of national community. But such policies are anathema to the neoliberal orthodoxy that both major parties largely accept and the mainstream media vigorously promotes. Instead of collective *inspiration*, politics now focuses almost entirely on individual *aspiration*, ignoring the social contract in favour of a perpetual rat race and a fear of missing out.

This is the tragedy underlying Australian democracy today: a political culture so dominated by market dogma and corporate media interests that even modest reforms are treated as radical, and the language of collective responsibility is increasingly absent from the national conversation. Political debates, as a result, have become risk-averse exercises in messaging discipline, not moments of inspiration: leaders don't inspire anymore because they're not trained to do this.

It's not that individual ambition and entrepreneurialism have no place—*they do*, and can flourish within a broader social framework. But without public investment, functioning health and education systems, decent infrastructure, and a vibrant middle class, individual success stories are nothing but shallow myths. Even billionaires owe their fortunes to collective efforts—roads, education systems, stable governments and *other people*—which they rarely acknowledge until their fortunes are at risk and they plead for bailouts.

These two debates, while marginally sharper than the previous two, ultimately changed little. Albanese reiterated his focus on health, Medicare, education, and the promise that "no one will be held back and no one left behind," a refrain from his 2022 campaign. Dutton stuck to crime, law and order, and defence—ground he has retreated to repeatedly throughout this campaign. The media in *The*

Great Debate declared Dutton the winner by a margin of two to one—the studio jury in *The Final Showdown* was far more comprehensive for Albanese, registering 50 per cent in favour, to Dutton's 25 per cent—but winning or losing a debate in the dying weeks of a campaign, means little when much of the electorate has already voted, or made up their minds long ago.

And in truth, winning these debates has little bearing on winning elections. History is littered with leaders who dominated debates but lost at the ballot box: Kevin Rudd against Tony Abbott in 2013, Julia Gillard against Abbott in 2010 (that resulted in a minority government), Bill Shorten against Scott Morrison in 2019. These sterile, tightly managed performances don't sway elections—they just provide momentary grist for media spin cycles and a few viral clips for social media.

THE OPINION POLLS CONTINUE TO PROVIDE BAD NEWS FOR THE COALITION

A new round of opinion polls released this week has crystallised what has been obvious for some time: the Labor government is pulling ahead, and the Coalition is falling further behind. The Morgan poll showed the most dramatic movement, giving Labor a commanding 55.5 per cent to 44.5 per cent two-party-preferred lead over the Coalition—a gap that, historically, no opposition has ever managed to overturn in the final week of a campaign. YouGov and Newspoll results showed similar patterns, indicating not just a drift towards Labor, but a hardening of voter sentiment as pre-poll voting continues.

Comparisons with the 2022 election show that at the same stage in the campaign, the numbers are almost identical. Although opinion polls can never guarantee the final result—as the 2019 election proved—the current dynamics are even more daunting for the Liberal Party. Unlike 2019, where voters harboured deep doubts about the leadership of Bill Shorten, there is no clear rejection of Albanese. And unlike Scott Morrison's last-minute surge in 2019, Dutton has no pool of goodwill to draw upon: *there's just not much there*. His belated attempts at softening his image have come too late and too inconsistently to have any real impact.

It's often said during election campaigns that *it's never over until it's over*, but even seasoned political observers are scraping the bottom of the barrel trying to imagine a scenario where Dutton can pull off a reversal. Even traditionally hostile media outlets such as Sky News are struggling to put a positive spin on Dutton's performance, with some conservative commentators openly acknowledging the Liberal campaign has been a disaster.

Dutton has missed the opportunity not just to win government, but to position the Liberal Party credibly for the next election. Throughout the campaign, Dutton has oscillated between two personas: the aggressive ex-cop who seems constantly one question away from snapping, and the awkward, softer image briefly glimpsed during the debate after the death of Pope Francis. But even when Dutton tried to project calmness, it felt strained, temporary, and at odds with his broader political identity. The day after the debate, he reverted to form—aggressive, combative, defensive, and belligerent when challenged by journalists.

This inability to consistently reframe his public persona is a major failing, especially when it has been obvious for years that the 'hard man' image is almost impossible to sell to a broader Australian electorate. Dutton had nearly three years to soften his edges, to offer a new, more constructive vision. Instead, he remained trapped by his past, and by a party apparatus either unwilling or unable to modernise itself.

A SYSTEM IN DESPERATE NEED OF RENEWAL

As the federal election campaign enters its final week, the overall picture has become clearer: a more energised although cautious Labor government seems to be veering towards re-election, and a disjointed and disorganised Coalition struggling to remain relevant. It has been a lugubrious and turgid campaign in many ways, defined more by what was left unsaid than by bold promises or visionary ideas. Yet within that, the broader currents of Australian politics have been exposed—a deep aversion to risk, a media and political system reluctant to engage with real change, and a widening disconnect between the political class and the communities they are meant to serve.

The issues that have been ignored during this campaign—Indigenous justice, climate change, poverty, homelessness, gambling reform, structural inequality—will not vanish after the election. They will grow and eventually demand political attention, whether today's leaders are prepared for it or not, and whether they like it or not. This campaign has been a missed opportunity to address these issues; to lay the foundations for a renewed, fairer Australia. Instead, the political establishment has offered a holding pattern, a rearguard action *against* change rather than a bold leap *towards* it.

If Labor is returned to government, which according to all published opinion polls is the most likely outcome, the pressure will shift. An electorate that may have reluctantly endorsed stability this time around will, over the coming years, demand more: more *ambition*, more *action*, more *courage*. If Albanese's government fails to deliver it, a new generation of independents, minor parties, and community movements will rise to fill the void.

Australian politics is changing—slowly, unevenly, but inevitably: the old party duopoly is weakening. The demands for structural reform, democratic renewal, and genuine social progress are growing louder. This election might not be the evolution many have hoped for, but it may provide another small step towards a different political future—one where *inspiration* is not a dirty word, and where government is about building something bigger than the sum of its political calculations.

***

A HISTORIC LABOR VICTORY AND A DEVASTATING LIBERAL LOSS

5 May 2025

No-one really expected this. There were murmurs, some wishful thinking, a few outlandish predictions—but few expected quite this incredibly one-sided outcome. And yet, many of those wild claims were realised. A number of seats still remain too close to call, but their outcome will do little to change the broader picture: the Albanese Labor government has not only retained power—it has expanded its majority to that of a *landslide*. On election night, Jim Chalmers' attempts to suppress his delight on the ABC broadcast were only partially successful, while Liberal senator James McGrath did a 'Chemical Ali' job of avoiding awkward questions about his party's crumbling prospects, constantly suggesting that it was best to wait for more votes to come in, even though it was obvious to everyone that result was well and truly decided.

But perhaps the most striking moment of the evening came not from the winners, but the vanquished. Peter Dutton's concession speech was unexpectedly gracious. It was humble, even self-deprecating—he accepted full responsibility for the loss, acknowledged the personal journey of his opponent with an empathetic nod to Anthony Albanese's late mother, and gave his blessing to the incoming Labor MP in his former seat, Ali France. For a man whose political brand has for years been associated with hostility, authoritarianism and culture war skirmishes, the moment was disarming. This was not the Peter Dutton the electorate had come to know: it didn't undo years of his political brutality, but it did offer a note of dignity to what is likely the closing chapter of his political career.

The magnitude of the Liberal defeat, and the momentary humanity of Dutton's departure, calls to mind another dramatic reckoning: the election of 1943. The United Australia Party—a precursor to today's Liberal Party—suffered a historic loss at the hands of John Curtin's Labor Party. Like the Liberal Party of 2025, the UAP had once been dominant, governing from 1931 to 1940 under the leadership of Joe Lyons. But Lyons' death, and the flawed elevation of the young and unpopular Robert Menzies, precipitated a rapid decline. Menzies, too arrogant for the times, was soon forced to resign, retreating to the backbench in disgrace. The UAP floundered under uninspiring leadership, was seen as a servant of big business, and had become disconnected from the national mood.

The parallels are remarkable: a party led by unpopular and ill-suited leaders. A steady exodus of moderates. A loss of identity created by years of ideological games. The 1943 election wasn't just a defeat—it was an existential crisis. Menzies recognised this: in 1944, with a mix of business and conservative allies, he created a new party: the Liberal Party of Australia. It would spend the next several decades dominating Australian politics, with only a few interruptions.

That success now feels like ancient history. The modern Liberal Party has purged its moderate flank. The last remaining centrists, Bridget Archer and Keith Wolahan, were swept away in the Labor surge through Tasmania and Melbourne. Calls for introspection during these moments are usually drowned out by demands to shift 'further to the right'—a strategy that continues to produce diminishing returns, not just federally, but in state and local contests. Outside its echo chamber, the party's alignment with the fringe ideas of the Institute of Public Affairs is toxic. And much like the UAP of the 1940s, the Liberal Party of 2025 is beginning to resemble a political museum relic—one that needs reinvention and replacement, to remain relevant in an Australia that has long since moved on.

LABOR'S DISCIPLINE AND THE POWER OF INCUMBENCY

While the Liberal Party unravelled under the weight of internal discord, miscalculation, and ideology, the Labor Party ran one of the most disciplined and effective campaigns in recent memory. It wasn't flashy. It wasn't revolutionary. But it was relentlessly consistent, grounded in pragmatic messaging, and focused on projecting stability—exactly what a risk-averse electorate seemed to want in 2025.

Labor understood the strength of incumbency and used it carefully. Anthony Albanese positioned himself not as a radical reformer, but as a steady hand during uncertain times. His campaign leaned on achievements: real wage growth, declining inflation, a strengthened Medicare system, and modest gains in housing affordability—presented not as *solved crises*, but as challenges being actively and competently managed. It was a subtle, yet powerful narrative: *we know things aren't perfect—but trust us, they're getting better.*

Critically, Labor resisted the temptation to overreach. While the Liberal campaign descended into increasingly dystopian warnings about national collapse and social decay, Labor stuck to measured optimism. Albanese avoided major gaffes, kept controversial ministers largely out of the spotlight, and maintained a clear focus on kitchen-table issues: wages, health, cost of living, and economic certainty. Rather than getting drawn into culture war traps set by the Coalition—on nuclear power, race, gender, and immigration—Labor avoided them altogether. It was a deliberate and disciplined campaign, one that left the Coalition shouting into a void while the electorate turned away.

DUTTON'S UNDOING: MISSTEPS, MISJUDGEMENTS AND ALIENATION

Dutton's defeat was not the result of a single event or tactical blunder—it was the culmination of choices over the years that alienated the very voters he needed to win over. Much has been made of Dutton's overt embrace of Trump-style politics, from the hardline nationalism and race-baiting dog whistles to the stifling culture war rhetoric that felt increasingly imported from the worst of American public debate. But as the United States continued its slide into dysfunction, many Australian voters took a long, hard look and decided this was not an agenda they wanted to follow.

The more immediate blunder came even before the campaign commenced, when Cyclone Alfred struck Queensland. While thousands of residents braced for damage and disruption, Dutton—whose own electorate of Dickson was affected—chose to leave the state for a fundraising event in Sydney, surrounded by corporate donors and political elites. The optics were devastating: the man who wanted to lead the country appeared to abandon his constituents at a moment of crisis. Even for voters who may have tolerated his abrasive style, this act of detachment seemed to be a final breach of trust. For many in the seat of Dickson, this was the moment Dutton forfeited the right to represent them.

But his real downfall may have started much earlier, during the 2023 Voice to Parliament referendum. Dutton's decision to lead the "No" campaign was, at the time, widely seen as a political gamble—a chance to rally the base, weaponise division, and further isolate Labor from conservative and regional Australia. The campaign succeeded in defeating the Voice proposal, but the victory came at a steep cost. Public sentiment shifted rapidly in the months that followed.

Voters—particularly younger Australians, women, Indigenous communities, and urban moderates—began to view the "No" campaign as rooted in deception, fearmongering, and barely concealed racial undertones. Dutton, became the face of that campaign, and for many Australians, he came to embody a form of politics they no longer wished to be associated with.

Perception became reality. Even if Dutton was not personally racist—and by all accounts, many colleagues insist he is not—the image was indelibly stamped. The political stain was compounded by his dry, often sarcastic manner, which read less as wit and more as disdain. For younger voters and women especially, Dutton's style felt combative and cold. He was a man out of step with the country he wished to lead.

In the end, Dutton's concession speech revealed much about his political journey. He made no mention of his leadership, his years in opposition, or even his electorate. Instead, he claimed his career highlight was his time as defence minister—a position built on security, militarism, and fortress politics. It was an interesting admission: for a man who led his party through one of its worst defeats in decades, and who could never quite shake his image as a political enforcer, there was no prime ministerial grace note waiting for him. Just the final irony of a career defined by division, ending in a moment of unexpected humility. Dutton wasn't beaten by fate—he was, in many ways, destined never to lead.

REBUILDING THE LIBERAL PARTY RABBLE

By any sober measure, the Coalition was never going to win the 2025 election. Requiring a net gain of twenty-two seats, the path to majority government was just a mathematical fantasy. But that doesn't mean the campaign had to be wasted in this way. A smarter opposition could have used this parliamentary term to consolidate its base, target winnable seats, and prepare a compelling policy vision that could lay the basis for the next election in 2028. Instead, the Liberal Party drifted through the campaign with policy offerings and costings that were weak and barely held up to scrutiny, vague promises, and a strategy that seemed to rely more on media favours and culture-wars outrage than on genuine public engagement.

While Labor presented discipline, consistency, and policy credibility, the Liberal campaign often looked like a disorganised imitation of past mistakes. The old trick of 'muddling through'—which had worked to a degree in 2013, 2016 and 2019—had finally run its course. The political landscape had changed, and the Liberal Party hadn't kept up. In contrast, Labor had done the hard internal work: it cleared out underperformers, reconciled internal factional tensions, refined its policy program, and learned the lessons from the 2019 defeat and the Voice referendum debacle with a more cohesive, future-oriented identity.

The Liberal Party, by contrast, lacked discipline, clarity, and self-awareness. It seemed complacent—still convinced that culture war slogans and reactionary talking points could substitute for substance and be enough to win. Where Labor had learned and adapted, the Liberals had regressed. It no longer knew who it was fighting for. Menzies once spoke to "the forgotten people"—the middle class that felt ignored by elites and the working class alike. John Howard found resonance with "Howard's battlers"—aspirational blue-collar voters. Even Tony Abbott's crude appeal to "Tony's tradies" had, for a time, connected with a segment of the electorate.

Dutton's Liberals, however, built their identity around a hollow rejection: they were not *woke*, not *elite*, not *educated*. They defined themselves by opposition—against imagined enemies rather than for real constituents. But these enemies were never clearly defined, and the concerns they obsessed over bore little relation to the actual anxieties of the electorate. With cost-of-living pressures, housing insecurity, interest rate worries, and international instability front of mind, the Coalition chose to shout about gender identity and 'cancel culture'. *Anti-woke*. The disconnect was profound. And it was *political suicide*.

The Liberal Party now enters what could be a long, painful period of introspection. Dutton is gone, and the names being floated as successors don't inspire any confidence at all. What the party requires is not another media-friendly placeholder or another ideologue from the fringes—it needs a leader with the courage to dismantle what no longer works and build something new. That will mean staring down the far-right faction, which is already attempting to rebrand itself as centrist while pushing the party even further into irrelevance.

What is required is nothing short of a Menzies-style reimagination. When Menzies founded the Liberal Party in 1944, he correctly identified a growing middle class that wanted stability, autonomy, and dignity. But that middle class has all but vanished in contemporary Australia. A new Liberal leader will have to look more deeply, and honestly, at what Australia is now: fractured by inequality, energised by diversity, and far less tolerant of dogma. This leader must shape a party not for a fantasy electorate, but for the real one that exists today—and govern with a vision that appeals beyond donors, media backers, and culture warriors.

The right has failed to do this for decades. If it cannot now, the Liberal Party may fade into the same irrelevance that consumed the United Australia Party before it. While we can't focus too much on the losers in this election—this is a one-in-a-generation type of victory for the Labor Party and must be savoured as much as possible by their supporters—how the Liberal Party rebuilds itself will be one of the fascinating narratives of this next parliamentary term.

***

THE BIG COLLAPSE: WHAT'S NEXT FOR THE LIBERAL PARTY?

12 May 2025

If a federal election produces a once-in-a-generation victory for one side of politics, it usually comes with a matching catastrophe on the other side—and that's exactly what unfolded for the Liberal–National Coalition in the 2025 election. The scale of the Liberal Party's defeat was unprecedented in Australian political history and, at this stage, it's difficult to see how the party can quickly return to political respectability. Peter Dutton, delivering a sombre and funereal concession speech, acknowledged this reality with a tone of resignation on election night: "Tonight's not the night that we wanted... but we've worked hard every day over the course of the last three years to do our best for our amazing country." These were hollow words in the face of the devastating results—both for the Liberal Party and for Dutton personally, who became the first sitting Opposition Leader in federal history to lose his own seat at a general election.

This wasn't just a bad night for the Coalition; it was a *political disaster*. The primary vote collapsed to 32.1 per cent, the lowest ever recorded for the Coalition, and the two-party-preferred vote sank to 45.1 per cent—another record low. On a proportional basis, they managed to secure just forty-two seats, with the Nationals holding steady (15 seats) while the Liberal Party bore the full brunt of voter dissatisfaction. Sixteen seats were lost by the Liberal Party, its campaign was weak, uninspiring and incoherent, and the leadership of Dutton and his deputy, Sussan Ley—widely considered to be tone deaf and out of touch—received a terrible verdict from the electorate.

The Liberal Party's collapse was severe in the urban heartlands that once defined its base. The party lost its footing in both inner and outer metropolitan areas, transforming what was once a powerful national political force into a party with diminishing urban relevance to something that looks like a second-tier regional organisation—trailing behind even the Nationals in coherence and purpose. Such an electoral wipe-out not only makes a comeback in 2028 virtually impossible, but also raises the possibility that the party may not return to power until the 2030s—if then—and it's quite possible that the next Liberal Party Prime Minister hasn't walked through the doors of parliament yet, or even signed their party membership form.

The causes of this collapse are now being openly debated and will be carefully dissected, even among the party's traditional supporters. For years, the Liberal Party has followed a political and ideological compass that pointed sharply to the right—egged on by the Murdoch media and figures such as Paul Murray and Peta Credlin. Yet in moving further into the culture-war wilderness, the party abandoned the very people it was originally created to represent. Formed in 1944 as an urban and suburban middle-class party, the Liberal Party lost not only traditional strongholds like Kooyong, Deakin, Wentworth and McKellar, but also the outer-suburban aspirational seats that often decide elections. While the seat of Goldstein in Melbourne may have been clawed back, and

Kooyong came close, it wasn't nearly enough to offset the collapse elsewhere.

Even conservative commentators now admit the party must urgently refocus on urban Australia or risk permanent political irrelevance. The Coalition might be intact in name, but the Liberal Party's soul—and its pathway back to national leadership—has never been in greater doubt.

THE CULTURE WARS THAT ATE THE LIBERAL PARTY

The Liberal Party's catastrophic defeat in the 2025 federal election wasn't just a rejection of its campaign or leader—it was a rejection of an entire political identity that has decayed over the past thirty years. This election felt less like a change of government and more like a mass flushing of the political drain—an emphatic rejection of the hard-right, culture-war-driven politics that has defined the Liberal Party since the Howard era. What began in the mid-1990s as a purge of moderates and a consolidation around conservative values has finally reached its logical endpoint: irrelevance in the very electorates that once formed the backbone of Liberal power.

And then, a dangerous complacency set in: the Coalition convinced itself that because it had managed to scrape through elections in 2016 and 2019—largely with the aid of fear campaigns, divisive rhetoric and political luck—it could keep reusing the same formula indefinitely. When it lost in 2022, it treated the result as a temporary setback rather than a structural warning and, instead of recalibrating its offerings to the public, it doubled down. Instead of reflecting, it retreated further into its ideological bunker. Rather than modernising or making peace with shifting social norms and community expectations, the Liberal Party continued to indulge in reactionary culture war tantrums, hoping that the outrage would mask its deficiencies in policy development.

THE BIG COLLAPSE: WHAT'S NEXT FOR THE LIBERAL PARTY?

And still, after the thumping loss in 2025, some within the party's ranks are pushing for *more* of the same. Sky News' Rita Panahi and former party vice-president Teena McQueen became outraged by the party's supposed slide toward "Labor-lite" politics. Incredibly, they framed the failure not as a result of Dutton's relentless negativity or his lack of vision, but as a consequence of him not being *right-wing enough*. McQueen lamented that the executive was "spooked" into softening their messaging on areas such as immigration and Welcome to Country announcements, as if doubling down on Trump-style culture wars could have saved the campaign. That this sort of commentary still finds a receptive audience within the party is a clear indication of how disconnected it has become from mainstream Australia.

At many levels, the Liberal Party appears dysfunctional. While it holds power in Queensland, Tasmania, and the Northern Territory at a state and territory level, these are anomalies rather than signs of vitality. Federally, it has become a hollowed-out shell: bereft of ideas, devoid of vision, and addicted to wedge politics. There is no forward-looking agenda, no appeal to the future—just an endless recycling of fear, resentment, and scapegoating. Its targets were predictable and uninspiring: attacks on the left and "wokeness", Indigenous communities, migrants, China, and anyone vaguely "different": *the other*. And yet somehow, the party leadership seems to think a narrow win in Goldstein or a near-miss in Kooyong justifies staying the course.

But this is a false hope built on fragile foundations. If Tim Wilson is now considered a core part of the party's future, it really is a bleak future. His record as a local member in Goldstein was marred by controversy, arrogance, and underperformance—hardly a signpost for renewal. That he is now reportedly eyeing the position of Shadow Treasurer—or even the leader—highlights just how shallow the Liberal talent pool has become. The higher the ambition, the more intense the scrutiny will become—and Wilson's past doesn't suggest he's built to withstand it.

At the heart of the matter is a crisis of purpose. The Liberal Party no longer seems to know what it stands for, beyond the protection of its own elite and the preservation of privilege. Certainly, the wealthy classes deserve representation, like everyone else in the community does, but the seats they hold at the table are far bigger than everyone else's: a mainstream party that fails to listen to and reflect the broad interests of the electorate ceases to be a mainstream party: it becomes a niche faction masquerading as a movement. In refusing to listen—to *really* listen—to the Australian public, the Liberal Party has shown more about its own insularity and denial.

A LEADERSHIP VACUUM IN THE POLITICAL WRECKAGE

With Dutton losing his seat, the Liberal Party ended the election not just demoralised, but without a leader—and without a clear pathway forward. What remains of its leadership cohort is uninspiring at best: the contest for the top job has narrowed to Angus Taylor, currently the Shadow Treasurer, and Sussan Ley, currently the party's deputy leader. Senator Jacinta Price, who defected from the National party room to the Liberal Party, has also placed herself as a joint ticket with Taylor, even though she's only been in the party for less than a week, a move that isn't likely to go down well with the more established and longer-term MPs within the Liberal Party.

There are also murmurings that Wilson, after narrowly won the seat of Goldstein, might raise his hand as well for the leadership contest. Of course, every party needs to have a leader, but even discussing leadership at this point feels like a pointless exercise, a distraction from the deeper existential work the party must do to avoid long-term irrelevance.

This isn't just about choosing a new figurehead. It's about rebuilding from the ground up—something the party should have begun after its defeat in 2022, but stubbornly refused to address. The Liberal Party has shrunk to a conservative rump: of the forty-two seats retained by the Coalition so far, only twenty-seven belong to the Liberals. Their identity is fractured, their membership base is ageing, and their unbreakable connections to bodies such as the Institute of Public Affairs and media echo chambers such as Sky News and News Corporation have stifled any capacity for genuine renewal. These partnerships might have once served as sources of influence and policy development, but they now act more like ideological anchors dragging the party away from mainstream Australia.

The scale of the rebuild ahead is massive—and might not bear fruit for a decade or more. While it's unwise to rule out anything in politics—remembering that Labor returned to office in 2007 after the 2004 electoral wipeout—the 2028 election seems to already out of reach for the party. Even 2031 feels optimistic and it might be 2034 before the Liberals can even think seriously about forming government again. But to get there, the party needs to undertake a brutal reassessment of what it is, who it represents in the electorate, and whether it can be something more than a political receptacle for resentment and privilege.

Right now, it doesn't matter who the leader is; Taylor, Ley, Wilson, Price or some other unknown figure. The party needs to stop obsessing over personalities and start doing the hard background work it's neglected for years. Policy development, community engagement, renewal of local branches, outreach beyond the ideological base of young hyperactive MAGA wannabes and crusty old men who think *political correctness has gone mad*—these are the fundamentals the party has failed to invest in. Dutton was, at best, always going to be a leadership placeholder, and though his exit from Parliament may spare him the brunt of internal blame, his legacy is one of strategic failure and political delusion. That he genuinely believed the commentary from Sky News about his prime ministerial destiny only highlights how deeply cut off from reality the leadership had become.

Looking back, this trajectory has been long in the making. After John Howard purged the party of moderates in the mid-'90s, a pattern emerged. Tony Abbott took the party further right and weaponised ideological conflict. Malcolm Turnbull, though personally progressive, failed to bring the party with him. Scott Morrison replaced substance with slogans and ran a government mired in secrecy, incompetence and scandal. And then came Dutton—a figure more feared than respected, and unable to bring the party out of its culture war death spiral.

Now the blame game has begun. It's evident from their past behaviours that Taylor is unsuitable and politically compromised, and Ley lacks charisma or strategic instinct, while also being politically compromised with previous scandals over misuse of travel allowances. Former staffers and insiders point to the lack of economic credibility, the absence of serious policy costings, and an election campaign that felt reactive and unfocused. There's plenty of blame to go around—and while Dutton is an obvious target, he shouldn't be the only one. The rot has been systemic, stretching back over a decade or more, across multiple leaders and factions.

The Liberal Party's fall was not inevitable—but it has been well deserved. Unless it faces up to the full scale of its collapse, it will never recover as a major political force. And perhaps the hardest part of all: the Liberal Party must learn to *listen*. Listen to the electorate, not just the loudest voices in the media, and then go on to regurgitate the noise from these voices as political garbage. Listen to communities. Listen to critics. Listen to those who have left the party, and those who might be willing to return—if there is something worth returning to.

***

THE LIBERAL CHALLENGE: A NEW ERA BUT WHO'S READY TO LEAD?

19 May 2025

One of the most dramatic and consequential federal elections in Australian political history is done and dusted and the main parties have all finalised their new leadership teams, setting the stage for what should be a transformative parliamentary term. Of course, Anthony Albanese, boosted by an emphatic victory of ninety-four seats, remains Prime Minister with his authority unchallenged: this was never in question, after such a massive win.

In contrast, the Liberal Party, after its worst election result ever, has chosen Sussan Ley as its new leader, with Ted O'Brien as deputy, following a failed challenge by Angus Taylor, and the last minute no-show of Senator Jacinta Price in the party room. The Australian Greens, having suffered the shock loss of their leader Adam Bandt's seat of Melbourne, have chosen to Senator Larissa Waters as the new leader; and within the Nationals, internal tensions fired up as Senator Matt Canavan launched an unsuccessful leadership challenge against David Littleproud, who managed to win after a secret ballot and undisclosed final numbers.

This batch of leaders for the new parliamentary term face vastly different challenges: for Labor, the task is one of *delivery* and *momentum*—translating their electoral dominance into meaningful reform. For the opposition parties, it's far more complicated. They need to contend with irrelevance, reinvention and the uncomfortable electoral truths that were revealed in the election. A massive parliamentary mandate should allow the Labor government to push through its legislative agenda, but it will also raise the stakes: a government with this much political capital can't rely on excuses or the caution that it so obviously displayed during its first term.

What role can the opposition play in a parliament where the scale of Labor's win has reshaped the balance of power? For the Liberals, the decision to choose Ley as their leader signals a potential shift in tone and style, but does little to answer whether the party really understands why it lost so comprehensively. The Nationals escaped relatively unscathed in the election, losing just one seat to the independent Andrew Gee, yet their alignment with a Liberal brand in crisis might end up being damaging in the long run. The Greens, with their new leadership, will need to rework their strategies, particularly after losing the flagship seat of Melbourne and will need to manage the contradictions between grassroots activism and federal parliamentary politics.

WILL THE LIBERALS LISTEN TO THE MESSAGE FROM THE VOTERS?

Two weeks have passed since the 2025 election and the wounds inside the Liberal Party are still raw. The party will need to shake of the tag of what RedBridge Group strategist Tony Barry referred to as "the nasty party"; there's talk of renewal, of soul-searching, of modernisation—but early signs suggest the party is still holding on to the same policies, point-scoring and the benefactors that helped drive this electoral disaster.

The main issue at the moment is the Coalition's stubborn fixation on nuclear energy, a policy platform came out of nowhere under the leadership of Peter Dutton: it failed to inspire voters and seems to have actively repelled them. It's not just a question of policy misjudgment—it's also about the perception: that the Liberal Party is still too heavily influenced by fossil fuel donors and figures such as Gina Rinehart, whose interests lie in preserving the old economy, not building a new one. Why would the Liberal Party cling on to a scarcely believable policy that failed so badly, or continue to take advice from from a benefactor who can offer a massive supply of funds, but little in the way of political intellect?

Rather than turning the page on the climate wars that have paralysed Australian politics for over a decade and moving forward, it appears the Coalition wants to keep the conflict alive, against what appears to be the clear will of the electorate. The 2025 election didn't just deliver a mandate for Labor; it delivered a strong message—a message that rejects the mindless culture war politics, ideological obstructionism and the relentless negativity.

If the party is serious about gaining credibility again, it needs to look closely at Labor's actions and behaviour in opposition between 2019 and 2022. Rather than lashing out or descending into reactive politics, Labor focused on discipline, policy development, and restoring trust. It lost the 2019 election despite being ahead in the polls, learned from that defeat, and returned with a quieter, more strategic approach—ultimately winning in 2022, and then again in 2025 with an even larger majority. The lesson is there, if the Liberals are prepared to see it: the road back to power is long, slow, and requires a lot more than just repeating failed tactics from the past and listening in to the dilettantes.

REBUILDING THE GREEN WALL BY PLAYING THE LONG GAME

The election was a painful result for the Australian Greens. After briefly tasting genuine lower house influence in the 2022–25 parliamentary term—with three seats held in Brisbane and one in Melbourne—the party has now been reduced to a single seat once again, this time it's the seat of Ryan in Queensland.

Under their new leadership, the Greens face a decision over whether should they continue to concentrate on the Senate—where they hold eleven seats and enjoy considerable influence—or redouble their efforts to gain seats in the House of Representatives, where electoral traction is a lot harder to obtain.

There are precedents for lower house success for the Greens. It's often forgotten, but the first breakthrough for the Greens came in the 2002 Cunningham by-election, when Michael Organ won in an upset result. Then came Adam Bandt, who held Melbourne for fifteen years from 2010 onwards, becoming the face of the lower house ambitions for the Greens. The 2022 election delivered a further breakthrough with the so-called "Greensland" across Brisbane, picking up Ryan, Griffith, and Brisbane. But this momentum proved hard to maintain. By 2025, only one lower house seat remains, and those promising gains in inner-Melbourne didn't materialise.

Yet the potential is still there. The party has demonstrated that, with the right political strategy and electoral messaging, it *can* win in the House of Representatives. But it requires a longer-term view—one that goes past individual electoral cycles. It means targeting winnable seats with precision, building strong local campaigns over multiple elections, and connecting with communities beyond the traditional environmental base. The Greens know how to do this—they've done it before—but what's needed now is a renewed commitment to that approach.

What would success look like for the Greens in the lower house? Winning 10 seats would be fantastic, but fifteen seats would make them a real force—perhaps giving them the balance of power in a minority parliament, in the same way that they operate in the Senate. Of course, that didn't happen in 2025, despite more favourable conditions for a minority government than at any point in the last decade. But it's not out of reach.

The Greens are not at the same crossroads that apply to the Liberal Party. They will continue to be a powerful force in the Senate—scrutinising legislation, shaping climate policy, and holding governments to account. Or they can begin the difficult but essential process of re-establishing themselves as a genuine third force in the lower house. The question is not whether they can do it but whether they are prepared to commit, again, to the long, often unrewarding task of building up electoral power over a longer period of time.

THE CONTINUING GENDER DIVIDE FOR THE CONSERVATIVES

One of the underlying issues of the 2025 election was gender equity—and it's clear which parties took the issue seriously, and which ones still have a long way to go. Labor now has a federal caucus that is 57 per cent female and a Cabinet with 51 per cent women—it's more than symbolic, and this gender balance has translated into real influence and leadership. While Prime Minister Anthony Albanese and Deputy Prime Minister Richard Marles remain in these two senior positions, it's women such as Senators Penny Wong and Katy Gallagher who are at the heart of the government's policy direction and Cabinet authority.

For the Greens, the issue is even more settled. With Waters and Mehreen Faruqi leading the party, and three-quarters of their parliamentary party identifying as women, gender representation has never been a challenge. Their politics are built on inclusion, and the electorate recognises this—particularly younger voters, for whom diversity and equality are non-negotiable issues.

But the Liberal and National parties remain stuck in another era that we thought might have been well and truly over. Only 21 per cent of Liberal MPs and 31 per cent of Nationals MPs are women—a contrast that will continue to cause problems for them at the ballot box. The elevation of Sussan Ley to the Liberal leadership is, at face value, a step forward. Yet it's hard to ignore the deeper structural and cultural barriers within the party that routinely keep women out of winnable seats and leadership positions. The Liberal Party remains captive to internal power blocs, particularly the men on the hard right, and if Ley wants to survive in the role—and do more than just symbolically hold the position—she will have to navigate constant destabilisation from within.

And then there's the media ecosystem. Sky News and aligned voices on the party's fringes have already started megaphoning their dissent at the choice of Ley and suggesting that any move away from the aggressive, reactionary politics of the recent past is a betrayal of Liberal Party. Ley is caught between two irreconcilable imperatives: to modernise the party and bring it back to the political centre where most voters now sit, or to appease the angry, ideologically rigid forces that dominate its internal narrative and external media messaging.

This leadership path is narrow: if the Liberal Party is serious about survival and success in the future, it needs to rapidly and comprehensively reform. That means building a talent pipeline for women, backing them with resources, and placing them in seats they can win: *quotas, targets, allotments*; whatever they want to call it, mechanisms for getting more women into the Liberal Party need to be introduced. It also means abandoning the stale 'blokesville' formula of climate denialism, culture war posturing, and economic policies designed for donors and friends in the right-wing media rather than voters. Certainly, there are many women in the community who champion these right-wing issues, but there just isn't enough of them to achieve electoral success.

THERE'S ALSO A LEADERSHIP TEST FOR THE PRIME MINISTER

For Prime Minister Albanese, the 2025 federal election result was not just a political victory—it was a generational *landslide*. With ninety-four seats, a commanding nineteen-seat majority, and a fifty-one-seat gap between Labor and the shattered leftovers of the Liberal Party, Albanese now leads a government with more power and political capital than any in recent times. The question that looms is not whether he has the numbers to govern decisively, but whether he has the *conviction* to use these numbers.

In the immediate aftermath of the election, Albanese coined the previously unheard phrase of "patriotic progressiveness" to explain the Labor Party's appeal to the electorate—a fusion of national interest with progressive values. But what does this slogan actually mean? Is it the beginning of a new political philosophy, or just a rhetorical shield for caution dressed up as principle? If "patriotic progressiveness" is simply the next iteration of *softly-softly* centrism, it will fall far short of the demands of the here and now—best to leave this sort of rhetoric behind, because this is not the time for political timidity and sloganeering; it's time for moral and political clarity.

The Albanese government was warned by powerful Zionist lobbyists and sections of the media that its failure to enthusiastically support Israel in its ongoing war in Gaza would cost it dramatically in the election—especially in electorates with significant Jewish communities or strong pro-Israel sentiment. But those predictions did not materialise: as it turned out, the Zionist and pro-Israel lobby groups are essentially paper tigers and use bullying and intimidation to achieve their goals and harass governments of the day.

Labor retained and gained seats in diverse electorates and it seems that the public was far more focused on the cost of living, health, housing, and climate change than whether the government passed the litmus test of overt support for the state of Israel. A good government would realise this and cut the pretence.

Despite this, Labor's official position still remains muted—at best cautiously critical of Israel's conduct, at worst complicit in silence. Since the election on May 3, the credible reports of war crimes have continued to emerge, the humanitarian catastrophe of indiscriminate killing and starvation in Gaza continues as a genocide, yet the government is still offering only vague appeals to restraint and "both sides" diplomacy. If "patriotic progressiveness" is to mean anything beyond a campaign slogan, it must start with telling the truth about what is happening in Gaza.

Australia can't claim to stand for progressive values—*patriotic* progressive values—while continuing to arm, support, and provide diplomatic cover for a state engaged in the systematic destruction of an entire population. It cannot claim the moral high ground on human rights while refusing to recognise the humanity and nationhood of Palestinians.

This is the test of leadership. Not just managing inflation or balancing the budget, keeping the Caucus calm, or the media cycle quiet. Leadership is about principle in the face of pressure and about choosing justice over convenience, just as Albanese did as the co-founder of the Parliamentary Friends of Palestine in 1999 (incidentally, Sussan Ley was the leader of this group in 2003, as was former conservative Liberal MP, Ross Cameron). And with the kind of electoral mandate this government now holds, there are no more excuses for deferral or delay.

If Albanese chooses to govern as though the election was just a congratulations on a job done well, he will squander an opportunity that might not ever come again. But if he sees this for what it truly is—a once-in-a-generation mandate for meaningful, values-driven reform—then he has the chance to reshape the political landscape and Australia's place in the world. That would be *real* leadership.

***

FIGHT FOR FAIRNESS: REFORMING SUPERANNUATION

26 May 2025

It's been said that one should never stand between a politician and a bucket of money, but the adage also applies to Australia's wealthiest individuals and the ultra-rich. The proposed Better Targeted Superannuation Concessions Bill—presented to Parliament in 2024—has set off massive debate from the usual suspects in the mainstream media and, if passed, the legislation will come into effect on 1 July 2025 and impose a 15 per cent tax on the portion of superannuation balances *over* $3 million, but only on the annual gains above that threshold.

For example, if a superannuation account grows by the average 10 per cent in a year (as it did in 2024), an account holder with $3 million or more would be taxed 15 per cent on the increase of $300,000—a tax of $45,000 on a wealth gained of $300,000 in one year—which seems like a very fair result and one that's in the interests of equity within the taxation system: if anything, these gains should be taxed even further but, at the least, they will be taxed *something*.

This measure also addresses a genuine problem within Australia's tax and retirement system: the disproportionate benefit that the wealthiest Australians gain from tax concessions that were supposed to support people in retirement through additional financial security, not as a tax shelter for extreme wealth. Yet, as is so often the case with reform in Australia, especially when it's proposed by Labor governments, it has sparked a ferocious campaign of misinformation and fearmongering, led by vested interests and amplified by sections of the mainstream media—most notably, the *Australian Financial Review* which, despite its claims of neutrality, still functions as a financial newsletter for the Liberal Party and other conservative interests.

It's an old pattern that's very familiar: the mainstream media, pretty much across the board, often blurs the facts, pushing misleading narratives or highlighting once-in-a-lifetime individual cases—someone with a complex superannuation setup who might face an unusual tax bill or, *for goodness sake*, be forced to sell their yacht or seventh holiday house—and then presents this as though it reflects a widespread problem. These narratives muddy the waters, and give cover to the powerful who stand to lose the most from change.

The Superannuation Guarantee was introduced in 1992 by the Keating government to ease financial burdens for an ageing population, and reduce the reliance on government-funded pensions. It was never intended as a tax minimisation scheme for the wealthy elite, which is what it has become almost thirty-five years later—a vehicle for those with significant means to accumulate vast wealth with advantages gained through the tax system.

Australia faces a range of pressing policy challenges that require serious, sustained reform—from funding of aged care and public health, to addressing the climate crisis and rebuilding the social safety net while, at the same time, the government needs to deal with the Coalition's legacy of structurally unsustainable Budget deficits. Reforming the tax treatment of superannuation balances over $3 million—

by reducing their highly favourable tax concessions back to something that's more modest—is a small but necessary step towards fairness and Budget responsibility. It's not radical and it's definitely not punitive. It's just common sense and obvious. And it's long overdue.

A SYSTEM EXPLOITED BY THE WEALTH CLASS

There's a persistent and emotionally charged argument that changes to superannuation rules somehow 'punish' those who have *worked hard all their lives*—as if nobody else except self-funded retirees works hard—it's a well-worn cliché, used to protect the interests of a wealthy minority, but completely misses the point. Everyone works hard in their own way, especially those delivering Uber Eats on small scooter-bike to the tree-lined avenues of Dalkeith, Toorak and Vaucluse at dinner time. What separates those with multi-million dollar superannuation balances isn't the effort or diligence—it's privilege. It's the access to better financial advice, the resources to navigate and exploit loopholes, and the capacity to contribute large sums while others can't even afford the basics. Not everyone is a commerce-degree mastermind, or good at finance and business, but they might be good at *many other things*. Hard work isn't the dividing line in these cases—wealth is.

This idea that people with $3 million in superannuation are victims of unfair policy change is a fiction that blatantly ignores the broader reality. Many Australians work hard all their lives and will never own their own home, let alone accumulate $3 million in their superannuation account. The system has been rigged for decades to reward those who already have the means to maximise the benefits—superannuation concessions were designed to assist those on low and middle incomes build a decent retirement and not as a tax shelter for the wealth class.

It's these same individuals who often cry poor, while asking for even more favourable treatment from the government, demanding that tax breaks for the wealthiest be maintained, even as the broader community struggles with stagnant wages, rising costs, and an overstretched public sector. And it's not a large group of people: out of approximately 18 million Australians with superannuation accounts, around 80,000—less than half a percent—have balances of over $3 million. This is a policy that affects a very small, very privileged segment of the population, yet the noise generated by the wealth class and their media allies makes it seem like it's a mass uprising of struggling retirees who are just about to cast out onto the street to left to their own devices.

Successive governments have provided incentives for more contributions into superannuation, and in principle, this is a good thing—more self-funded retirees mean less pressure on the age pension system. But somewhere along the way, the system has been hijacked by a wealthy elite who use it not as a retirement savings plan but as a tax-avoidance scheme. Through complex structures implemented within self-managed superannuation funds, they can purchase commercial properties, shelter capital gains, and avoid personal income tax rates of up to 49 per cent, and replace them with a flat 15 per cent tax—or in some cases, no tax at all.

This pattern is also a reflection of what's happened with franking credits. When the Hawke government introduced the dividend imputation system in 1987, it was designed to stop double taxation on company profits paid to shareholders—but offered a credit only to those who paid income tax. Then, the Howard government broadened the scheme so that even those who paid no income tax could still claim a refund. What started as a sensible reform became, over time, a massive and unsustainable tax giveaway. In 2024, franking credits cost the federal budget around $6 billion—part of a $30 billion annual payout, most of which flows to people who don't pay income tax in the first place.

Superannuation concessions have followed the same path. It's not just a technical issue—it's a question of fairness, of equity, and of whether our tax system serves the public good or the interests of a few. Reforming the system isn't about punishing hard work—it's about ensuring that the benefits of Australia's tax and retirement policies aren't overwhelmingly skewed towards those who need them the least.

A TEST OF POLITICAL WILL FOR THE LABOR GOVERNMENT

The narrative now being pushed against this policy is very similar to the one pushed during the 2019 federal election campaign, when Labor leader Bill Shorten's proposed to reform franking credits—another tax break overwhelmingly benefiting a small cohort of wealthy retirees—was weaponised by the Liberal Party and the financial sector, and succeeded in whipping up fear among people who would never have been affected by the changes anyway, and created a moral panic that Labor was out to rob pensioners and steal their retirement savings.

It's the same fear campaign that's being revived now and it's almost the same voices. The risk is that many Australians who won't be impacted at all by these changes will be misled into believing that their own relatively small retirement savings are under threat, when in fact, the changes only apply to the top 0.5 per cent of people. And if the issues aren't clearly communicated, and if the vested interests are allowed to push their self-serving agendas without any blowback, the public debate risks being hijacked yet again.

But it's about fairness, equity, and the future sustainability of Australia's tax system. Why should the people those who will never have the means to realise a $3 million superannuation balance continue to support the tax breaks of the wealthy few? It's also a reform with a clear democratic mandate. The Labor government campaigned on a platform of fairness and fiscal responsibility, won a resounding majority at the election, and now has the authority—*and the obligation*—to implement the changes it proposed. The Liberal Party, weakened, divided, and preoccupied with its own navel gazing and internal conflicts, is barely an effective opposition, at least in the short term. The policy isn't a surprise; it has been discussed, debated, and openly canvassed for over a year. The public voted just a few weeks ago and they now expect action, not capitulation to the same old voices of entitlement.

If Australia can't even implement a modest reform that affects only the wealthiest 0.5 per cent of the population, what hope is there of achieving the deeper, more systemic tax reforms that are urgently needed? The media and business elite have long championed the idea of tax reform—until it threatens their own interests, or those of their constituents, or if it's proposed by a Labor government, even if it's something that it would support if it was ever proposed by a Liberal Party government.

The reality is that Australia's budget needs fundamental restructuring to ensure long-term sustainability, to deliver the services people expect, and to address the pressing challenges of an ageing population, the climate crisis, and growing inequality. But if every attempt to make the system fairer is met with a massive roar from the wealth class, backed by a compliant media and a frightened political class, how will the desperately needed and meaningful reform ever happen? This is a test for the Labor government—not just of policy, but of political will. And it's long overdue.

***

THE GOVERNMENT'S BETRAYAL OF THE COMMONWEALTH

2 June 2025

During the recent federal election campaign, climate change barely rated a mention—and it seems that this omission suited the Labor government perfectly, as any meaningful discussion would have exposed the uncomfortable reality of Australia's weak environmental credentials: despite a legislated target to cut emissions by 43 per cent below 2005 levels by 2030, the country is not on track to meet this goal, and there's less than five years to go. The omission also meant the government could avoid questions about its approvals for a wave of new coal and gas projects during the last term, quietly enabling the fossil fuel industry to expand while presenting itself as a supposedly responsible climate actor.

Perhaps the most egregious example of this contradiction is the recent decision to extend the licence for the North West Shelf gas project—Australia's largest fossil fuel operation—until 2070, another forty years. Of course, the delay was a deliberate decision: the government extended this licence *after the election*, because it knew that it would have been political toxic to announce it before or during the campaign. The current licence was due to expire in 2030, and there were expectations that the project would begin to wind down, so the Labor government could meet climate targets and provide for a transition away from gas. Instead, Australia will depend on more fossil fuels for decades to come, as well as adding around six billion tonnes of emissions into the atmosphere.

For many years, the North West Shelf project has also been Australia's largest industrial emitter of greenhouse gases and in 2021, accounted for 5 per cent of all emissions in Australia. The extension guarantees that this environmental burden will continue, making a mockery of Australia's international climate commitments under the Paris Agreement.

And in addition to these emissions, the gas project has already inflicted catastrophic damage on the Burrup Peninsula's cultural heritage, with more than 5,000 sacred Aboriginal sites destroyed over the past few decades—carelessly and in some cases, *deliberately*—and the gas plant in Karratha is positioned precariously close to Murujuga rock art, a collection of over a million rock carvings, making it the largest and oldest outdoor art gallery on the planet. These ancient artworks are now threatened by acid emissions, industrial expansion, and the negligence of governments prioritising corporate profits over heritage protection.

This extension also raises serious questions about corruption within Australia's political system. Aside from its program of 'sportswashing' through the AFL's Fremantle Dockers, Woodside has long been a generous donor to both major parties, and between 2010 and 2025, it contributed over $5 million to the Liberal and Labor parties—an investment that, for the company, has obviously paid off handsomely. This is just one in a series of decisions where government approvals for fossil fuel projects have been linked to political donations, exemptions from regulations, and a revolving door of former politicians and bureaucrats joining the fossil fuel sector as consultants or lobbyists. The Labor government's approval of this extension *after the election*—made with little public consultation and transparency—erodes public trust in Australia's democratic institutions and shows how much influence fossil fuel interests have within local politics.

Australia has committed to net zero emissions by 2050, yet this single project will continue to emit greenhouse gases into the atmosphere well beyond that date, undermining the national and global efforts to reduce the effects of climate change. This isn't just a policy decision—it is a choice to sacrifice environmental integrity, cultural heritage, and the wellbeing of future generations in favour of short-term political convenience and corporate profits. And it's obvious that the Labor government with its freshly minted 50-seat majority in Parliament, despite its rhetoric on climate action, has made its priorities very clear for the next term.

THE FIRE SALE: HOW AUSTRALIA'S GAS WEALTH IS SQUANDERED

Aside from the environmental scandal, the extension of the North West Shelf gas project is also a monumental economic failure. For years, Australia has practically given away its vast mineral and energy resources, collecting only a fraction of the revenue that other gas-rich nations extract from the same industry. The Labor government, in approving this extension and maintaining a broken tax regime, is continuing the very practices it once condemned when the Coalition was in power: the quiet, ongoing sell-off of national resources to corporate interests for next to nothing.

During 2023-24, the Australian government collected $1.1 billion on natural gas exports of $70 billion through the petroleum resource rent tax, a tax which was created to supposedly collect a fair share of profit from the non-renewable resources sector. This is less than 1.5 per cent of the value of the gas. In contrast, Qatar had a similar level of exports—77 million tonnes, versus Australia's 84 million tonnes—yet collected $26 billion in royalties, or almost *twenty-six times more*.

To add further insult to injury, around 80 per cent of Australia's LNG is shipped overseas, with no royalties paid on around 56 per cent of this gas. In effect, vast quantities of the country's natural wealth are being extracted, processed, and sold for massive profits by multinational energy companies, while the Australian public sees almost none of the benefits. The government's own reports have repeatedly shown that the current resource rent tax system has too many loopholes that allow gas giants such as Woodside, Santos, and Chevron to offset their profits through deductions, inflate development costs, and avoid paying a meaningful share back to the Australian people.

Defenders of this ludicrous arrangement—primarily from the resources industry—argue that raising royalties or closing tax loopholes would scare off investment, yet Qatar imposes far higher tax rates and royalty charges on its gas sector, and its industry is booming. In fact, Qatar has successfully leveraged its gas wealth to fund social services, infrastructure, and economic diversification, while Australia has let its own gas boom become a profit bonanza for corporations and shareholders.

The North West Shelf extension, and the failure of resource taxation and royalty scheme represents a historically and monumental failure of government. It's a case study in how public resources are transferred to private hands with next to no benefit to the nation. The Labor government, like its Coalition predecessors, has perpetuated this model: approving projects that lock in fossil fuel dependency, while ensuring that the financial windfall flows almost entirely to industry, and not to the public. At a time when governments around the world are rethinking resource taxation in the face of climate change—as well as addressing higher levels of public debt—Australia has signed away its wealth for another forty years and undermined its own environmental commitments.

ECONOMY AND ENVIRONMENT SACRIFICED AT THE ALTAR OF GREED

The seeds of Australia's gas disaster were planted many decades ago. The North West Shelf project—established in the early 1980s—was supposed to capitalise on the nation's vast gas reserves, primarily for export. The first shipments of liquefied natural gas left for Japan in 1989, but even then, the royalty and tax arrangements were hopelessly inadequate. The most ridiculous deal, however, came in 2002: a long-term contract facilitated by the Howard government to supply three million tonnes of LNG per year to China, worth $25 billion over twenty-five years—roughly $700 million to $1 billion per year, with prices locked in until 2031, with no increases allowed, no matter how much global LNG prices surged.

By 2015, the absurd nature of the deal became obvious: as international LNG prices kept on skyrocketing, Chinese buyers were paying around one-third of what Australian domestic consumers were forced to pay for the same gas, and from the same market. The situation was so ludicrous that Australian companies were buying back their own gas—and still doing so—from overseas markets in Japan and South Korea because it was cheaper than purchasing it domestically. It is, without a doubt, one of the worst commercial deals ever signed off by an Australian government—locking the nation into decades of underpriced exports while Australians faced rising energy costs at home.

In 2019, Woodside, along with its joint venture partners—Chevron, Shell, BP, and Mi/Mi—formally proposed to extend the life of the project, including the Karratha gas plant. Despite widespread warnings from scientists and environmentalists that have been provided over the past six years, the project has now been approved by the new Minister for the Environment, Senator Murray Watt. Independent analyses suggests that due to the additional six billion tonnes of greenhouse gases released over its lifetime, this will make it almost impossible for Australia to achieve net-zero emissions by 2050.

This approval is a betrayal by the Labor government—a sell-out of both the environment and Australia's economic future. Labor was swept into office in 2022 on the back of promises made on climate action and renewable energy investments but it has reneged on so many of these promises. The government also abandoned plans to establish a federal Environmental Protection Agency in the lead-up to the Western Australian state election, fearing a backlash from powerful fossil fuel interests, and since its election in 2022, it has approved new gas fields, new coal mines, and now this—an extension of a project that locks in decades of carbon pollution, both here and internationally. And this is in the context of Australia already feeling the consequences of climate *inaction*: a summer of record-breaking heat, unprecedented cyclones battering Queensland, and severe flooding for New South Wales.

It's a strange political dissonance and surely one that will catch up with the government at some point, despite the fact that they're up against a weak Coalition opposition. It's becoming clear, however, that this government, despite its promises, is not serious about climate change. There's the ongoing rhetoric, but it continues to prioritise short-term fossil fuel profits over long-term environmental survival and economic fairness. The extension of this project is not just another economic blunder on behalf of the Commonwealth—it's a deliberate decision to sacrifice Australia's climate commitments, its Indigenous cultural heritage, and the interests of future generations for the sake of corporate greed. And once again, it's the public who will pay the price: through higher energy costs, a destabilised climate, and the irreversible loss of the nation's natural and cultural treasures.

***

THE HONOURS SYSTEM OR A SYSTEM IN DISHONOUR?

9 June 2025

When the Order of Australia awards were announced in 1975 as a replacement for the antiquated British honours system that Australia had held for decades, conservative thinkers were incensed. Monarchists were similarly outraged and openly hostile, suggesting the new system was a "Bunyip Aristocracy", and deplored its lack of historical legitimacy.

Others claimed that honours needed to be rooted in long tradition to carry *real* gravitas, questioning whether a new local system could ever match the centuries-old British awards in symbolic power.

Meanwhile, on the left, there were deeper concerns about the very existence of an honours system in a nation that prided itself on egalitarian values. Critics such as historian Humphrey McQueen noted that many prominent Australians—Alfred Deakin and Rupert Murdoch among them—had refused such honours, arguing either that they had already been sufficiently rewarded or that such recognitions were better suited to others. Paul Keating, widely regarded as one of Australia's more transformative prime ministers, also declined the award, despite his substantial achievements in economic reform, Indigenous affairs, and foreign policy.

The Order of Australia was designed to function alongside the British system initially, but from 1992 onwards, it stood alone. It consists of four tiers: the Medal of the Order (OAM) for local service, Member (AM) for more significant contributions, Officer (AO) for national-level impact, and Companion (AC), intended to recognise those whose work has had a profound effect on the nation or the world.

Yet the process, though meant to be rigorous and independent of government influence, has not always functioned as intended. Nominations are supposed to be anonymous, community-driven, and vetted with stringent checks on referees. The system works well—recognising tireless community workers whose names would never appear in headlines, but who gave decades of unpaid, often invisible labour to others. For them, the award was a simple gesture of gratitude—an official pat on the back from the state.

But the integrity of the system has been repeatedly tested. If a nominee becomes aware of their nomination prematurely, or if they attempt to nominate themselves, their eligibility is voided. And yet, when you examine the list of past Companions, the suspicions raised by conservatives back in the 1970s appear eerily prescient.

Among the honoured are figures of dubious moral standing—crooks, spivs, political hucksters and corporate shonks—some of whom eventually relinquished their awards under pressure or scandal, such the former High Court judge Dyson Heydon, who resigned from the Order of Australia in 2022 following findings of sexual harassment. It's a list that, while including many admirable Australians, increasingly resembles the kind of club Groucho Marx once joked about: one you'd rather not be part of, precisely because of who else is in it.

THE REWARDING OF FAILURE

The revelation that Scott Morrison is to be appointed a Companion of the Order of Australia should mark the end of the honours system altogether. For many, Morrison stands as the most underwhelming, divisive and damaging prime minister in the history of the federation—a leader whose tenure was marked not by distinction, but by secrecy, cruelty, and profound misjudgement.

His management of the COVID-19 pandemic saw the virus spread rapidly and with devastating consequences. He infamously claimed "it's not a race", and delayed the delivery of vital medications and supplies. His role in disembarking passengers from the *Ruby Princess* in March 2020 remains unclear, but it's a decision that allowed infected people to go into the community, and the spread of the virus from this case resulted in twenty-eight deaths and over 900 infections. The management of the pandemic, under Morrison's watch, proved to be a disastrous failure.

His crowning "achievement", the AUKUS deal, locked Australia into a decades-long strategic and a $380 billion financial commitment, funnelling vast public funds into the American defence industry with little more than speculative promises in return. His secret self-appointment to five additional ministries not only undermined cabinet government but also made a mockery of democratic norms and transparency.

Worse still was his economic management. As Treasurer, Morrison oversaw policy decisions that widened inequality, ignored structural issues, and pursued ideological rigidity over evidence-based action. And as Prime Minister, he presided over Robodebt—a scandal now infamous not only for its illegality, but for its cruelty. This automated welfare scheme unlawfully pursued vulnerable citizens for debts they didn't owe, leading to widespread trauma, financial despair, and, tragically, suicides. Morrison has neither apologised nor faced true consequences for the policy. And now, someone has decided he deserves the nation's highest civilian honour.

His appointment stains the awards system. It diminishes the meaning of every medal handed to a humble community volunteer, an unsung teacher, a lifelong carer. It tells Australians that failure, dishonesty, and cruelty in high office will still be rewarded—if not by the public, then by a panel cloaked in respectability. It casts the entire honours structure into disrepute. There is a deeper philosophical question too: why should already prominent and well-compensated individuals receive even more praise, when so many Australians who live lives of quiet service go without recognition? In a society that values equality, should we be showering political elites—especially those who used their power to diminish others—with vainglorious validation?

What exactly are we rewarding Morrison with? His flagrant abuse of power? His botched pandemic management? His callous response to natural disasters? His vanishing act during national crises? Or is it simply the hollow idea that holding high office, no matter how badly is, in itself, enough cause for celebration?

Scott Morrison deserves no honour. He should be remembered not for leadership, but as a reminder of how far Australia can fall when competence and accountability are thrown out the window. To grant him the Companion is not just tone-deaf; it's an insult to the lives he failed, and to the very idea that honours should reflect integrity, service, and sacrifice. His name does not elevate the Order of Australia—it drags it into the dirt. He may have been prime minister, but he brought no honour to the role and, as such, does not deserve any honour at all.

**

AMERICAN FASCISTI: IS IT THE END OF AN EMPIRE?

16 June 2025

The political and social situation developing in the United States is increasingly chaotic and authoritarian, marked most recently by the ongoing unrest in Los Angeles. These protests—triggered by the sweeping and draconian immigration ICE raids ordered by U.S. President Donald Trump—have reached a level of dystopian aggression not seen in America for decades. Nearly 5,000 National Guard troops and marines have been deployed across the city, and the result has been widespread civil rights violations: tourists incorrectly detained and deported, legal residents unlawfully removed, and individuals targeted just for their viewpoints offered online. Social media is now under widespread scrutiny, and the expression of views such as "Free Palestine" or even mild criticism of the Israeli state has become a deportable offence. The scale and brutality of the crackdown in Los Angeles—rubber bullets, tear gas, pepper spray, and stun weapons deployed indiscriminately—have shocked many observers.

This is not the behaviour of a confident or stable democracy—it's the erratic violence of a crumbling regime and resembles the actions of an autocratic tin-pot dictatorship, further magnified by the first military parade since 1991, which coincided with Trump's birthday on June 14. Of course, American history is riddled with moments of state violence, from the 1992 L.A. riots to the shootings at Kent State University and other campuses, and systemic and historical violence perpetrated against people of colour. These events have never been isolated—they have risen from a deeper structural brutality, one that's often racially charged, and from a leadership class that is increasingly obsessed with control as their grip on reality weakens. Trump's impulsive declarations, such as calling for the arrest of California Governor Gavin Newsom, only highlights this insecurity, and there's no real logic behind this administration's actions—just a high level of paranoia, volatility, and a creeping embrace of American fascism.

While it might be so evident right now, Trump is *not* the disease, but a *symptom* of the ills of the United States. The deeper sickness is the slow but unmistakable decay of the American system itself. Trade policy under Trump lurches erratically from one direction to another, gaining applause and cheers from an equally maniacal Republican Party. Allies are cast aside on a whim, including Australia. Iran is attacked through America's vassal state, Israel. The United States no longer functions with strategic clarity—only tactical knee-jerk reactions that end up hitting everyone in the face. It's not a sustainable situation, and the world, especially countries such as Australia, need to wake up to what is happening. The alliance once based on shared values and global stability is now increasingly becoming compromised by America's Trumpist dysfunction and Australia needs to start charting an independent path and diluting its alliances, not out of hostility, but for the sake of due diligence and self-preservation.

Since the late-1800s, the United States has brought immense harm to the world through belligerence, self-interest and an unchallenged belief in its own exceptionalism. For sure, the United States has also provided the world with profound beauty—jazz, blues, cinema, television, and literature that shaped a century—but these cultural gifts mask the disastrous face of an interventionist U.S. military, which has had a role in almost every conflict around the world since 1945, either through direct military involvement, clandestine CIA-backed operations, indirect proxy involvement and arms trades. The U.S. has been the out-of-control behemoth for many years, but it's going through a natural and slow decline which has been building up for some time.

Empires don't last forever; history has shown that. We watched the Soviet Union collapse in the late 1980s; now we are watching the United States decline in full view. Of course, it won't vanish overnight, but the trajectory has been set: we've seen this happen in history before and it's happening again, and the sadness of watching something so influential falter is tempered only by the inevitability of it. Power fades; it always does, once its replaced with complacency. And for now, the wisest course for countries such as Australia is to stay alert, stay detached, and strategically prepare for what comes next.

AUSTRALIA'S SUBSERVIENCE FAILURE TO SPEAK TRUTH TO POWER

What's just as disturbing as the events in the United States is Australia's muted, almost embarrassed response to it. The spectacle of our national government and media tiptoeing around American brutality—this time, a U.S. National Guardsman shooting rubber bullets that hit Australian journalist Lauren Tomasi in Los Angeles—has been disheartening but predictable. There isn't a dispute about the facts: she was clearly identified as media, obviously doing her job, standing at a reasonable distance from any confrontation, yet was deliberately targeted. The footage that went viral all around the world is very clear. And yet, the initial reporting by Australian outlets was almost apologetic and submissive—portraying Tomasi as "caught in the crossfire", as if her injury were some unfortunate but understandable accident, rather than an act of calculated intimidation.

The response reflects a broader trend of Australian deference to the United States, particularly under the Albanese government. Last week it was Defence Minister Richard Marles fawning over U.S. military might, practically grovelling in public. This week, it's the media unwilling to defend one of their own, for fear of offending a dangerous ally. At first, Prime Minister Anthony Albanese seemed to follow suit, issuing a vague and mealy-mouthed statement about "democratic institutions" and "global uncertainty". What does that even mean in the face of a soldier turning a weapon on a clearly marked journalist?

Perhaps realising the errors of his ways, Albanese later clarified his position with stronger language, calling the incident "horrific" and noting that the footage made it clear she was just doing her job as a journalist, also stating that the government had raised the issue with the U.S. administration and considered the action unacceptable. But even this firmer stance still had the air of damage control, rather than a bold defence of press freedom and police brutality meted out to an Australian citizen.

The idea that this was an *accident*—or just "rubber bullets"—is itself part of the problem. Rubber bullets can do some serious damage to people. They can kill. They're designed not for gentle deterrence, but for violent crowd suppression. This was a direct shot to the leg, fired with intent, by someone who likely resented her presence as a journalist bearing witness to what was happening on the ground. If the price of maintaining the American relationship is silence in the face of violence, or when media freedom is under attack, then Australia needs to ask itself whether it is protecting a friendship or enabling a descent into fascist tyranny.

A MAD KING AND THE ALLIANCE OF ILLUSION

There's no longer any serious argument that what's unfolding in the United States is normal politics. It has become a theatre of the absurd in power and dysfunction, but its consequences are real and global. The latest drama in the fallout between Donald Trump and Elon Musk—which appears to be more of a battle of two ego-driven Alpha males in an episode of the TV soapie *Bold and Beautiful*, than an ideological contest to arrive at the best outcomes for the United States. But it's also important to remember that *this ain't no soap opera*: one of them is the elected leader of the most powerful country in the world—at this time in history but, perhaps not for too much longer—the other is the wealthiest man on the planet, who holds incredible influence in technology, communications and space infrastructure. Neither of them are grounded within the tradition of democratic accountability, neither behave in ways that inspire global confidence, and come directly from the world of crony capitalism.

Imagine the outcry and ridicule if China's President Xi Jinping had a very public feud with Jack Ma or spent his time posturing on social media, quoting obscure song lyrics, dancing to a Chinese version of the Village People or waging personal vendettas. We'd rightly call it erratic and dangerous, and China would lose all credibility on the world stage. But when Trump does it, the Australian media too often shrugs and dismisses it as *Donald being Donald*. He now carries the nickname "TACO"—Trump Always Chickens Out—after requesting a call with Xi Jinping, only to refuse it once it was granted. This is not *strategy*. It's not *diplomacy*. This is chaos dressed in a presidential suit.

And yet, here we are—watching the United States spiral out of control, while Australia waits awkwardly in the wings, unsure how to act. It's been nearly a decade of degraded leadership in Washington: from the first Trump term's scorched-earth populism, to Joe Biden's stumbling centrism, and now Trump 2.0—a return to volatility without even the pretence of governance. Australia is caught somewhere in the middle, clinging to old certainties in a world that no longer resembles the post-war order we built ourselves around. We're no longer a part of the British Empire that Menzies always wanted to reach out to; we're no longer a part of the U.S. exceptionalism that John Curtin felt Australia could use to its strategic benefit. It's clear that stronger relationships with China would be of greater benefit to Australia, but the Anglo-U.S. connection keeps denying us the clear direction that we need to travel towards.

The sensible course would be to begin the slow, strategic decoupling from American military dependency. Instead, we remain wedded to a fantasy of permanence—none more evident than our silence over the AUKUS agreement. While the United States has launched an internal review of AUKUS, and the United Kingdom is reassessing its commitment, Australia refuses even to discuss the possibility. It's total *madness*. If two out of the three members of a tripartite alliance are having doubts, it defies logic not to review the deal. You cannot cling to the "A" in AUKUS if the "UK" and "US" walk away, or continue to believe the deal is a reliable one if the other two parties are critically assessing the merits of it.

There is growing political pressure to reassess or cancel the AUKUS deal. Former Prime Minister Malcolm Turnbull, while he's been a long-term critic of the AUKUS deal, is now calling for a review, along with the Australian Greens who are also demanding transparency and parliamentary approval for these kinds of military and security deals. But what do we get from the Australian government? Silence and a government still caught in the inertia of old alliances and Cold War ghosts.

The Prime Minister has recently talked about "Australia making its own decisions". If that's the case, now is the time to prove it. It is not radical to say that Australia's defence and foreign policy should be developed and created in Canberra, not in Washington or London. We no longer owe anything to the Anglosphere's geopolitical fantasy. The Pacific is our neighbourhood, and the Indian Ocean is our future. Our attention must turn to the region we live in, not to the dying empire across the Atlantic or, as former Prime Minister Paul Keating said, Australia needs to "seek its security *in* Asia rather than *from* Asia".

For decades, Australia's relationship with the United States has operated on loyalty rather than strategy. John Curtin turned to America in 1941 because Britain had failed us. Harold Holt declared we were "all the way with LBJ" in 1966. But the time for declarations is long over. Today's alliance is unbalanced. Australia is treated as a client state—militarily compliant, economically pliant, and politically submissive. We house U.S. bases. We commit to their wars. We accommodate their spies. And when a journalist is shot by an American soldier on U.S. soil, our first instinct is not to protest—but to defer and explain it all away, as if nothing really happened.

It's no longer enough just to be the so-called good friend or rely on this jingoistic notion that we are "all mates". Australia must now be a sovereign friend. That means asking hard questions, reviewing dangerous deals, and breaking the habit of obedience and subservience. The mad king is back on the throne in the U.S. It's just that we can't afford to be his loyal jester for too much longer.

***

THE REAL AGENDA BEHIND THE BOMBING OF IRAN

23 June 2025

The world moved closer to complete catastrophe in Middle East this week, when Israel launched a series of unprovoked attacks on Iran's nuclear facilities and missile sites, resulting in the deaths of 224 people—most of them civilians. Iran then responded with missile strikes of its own, leaving twenty-four Israelis dead and, to round off the week, the United States bombed three nuclear sites within Iran under Operation Midnight Hammer, at the behest of and with the full co-operation of Israel.

The official rationale for Israel's assault and the follow-up U.S. bombing was the now-familiar claim: Iran is "weeks away" from developing a nuclear bomb, a false claim repeated by Israel, Prime Minister Benjamin Netanyahu—without any evidence—for well over twenty years. But this justification seems to be a repeat of the infamous lies about Iraq's weapons of mass destruction—a convenient fiction that hides far more cynical motivations, just as it did back in 2003.

Behind the air raids and retaliatory fire lies a large dose of political desperation. Both Israel and the United States are struggling with internal political crises—in Israel, Netanyahu is besieged by ongoing legal battles, mass protests, and a collapsing far-right coalition. In the United States, the political system is paralysed by dysfunction and ineptitude, as a result of a second Trump presidency and a deeply polarised nation. A foreign crisis—especially one framed as a supposedly righteous pre-emptive strike—offers both governments a perfect distraction and a chance to change their respective political narratives. But the stakes are also dangerously high, and this reckless brinkmanship could ignite a regional war with no winners, and only leaving behind a trail of destruction.

As always, there's an obvious level of hypocrisy and duplicity at play here. Israel does not allow visits from the International Atomic Energy Agency and has not signed the Nuclear non-Proliferation Treaty. In contrast, Iran *has* signed up to the Treaty, allows inspections into its nuclear program, and was holding negotiations with the United States, just as Israel was firing rockets at Tehran, and decided that it was best to kill Ali Shamkhani, Iran's chief negotiator in these talks. Just *who* exactly are the real terrorists here?

Yet the Western narrative insists that it's Iran poses the nuclear threat. For over two decades, Israel has claimed that Iran is on the verge of acquiring nuclear weapons—an imminent danger that never materialises, and is always used to justify the next act of aggression. Iran's uranium program remains well below the 90 per cent enrichment threshold that's needed to develop a nuclear weapon—even the U.S.'s own intelligence agencies have confirmed this—and yet it's Iran that's portrayed as the villain in this geopolitical game, not Israel.

While there is still some way to go on this conflict, the United States and Israel will be in for a rude shock if they think they will emerge from this war victorious and unscathed. Iran is not Libya. Nor is it like Iraq, Gaza or Syria. It's a nation of 94 million people, with a larger and formidable geography that makes conventional invasion a logistical nightmare. The Iranian plateau, like the highlands of Afghanistan or the beaches of Gallipoli, is difficult terrain for military warfare. And no nation has ever been conquered by air strikes alone, a fact that any student of military history would understand. The United States learned this lesson the hard way in Vietnam, and then again in Afghanistan. A motivated population defending its homeland cannot be broken by bombs. Pentagon analysts would also understand this, and they have reportedly warned against any such incursion, recognising that the cost in lives, equipment, and the damage to the credibility of the United States would be immense and futile.

What we're witnessing, in all likelihood, is a game of *distraction*, for ulterior motives, and none of them are good. For Netanyahu, war is political capital—the 'forever wars' are a means of survival for his leadership, a diversion from courts and corruption trials. For Washington, it's a convenient distraction from its economic woes, the debacle of the Trump's tariffs war, electoral disarray, and policy paralysis. But the collateral damage isn't just Iranian or Israeli lives—the entire region is precariously balance on the edge of chaos.

The only hope—if that's what we can call it—is that this latest escalation is not much more than a cynical ploy by two failing governments and two inept leaders to manufacture relevance, or at least provide a short-term distraction. But if they really do believe they can impose regime change in Iran through force and, as Trump suggested, "make Iran great again", they are deluding themselves. Most leaders in the West would realise this, and it's about time they started saying the quiet bit out loud, before it's too late.

THE RIGHT TO DEFEND: WHO HAS IT AND WHAT ARE THE RULES?

War should never be the first response in any circumstance—it *must* remain the last line of defence. If peace is the product of hard work, wise and capable leadership, and war is the easy and final refuge of scoundrels and a game played by leaders of low intellect, then Trump and Netanyahu are obvious candidates to lead this feckless march toward destruction.

Wars *should* be avoided at all costs, yet here we are again, as if the lessons of Iraq, Libya, and Syria have been erased by collected amnesia and a lobotomised Western community, with leaders choosing escalation over diplomacy and provocation over diligence.

Senator Penny Wong—surely up there as one of Australia's most unprincipled Foreign Ministers—condemned Iran's missile strikes on Israel as a "dangerous escalation," while reiterating Australia's commitment to international law and the supposed right of Israel to defend itself. And yet, in these carefully worded statements lies the big omission: if Israel has a right to defend itself—surely a standard part of statehood, irrespective of how that statehood was achieved—then why is there no equal recognition of Iran's right to respond to what was, quite clearly, an unprovoked assault by Israel? If international law is so important for Israel, why was it not important when Israel was attacking Iran? Or for the eighteen months Israel has been perpetrating a genocide on the peoples of Palestine? Where is the application of international law in those cases?

This selective framing has become *so* predictable and disgustingly outrageous and disingenuous. It would be more intellectually honest, although politically inconvenient, for Wong to acknowledge that Iran's strikes were retaliation for an initial Israeli attack, itself part of a broader campaign sanctioned and materially supported by the United States. But to say that plainly would involve uncomfortable diplomatic contortions, and so Wong's narrative remains obtuse and untrue—Israel *defends*; Iran *provokes*. Iran is a *regime*, after all, so of course, for Wong and her Western friends, it's always going to the one that provokes, even when it doesn't.

Geopolitically, it's not helpful to claim who fired the first shot—like the shot fired by Gavrilo Princip at Archduke Franz Ferdinand that led to war in 1914—because these are deeply complex tensions rooted in decades of covert operations, sanctions, proxy wars, and ideological antagonism. But moral clarity could be found in calling out what is obviously being ignored: no one in Canberra or Washington is speaking about Iran's right to self-defence. Nor Lebanon's. Nor Palestine's.

For all the talk about adhering to international law, the law seems to be selectively applied in only the one direction: Israel. And, who knows, if international norms had been consistently applied over the past eighteen months—and if Israel's bombardment of Gaza, incursions into Lebanon, and now direct strikes on Iran had been called out with even a fraction of the outrage reserved for their retaliation—we might not have reached this point.

International law, like diplomacy, is imperfect. It hasn't prevented wars in the past, but when applied, it has delayed them, restrained them, and sometimes even stopped them. The erosion of these protocols happens not through a single violation, but through the steady silence that follows every breach. And when silence follows one side's actions—Israel's—and the other side takes all the blows without sanction, it's obvious that retaliation will become the only remaining language of power.

FALSE WORDS AS A WEAPON OF WAR

This conflict hasn't been fought just through missiles and drone attacks—it's also been waged with words and rhetoric—and the language used in Western media, as well as by its political leaders, has become a weapon in its own right. The pattern is the usual one, and uses a clear formula: Israel has a *government*, Iran has a *regime*. The United States has *allies*, Syria and Lebanon have *proxies*. Britain and Australia support *democracies*; Russia and China prop up *despots*. It's the old Cold War rhetoric of moral superiority, where "regimes" is the code-word for any nation not aligned with Western interests and any country that we don't like: Iran, Cuba, China, North Korea, Venezuela—if they won't bend to the American-led order and go on to resist in any way, they are labelled *regimes*. And regimes in the eyes of the United States, of course, are there to be toppled, not to be reasoned with.

This weaponisation of language doesn't only shape perceptions, but also directs policy. It dehumanises the enemy and simplifies the conflict to fit an easily digestible narrative. Saddam Hussein, once a key United States ally during Iraq's war with Iran between 1980–88, was referred to as *a leader* then. But when he outlived his usefulness, he became a dictator heading a *brutal regime*. It was the same man, and the same country. But, a different spin was applied. And that spin paved the way for one of the most catastrophic foreign policy failures of the modern era—the 2003 invasion of Iraq. Over 200,000 civilians died. The country was destroyed. And the justification, parroted by George W. Bush, Tony Blair, and our own John Howard, was a complete fiction: the weapons of mass destruction didn't actually *exist*, it was a falsehood to justify an invasion of a sovereign country.

Today, the same narrative is coming back to life. Iran is once again being framed as a rogue power on the verge of nuclear capability, while the lies of Iraq's "weapons of mass destruction" has faded into the background for those who conveniently benefit from public amnesia. But the objective remains the same: dominance over the Middle East. It's not about nuclear weapons, it never has been. It's about punishing Iran for rejecting American control in 1979; it's a payback for the hostage crisis between 1979–81; for the removing the United States-installed puppet ruler, the last Shah of Iran, Mohammad Reza Pahlavi—and for nearly half a century of

Iran refusing to play by the rules of Washington. What we are seeing here is the long tail of imperial resentment by the United States, just like a spoilt child, in the same way it punished Cuba and Vietnam for decades after humiliating and well-deserved defeats.

While many still accept the political framing—*Iran is a regime and must be stopped*—more and more people are beginning to question this ridiculous script. What does "regime" even mean? Is it really any different from right-wing strongman war mongers like Trump or Netanyahu, whose own governments have embraced authoritarianism while still cloaking themselves in the language of democracy?

People have become more cynical, and more literate in the output of propaganda pushed forward by the state. They've seen how words have been twisted to justify Iraq, Libya, Syria, Afghanistan—and now Iran—and they're less likely to accept it this time around.

WAR AS A LIFELINE FOR LEADERS IN TROUBLE

The recent escalations in Gaza, Lebanon, Syria, and now Iran appear less like strategic military operations and more like calculated political theatre, just like we saw in the movie *Wag The Dog*. A common thread in all of this is Netanyahu, a leader clinging to power by any means necessary, including manufacturing wars to keep a hold of power. With an Israeli election looming in October 2026 and a right-wing coalition as fragmented as ever, Netanyahu's survival strategy seems to rest on keeping the country in a state of permanent war, just like Orwell's *1984* concept of the "forever war".

But that election is still over a year away: can Netanyahu really keep up this charade for another fifteen months without plunging the region into deeper chaos? Can the world afford to pander to a leader such as Netanyahu when global peace is at stake? Across the Atlantic, Trump is reading from the same script—using inflammatory threats and foreign policy bluster to distract from his own mountain of legal troubles and authoritarian fantasies, and "peace through strength". It's not a ridiculous as "we had to destroy the village in order to save it" that the U.S. applied in the Battle of Ben Tre in Vietnam, but it's getting there.

Just this week, Trump publicly threatened to assassinate Iran's leadership, and fresh from bombing three nuclear sites in Iran—against international law—is now openly calling for "regime change". This isn't strategy: it's just tough-guy recklessness dressed up as resolve, like a bumbling G.I. Joe character with orange hair. And it highlights a frightening reality: two of the world's most powerful and nuclear-armed states are being steered by two foolish old men who are using war as a tool of self-preservation.

For sure, Iran has its problems, but it's not an isolated rogue state, like North Korea. It is a major power in the Middle East with long term alliances and strategic importance. India has a strong diplomatic relationship with Iran, and Russia views Iran as a partner in its anti-Western bloc. China has long courted Iran for economic cooperation. This isn't Libya or Afghanistan. An attack on Iran risks detonating a regional war, if not a global crisis.

This use of "regime change" rhetoric from Washington and Tel Aviv is, clearly, far removed from any strategic logic. The Iranian state is entrenched, not just militarily but socially. The leadership might not be universally popular, but as history has shown—most recently in Iraq—foreign intervention has the uncanny ability to unite even a fractured population against a common external enemy. To remove Iran's government by force would require a ground invasion of a mountainous nation with 94 million people. Even the United States—the world's largest military power—knows this is not viable, yet, just as Colin Powell did over Iraq in 2003, its military leaders are playing along with this charade, despite the madness of their commander-in-chief. And yet, leaders like Trump and Netanyahu float these ideas like they're part of a cheap political campaign, not a dangerous geopolitical gamble where many people will die.

It all circles back to a poignant irony: the men maniacally shouting out about threats to global peace—Trump and Netanyahu—are, in fact, the ones threatening it most. The self-proclaimed "stable genius" of Trump is now openly baiting nuclear powers and destabilising entire regions, and the Israeli Prime Minister is turning war into a form of personal immunity. If this isn't madness, what is? Why can't world leaders see what is plainly evident to everyone else? Why are so many naked emperors wearing the invisible cloaks and nobody dares to call them out?

This is where international diplomacy should step in—otherwise, what's the point of it—but will it? Perhaps there more sane and measured voices from France, Germany, Britain, or even South America and Africa might still intervene against the Idiot King and talk this down. This might be a naïve hope because, so far, the loudest voices have been the ones pushing us toward the brink.

Australia, too, must reckon with its role in this. Our history with Middle Eastern conflict is long, bloody, but poorly remembered. We've followed allies into the region before, from Gallipoli in 1915 to Iraq and Afghanistan in the 2000s. And each time, we have emerged with little more than body bags, broken veterans, and a vague sense that we were helping to uphold Western ideals—ideals that looked like imperial delusions then, and will continue to do so now.

The Middle East region now stands on an extremely precarious edge. Trump's Operation Midnight Hammer marks a bold departure from previous United States policy: direct strikes on Iranian nuclear sites which breach international law, coordinated with Israel, and grounded in a doctrine of preemptive national defence. This is an international disaster. Whether this reckless ruse brings Iran back to the negotiation table—and why would they—or ignites a broader conflict involving proxy forces and allied nations, is a difficult question to answer at this stage. We can only hope this time is different but history, sadly, is not on the side of peace.

***

A GREAT AUSTRALIAN SILENCE

30 June 2025

Sometimes, it's the words that *are* not made that make the biggest impression, and Australia's great silence after the United States bombed Iran's nuclear facilities with stealth bombers last week gave the biggest indication of where the Australia–U.S. diplomatic relationship stands: it's *subservient* and guided by a lack of principles. When Prime Minister Anthony Albanese and Foreign Minister Penny Wong finally emerged from their 24-hour silence, their words just repeated Washington's talking points, framing the strike as unfortunate—but necessary—and an extension of obligations of the alliance. This pantomime felt familiar: in 1966 Harold Holt promised to go "all the way with LBJ", and in 1999, when John Howard first boasted that Australia would act as America's "deputy sheriff" in the region. Half a century on, the deference from Canberra remains: different players and different words, but the sentiment remains the same.

What makes this particularly offensive is the contrast with Australia's post-war record as a multilateral player and a force for positive change, being one of key voices in the creation of the United Nations, the Genocide Convention and the Non-Proliferation Treaty, the frameworks that were designed to prevent the types of military adventurism that we often see from the United States. And by supporting this

U.S. bombing, Albanese has sided with a unilateral action, rather than the "rules-based international order" that his government frequently talks about.

The official justification—that the attack stopped an imminent Iranian breakout of nuclear weapons—sits uncomfortably with the flood of facts coming out of Vienna and The Hague. International Atomic Energy Agency inspectors have not found fresh evidence of weaponisation, and Tehran's foreign ministry insists enrichment remained within thresholds of the Iran nuclear deal (JCPOA)—even though Wong is now claiming the opposite. Where did these alternative facts come from?

Meanwhile, U.S. officials privately concede that this operation was hastened by domestic politics: the survival strategy of Israel's Prime Minister, Benjamin Netanyahu, Donald Trump's mid-term election politics, and lucrative deals and contracts in the arms industry. Australia's endorsement risks entangling it in a conflict driven more by American primaries and Israeli politics than by any genuine threat to regional security, so why do it?

Domestically, the episode has also reignited the long-simmering debate over autonomous defence policy. Polling since the AUKUS deal was created in 2021 already shows a majority of Australians favour a more independent foreign strategy, and Labor's progressive base is openly asking why the government condemns violations of international law in Moscow or North Korea yet stays silent when they originate in Washington. Albanese's reluctance to criticise the United States has also undermined his own narrative of pursuing a "middle-power diplomacy" that should be placing human rights at heart of its actions.

For now, a fragile Iran–Israel ceasefire is holding, but Israeli defence spokespeople are already claiming a "broken truce"—without providing evidence—and hinting at the need fresh attacks on Tehran. The real question is whether Australia can still draw on the moral imagination it displayed in San Francisco in 1945—when H. V. Evatt insisted even great powers needed to be bound by law—or whether it will just settle for the quiet comfort of U.S. subservience.

THE ABC OF MANUFACTURING CONSENT

In the aftermath of the United States' bombing of Iranian nuclear facilities, Western media coverage quickly fell into its well-worn cliches and talking points: Israel and the U.S. were cast as defenders of peace and democracy; Iran was framed as the unpredictable villain and rogue. Of course, these tropes are not new, but their repetition in the wake of such a serious escalation reveals a Western information ecosystem that's more invested in narrative control than independent scrutiny. While many non-Western media outlets reported the strike as a violation of international norms and gave airtime to Iranian officials articulating the legal basis for self-defence, most of the Australian and U.S. mainstream media doubled down on their binary worldview, just like in a Hollywood action movie, where American power is always legitimate and on the *side of right*, and its enemies always irrational and on the *side of wrong*.

Iran's foreign minister Abbas Araqchi, in a sober and legally grounded statement, condemned the attack and invoked the UN Charter's provisions on self-defence. He was one of the few adult voices in a room increasingly dominated by partisan Western war rhetoric and military fanfare. Yet voices like his were almost entirely absent from Australian media coverage, replaced instead by recycled commentary from embedded Western correspondents and a handful of dubious "expert" guests—most of them with longstanding ties to the political establishment or the arms industry.

The ABC, Australia's national broadcaster, did itself no favours by inviting former Prime Minister Scott Morrison to offer his perspective on the bombing—without disclosing that he now has advisory roles with American Global Strategies and DYNE Maritime, major players in the arms manufacturing and defence industries. Morrison offered a predictable defence of the U.S. strike, painting it as reluctantly necessary, restrained, and justified. His commentary was more like a press release than real analysis, and while as a former Prime Minister, he's entitled to speak in public, the ABC's decision to platform him without even a passing reference to his role in the arms industry undermined its duty of transparency.

But it wasn't only Morrison: ABC viewers were also regaled through a lengthy interview with Mike Pezzullo, the former Home Affairs Secretary removed by the Labor government for political interference and leaking. That the ABC would prioritise a disgraced bureaucrat—as well as a disgraced former Prime Minister—over any number of available legal experts or seasoned foreign policy analysts is bewildering at best, and absolutely cynical at worst.

Australia is not short of foreign policy experts— international lawyers, retired diplomats, experienced journalists, and even former ministers could have offered context, insight, and critique. But these people were all bypassed in favour of Morrison and Pezzullo—two players with reputational baggage and clear conflicts of interest. This isn't a call to ban figures like this from public debate, but it is about presenting their words appropriately and offering audiences the disclosures they need to evaluate opinions critically.

Of course, the ABC is a complex institution. While it continues to produce standout investigative journalism and informed commentary in some areas, the rot of managerial confusion and political appeasement is quite obvious, and evident whenever issues do arise from the Middle East, and within Israel and Palestine. It's a 1980s-style broadcasting strategy, compromised by political obedience, that is ill-suited to the complex media landscape of 2025. The result is an uneven output: excellent at times, but increasingly riddled with soft propaganda and unexamined privilege.

Scott Morrison may eventually attempt to rewrite his legacy—as many failed leaders do—but the historical record is already very unkind. Robodebt alone should have sealed his fate as one of the least respected prime ministers in Australia's modern era, and attempts to resurrect his authority through appearances on the national broadcaster serve no one, least of all the Australian public.

During times of conflict, facts matter, and so do the voices that are coming out to discuss these conflicts. And right now, Australia's national conversation is being warped by the reappearance of discredited men in suits, whose past failures should disqualify them from setting the agenda of such difficult international discussions.

THE BROKEN WORLD ORDER

In 1945, "Doc" Evatt didn't just represent Australia at that San Francisco Conference—he fought to ensure that smaller nations had a voice equal in principle, if not power, as a counterbalance to the giants of the postwar world structure. Australia also played a founding role in shaping the International Monetary Fund and the Bretton Woods system—tools meant to rebuild and stabilise a devastated global economy and prevent future wars through economic interdependence and rules-based diplomacy.

Australia's legacy now lies in ruins.

Australia today is no longer provides a pathway for cooperative multilateralism. Instead, it has become a muted appendage to a crumbling hegemon in the U.S. With each American airstrike justified in the name of "self-defence" and each Israeli bombardment reframed as necessary "retaliation",

Canberra justs nods along. Penny Wong and Defence Minister Richard Marles just offer the words from a pre-packaged statement of alliance with the U.S., while Albanese seems to look the other way. The legacy of 1945 has given way to the politics of acquiescence.

Since October 2023, in the shadow of Israel's campaign in Gaza and now the U.S. strikes on Iran, Australia has failed to raise even the mildest public criticism of these Israel or the U.S. Instead, its silence is often coupled with an authoritarian response: protestors in the Australia are silenced and police are mobilised—as shown in the recent incident where former Australian Greens candidate Hannah Thomas suffered graphic injuries from police during a pro-Palestine protest in Sydney—cultural figures are hounded by Israeli lobby groups and forced into cancellation and submission.

The government that once championed the idea of a rules-based international order is now too timid—or too cynical—to defend its founding principles. When asked if the U.S. bombing of Iranian nuclear sites violated international conventions, Australia had no comment, perhaps because to comment would reveal an inconvenient truth: that the so-called rules-based order no longer exists, or at least not in any coherent or enforceable form.

The heart of the problem lies in the global system's cancerous and sclerotic architecture. The UN Security Council, designed in 1945 by the victors of a global war, has remained virtually untouched in the eighty years since. The world it was meant to manage just doesn't exist anymore. The United States is no longer the unchallenged superpower; the United Kingdom is now diminished in its post-Brexit shell; Russia is a declining, disruptive force locked in Cold War nostalgia; France does wield some cultural and diplomatic capital but has a limited strategic reach; and China has emerged as the only power with the capacity—and intent—to reshape global norms and, in the absence of true leadership provided by the U.S., probably will take on that role on international leadership. The Security Council today is like a diplomatic museum, and the permanent members are a snapshot of an era that ended decades ago.

Any proposal to modernise the Security Council—by bringing in countries such as Germany, India, Brazil, Nigeria, Japan and Indonesia—would be opposed by these entrenched interests, as the existing permanent members would never voluntarily surrender their veto rights or their prestige. And yet the logic for change is overwhelming.

A more relevant structure wouldn't just reflect the demographic and economic weight of many countries around the world, but provide for a new legitimate global structure. And while it might not resolve everything, it would at least reflect the times that we are living in.

Until this type of change takes place, the world just seems to be stuck in a system that was designed for the *real politik* at the end of World War II, and not for the realities of the 21st century. And it's not a system that offers justice on the world stage, provides no guarantees for action against abuse of power and, as we have just seen with the U.S., has nothing in place to stop a rogue superpower.

This is how major wars begin: through old alliances, outdated treaties, and institutional paralysis. World War I was launched under the weight of decaying empires acting on long-expired commitments—a century-old promise to protect Belgium from Napoleon provided the catalyst for Britain to enter the war. World War II followed less than three decades later, fueled by the failures of a League of Nations which was unable to hold fascist powers to account.

We're repeating the pattern. An outdated international system that has once again lost control of the moment, and Australia—once a leader in building a new global order—

now appears too frightened to say so. If catastrophic war is to be avoided—in the Middle East or anywhere else—the world must not only confront the many failures of U.S. imperial overreach but also find the courage to reimagine the institutions that were meant to prevent exactly this kind of spiral. Australia can't afford to sit silent while history repeats itself.

***

CRIMINALISING PROTEST IN NSW

7 July 2025

The rain had barely cleared from Lakemba Street in Belmore when police descended on a peaceful protest outside SEC Plating, a modest factory that turns raw aluminium into the shiny finishes that are bolted on to Israeli F-35 fighter jets—which are then used to drop bombs over Gaza, killing innocent civilians, including children. This was meant to be a routine mid-week protest organised by Weapons Out of The West—a loose collective of teachers, students and shift workers who are furious that a secretive arms manufacturing network in the western Sydney region is exporting military parts to Israel and wanted to raise public awareness of this. Instead, it ended with Hannah Thomas, an activist and candidate for the Australian Greens at the 2025 federal election, beaten up by police, her face smashed into the bitumen, with her left eye bloodied and possibly beyond saving.

On this night in late June, scores of aggressive and angry police officers arrived, radios crackling with a response that seemed out of proportion to the handful of protesters holding a peaceful protest at a small suburban location. Thomas stepped forward as the police announced a "move-on" order—and when asked under what laws the police were acting on, officers dragged her to the kerb, struck her repeatedly, while dazed onlookers screamed out to "let her go!"—pleas that were ignored and quickly followed by more thumping of boots, arrests and the clatter of riot gear.

The charge sheet cited the newly amended anti-protest laws in New South Wales, the Minns Government's hasty response to Israel lobbyists who earlier this year claimed that anti-war action in Sydney and a "bomb scare" in Dural—that turned out to be a hoax—could result into attacks on synagogues. SEC Plating is located across the road from a youth-oriented church hall: there's no stained-glass windows, there's no sermons—it's just an old brick shell which is an annexe of the main church site in Punchbowl several suburbs away, and it's a hall that hosts workshops on Saturdays, with little indication that it might be a "place of worship". Yet the Act's wide definition of "religious precinct" gives the police a broad enough scope to criminalise a protest if someone, somewhere, might one day surreptitiously murmur a prayer nearby.

In the aftermath of this incident, NSW Premier Chris Minns regurgitated those same old talking points about "operational independence" and the "paramount importance of community harmony", but we all know what this is: it's the incremental drift towards state authoritarianism, one that the old NSW Liberal Party curmudgeon and former NSW Premier, Robert Askin, would have been proud of.

This law was always going to be political theatre—a concession to the Israel lobby rattled by large pro-Palestine crowds and a coalition of conservative clerics warning of sectarian spill-over—but it is *a law*. The Dural "caravan bomb" scare earlier this year provided convenient ammunition: outrage headlines about homemade explosives, later shown to be false when forensics found nothing but fertiliser and rust. But the truth didn't seem to matter to Premier Minns; by then the narrative of imminent terror had been lodged into the public consciousness: laws were enacted quickly, even when it became known to the government the Dural incident was a fabrication.

HOW THE DURAL HOAX BECAME LAW

It took just six weeks for a bomb scare hoax in the outskirts of Sydney to evolve into a legal assault on civil liberties. In January, NSW police were tipped off about a caravan parked behind a weatherboard cottage in Dural, and the vehicle supposedly contained mining gel detonators, a tangle of wires and a note naming the Great Synagogue as a target. Premier Minns called it "a terror plot against the Jewish community" and News Corporation tabloids splashed the headlines "Caravan of hate" across their front pages. Yet seasoned counter-terror detectives were sceptical from day one and, by March, the Australian Federal Police confirmed the whole thing was a criminal confidence trick designed to frighten Sydney—or to use the words of the AFP, a "fake terrorism" plot.

However, the official debunking came too late. On 11 February the Minns Government had already introduced the Places of Worship Bill, pitching it as a shield for synagogues, mosques and churches "under siege". The legislation sailed through both houses in nine days, granting police power to issue move-on orders, arrests without warrant and impose $22,000 fines on anyone protesting "in or near" a place of worship—a phrase so loose that it could cover half a suburb.

Civil-liberties lawyers did warn at that time that a prayer room above a convenience store, or even an *ad-hoc* Buddhist shrine in someone's loungeroom, now created an invisible and undefined zone where dissent could be criminalised. When the Human Rights Law Centre tallied the potential reach, they found virtually every major shopping strip in metropolitan Sydney contained at least one designated sacred site.

The political calculation behind this rush was pretty obvious. Although this legislation was developed within the jurisdiction of New South Wales, polling for the upcoming federal election suggested that Labor was losing votes in sections of Sydney amid a moral panic over anti-Semitic vandalism; these laws were drafted as much for optics as for public safety. Tony Burke, the federal Minister for Home Affairs—and member for the neighbouring seat of Watson—weighed in on breakfast television, applauding "urgent action to reassure faith communities," even though he had not read the final bill before endorsing it.

What the bill actually did was create a legal pretext ready-made for selective enforcement. Police command quickly circulated briefing notes describing pro-Palestine rallies as "events of heightened sensitivity", a euphemism that paved the way for heavy-handed police tactics. The government was quick to act: climate activists leafleting outside St Mary's Cathedral in Sydney were "moved-on" by police, while Palestine Action Group members holding candles across the road from a Lakemba mosque were monitored and threatened with arrest.

The biggest question is: who is all of this police power supposed to serve? In practice it insulates three constituencies: the property class, whose factories and showrooms are rebranded as "critical infrastructure"; the well-connected lobbyists who frame Palestine solidarity as a threat to Jewish safety; and a government anxious to look decisive every time a right-wing commentator on talk-back radio or Sky News claims that national security is "out of control". For everyone else, the message is unambiguous: speak against the war on Gaza in the wrong postcode—or *any* postcode, according to these laws—and the state will meet you with cuffs, fines, and, just like an Orwellian dystopia, provide you with a future of "a boot stamping on a human face—forever".

HOW NSW'S VAGUE WORSHIP LAWS ENABLE POLICE ABUSE

The protest in Belmore was more than one of the first test cases for the places of worship legislation—it was a warning about how a vague, discretionary law can morph into a blunt instrument of oppression when the government disagrees with certain political opinions. On the surface, the premise might seem reasonable enough: people of faith should be able to gather and worship *in peace*. But the legislation passed by the NSW Government offers no clarity on what constitutes a "place of worship," nor how "near" such a place is. And that ambiguity is the main reason that makes the law so dangerous.

There are over 4,000 officially recognised churches in New South Wales but that doesn't include the many other prayer spaces, meditation rooms, informal temples, suburban mosques, and *ad-hoc* faith centres that exist across the state. Under the law, any one of these can effectively create a protest exclusion zone with a radius known only to the officer enforcing it. "Near" can be interpreted as a few metres, a few blocks away or even in the next suburb.

This is the absurdity: the state can now declare your presence illegal if you're standing within earshot of a room that once might have held a Bible study session. If tomorrow someone holds a silent vigil on the footpath outside a warehouse used last month by a faith-based charity, police could conceivably declare the space sacred and the protest unlawful. That's not *law enforcement*; that's theocratic authoritarianism dressed up in legal niceties.

If this much force can be exercised at a protest near an empty workshop in a church annexe, what happens when the protest is actually about the religious institution itself? What happens when the issue is child sexual abuse perpetrated by the church, synagogues hiding paedophile teachers like Malka Leifer, or bigotry preached under the guise of doctrine? Are those forms of public criticism now to be silenced under the pretence of "protecting worship"? At what point do we acknowledge that the real aim isn't to protect faith communities from harassment—but to shield specific political, economic, and ideological interests from scrutiny?

The fallout from the Belmore protest shows just how quickly the public discourse can be manipulated. In the hours after the assault on Hannah Thomas, social media churned out the predictable accusations—she was anti-Semitic, she provoked the police, she somehow faked the injury, even though the bruising, swelling, torn skin and the real risk of permanent damage or the loss of the eye was obvious.

There needs to be protections for peaceful protest in a democracy, otherwise, it's *not* a democracy. A pluralist society can't be maintained if the right to dissent is confined only to "safe" targets approved by the state. Religious organisations, like governments and other corporations, operate in the public domain, benefit from public funding and rely on public trust and legal protections. Like everyone else, they must be subject to public criticism and scrutiny. After all, as Burke said when he criticised the protest actions of Hannah Thomas, rather than the police officer who inflicted the damage to her, "no one is above the law".

Yet the current New South Wales framework allows any officer to end a protest with force, without a warrant, based on nothing more than proximity to a poorly defined "place of worship". It's not a law for protecting prayer or religious beliefs—it's a law for criminalising opposition. And in that respect, it's already succeeded. The law created the *pretext*, and the police delivered the *violence*. It's a farce.

THE BILLION-DOLLAR PIPELINE THAT LEADS TO ISRAEL

What unfolded in Belmore becomes clear once you start following the money—and the links between bits of aluminium, carbon-fibre clips, micro-processors and spray-cured polymers that flow from suburban Sydney factories into the F-35 fighter jets that are bombing Gaza. SEC Plating is only one link in this extensive network: there are nearly twenty contractors in Sydney alone, and about seventy nationwide, all feeding the Joint Strike Fighter program the Albanese Government insists has "no operational nexus" with the Israel Defense Forces. Yet Australia's share of that program is valued at roughly $4.1 billion, under fifty-two export licences with Israel, underwritten by Australia's Global Supply Chain agreements. Every time a F-35 drops bombs over Gaza, Australian labour and tax subsidies are flying onboard with the pilot.

And what a wonderful example of "double-speak": the Labor government lectures protesters on "peaceful engagement" and claiming that "no one is above the law", while tacitly profiting from weapons that are destroying apartment blocks and aid convoys in Gaza. Ministers such as Penny Wong rinse and repeat their slogans about an international "rules-based order" but are outraged at the moment someone asks which rules offer a justification for selling war parts to a state accused of genocide by the International Court of Justice.

A state that would rather have its citizens remain unaware of a conflict and be complicit in that conflict—rather than be critics of that state—will always force violence upon those citizens who start connecting up all the dots and try to expose immoral and possibly illegal behaviour.

The footage of Hannah Thomas being slammed to the ground has been far more effective than any government-based denial. It combined two stories into the one that reveals the problem with this legislation: a peaceful protestor bleeding on the ground and possibly losing her eye, juxtaposed against a church annexe that barely looks like a "place of worship", yet used to justify vicious police brutality. A law ostensibly designed to protect worship has become the legal fig-leaf for protecting war profits—and the police who bashed Thomas were, effectively, the bouncers and pimps for a billion-dollar export scheme that Weapons Out of the West banner threatened to expose and embarrass political leaders with.

But the biggest question will always be: where does accountability begin? With the police officer who swung the fist and attacked Hannah Thomas? The commissioner who authorised the police attack? The NSW Government which enacted the places of worship legislation based on a lie? The Israeli lobby in Sydney that is always requesting more and more draconian laws that protect their own interests and silences dissent? Or the federal cabinet that keeps approving export licences to Israel and then denies that military parts are being supplied to F-35 fighter jets and then used to kill civilians in Gaza?

Until that chain is confronted and fully exposed, there'll be more peaceful protestors bludgeoned by the riot police, who are only too happy have laws that protect their thuggery, instead of the public interest, laws that were based on lies and should have never been enacted in the first place.

***

THE SEGAL REPORT, FREE SPEECH AND THE POLITICS OF FEAR

14 July 2025

There's something unsettling about the way political and media attention gathers with such immediacy and intensity whenever an act of anti-Semitism is reported—particularly when that act coincides with moments of increased scrutiny toward Israel's conduct in Gaza or the imminent release of a report concerning anti-Semitism in Australia. The recent incident in Melbourne is a perfect example: Angelo Loras, a 34-year-old man from Sydney, was quickly arrested after allegedly setting fire to the doors of a synagogue, an act Prime Minister Anthony Albanese immediately condemned as "cowardly", a "violent" attack with "no place in Australian society", asserting that those responsible would face the full force of the law.

But something in this case doesn't quite add up. First, the damage was minimal, and the synagogue, as it turns out, is located next to a fire station. No one was hurt, and while the act was unquestionably reprehensible, the media and political response seemed vastly disproportionate. Aside from a handful of photographs on Instagram, Loras has no digital footprint—there's no political activity, no signs of ideological motivation, and no attempt to disguise his actions in Melbourne, all of which were recorded on CCTV. It's reminiscent of a case earlier in the year in the outer Sydney suburb of Dural, where a supposedly politically motivated threat on synagogues was later revealed to be an elaborate hoax, a hoax which resulted in draconian police powers quickly introduced—powers that have already led to documented instances of police brutality, especially against pro-Palestinian demonstrators.

But what do we really know about this incident? It has already disappeared from the headlines, and no new facts have emerged since the arrest. Like other recent provocations—such as the bizarre case where Ofir Birenbaum and journalists from News Corporation entered the Cairo Takeaway in Newtown wearing a Star of David and attempted to bait the kebab shop owners into saying something anti-Semitic and incriminating—this case raises far more questions than it answers. Is there a co-ordinated international effort to generate these flashpoints, as the Australian Federal Police suggested in the Dural hoax? Are these isolated acts by "nobodies" being used to justify a creeping state authoritarianism under the guise of protecting faith communities?

There's also wider issues at stake: the government's reaction to this incident in Melbourne was quick and morally unambiguous. But when Islamophobic attacks occur—hate graffiti on mosques, women wearing hijabs harassed and attacked, or threats made against Palestinian Australians—the response is, at best, muted, or non-existent. There's a dissonance in a political culture that seems more outraged by a burnt door than by the daily incineration of children and aid workers in Gaza—where some communities are granted immediate empathy, while others are met with suspicion, silence and constant surveillance.

No one is excusing violence: *this point has to be made very clear*. But if dissent about Australia's foreign policy—or even basic support for Palestinian human rights—ends up being criminalised under new arbitrary "anti-hate" laws crafted in response to events like this, then the real danger isn't just from rogue arsonists, as bad as that is, it's from a political and media establishment willing to exploit fear on behalf of vested interests.

SELECTIVE OUTRAGE AND THE WEAPONISING IDENTITY

While the double standards are pretty obvious, it's no longer possible to ignore and do nothing about them. When acts of anti-Semitism occur—even those of uncertain origin or limited impact—governments at both state and federal levels move instantly, whether it's lighting up the Sydney Opera House with the flag of Israel, or implementing draconian new laws and police powers. Strike Force Pearl in New South Wales, Operation Anti-Hate in Victoria: these responses came with full media conferences, high-level political engagement, and sweeping new policies. The messaging is clear and consistent—there is zero tolerance for anti-Semitism, *as it should be*.

But when the hate is directed against other communities—Islamic, African Australians, Indigenous people or pro-Palestine people—there's no urgent media conferences, no task forces, and certainly no legislation rammed through parliament in late-night sittings. And this is not to minimise the very real threats that Jewish Australians do face—those should never be dismissed. But the inconsistency in response reveals something much deeper, and far more dangerous, about how political power in this country is being used—and misused—to benefit special groups with vested interests.

This pattern of selective justice doesn't just affect those directly targeted by hate crimes, it distorts the entire legislative and cultural framework of the country. As we saw in the wake of the Dural hoax earlier this year, bad laws are being rushed through parliaments in a panic, drafted poorly and with sweeping powers that end up hurting the very democratic principles they claim to defend. With the federal government now considering a sweeping national plan to combat anti-Semitism—one that appears to have been written less with justice in mind than appeasing powerful lobby groups—Australians are once again being asked to accept a framework of "protection" that is not based on universal rights, but on political expediency.

And it's reaching a point where even asking questions about these legislations and ambit claims—legitimate questions that need answers and transparency—risks the immediate accusation of anti-Semitism. It's now an accusation that has become a political weapon, and one that is used to shut down inquiry and criminalise dissent.

This is not how free societies are supposed to work. Justice can't depend on identity or specific religions—hate crimes against any community should be met with the same level of seriousness, the same legal scrutiny, and the same moral clarity. But a dangerous trend is emerging where criticism of Israel's government—no matter how valid or fact-based—is automatically recast as racial or religious hate, which stifles public discourse and actually undermines the fight against real anti-Semitism. And it becomes a case where if *everything* is labelled anti-Semitism, then *nothing* is.

PROTEST AND THE POLITICS OF MANUFACTURED OFFENCE

There was another incident in Melbourne which provided the mainstream media and the political class another moment in their ongoing campaign to conflate anti-Zionism with anti-Semitism. However, this one was not a mysterious act of arson by an unknown individual from another city; it was a public protest involving around twenty demonstrators who stood outside Miznon, an Israeli-owned restaurant in the Melbourne CBD. The protest wasn't directed at Jewish people, or Judaism, or the existence of Israel—it was a protest directed at the restaurant's owner, Shahar Segal. Segal isn't just a private citizen running a hospitality business; he has also been publicly linked to a private humanitarian organisation accused of corralling starving Palestinians in Gaza with promises of food, only for those areas to be targeted in subsequent bombings and shootings, with over 600 Palestinians reportedly killed in these so-called "safe zones". These are the facts the media—in its breathless reporting—conveniently ignored.

This was a protest about complicity in war crimes. The protestors were not targeting a religious group—they were opposing acts of state violence, and the individuals allegedly involved in supporting or facilitating it. But the media repeatedly described it as an "anti-Semitic attack," and conflated its reporting with the synagogue arson, and then going on further to claim that multiculturalism in Australia is collapsing under the weight of racial hatred.

This isn't just bad journalism—it's political propaganda disguised as reporting on behalf of the Zionist movement, and the conflation of legitimate political protest with racial or religious hatred was such a dishonest act. It removes any space for dissent, silences criticism of Israel's government, and equates protestors with bigots. But as Federal Court Justice Angus Stewart made very clear in the recent *Wertheim v Haddad* case, it is *not* anti-Semitic to criticise the Israeli government, or to protest against Zionism, or to oppose the policies that are causing a genocide in Gaza. These are not some made-up leftist or radical opinions—these are points of law, specifically made by Justice Stewart in a Federal Court.

The selective reporting, however, presented a different story. The ABC—once a public broadcaster with a reputation for independent public journalism—parroted the same lines as the Murdoch press: a "hate-filled protest," "anti-Jewish targeting," "a worrying escalation". But nowhere in the coverage was there serious engagement with what the protest was *actually* about. There was no mention of the accusations against the private humanitarian organisation in Gaza. No reporting on the Federal Court decision, and certainly no context: just the usual lazy, establishment journalism echoing the political class and shielding those in power.

In 2024, the former Attorney-General Mark Dreyfus, claimed that criticism of Zionism or Israel amounts to anti-Semitism. But that position is not only legally incorrect—it was an attempt to remove specific political opinion from public debate, one that is held by millions of people around the world, including many Jewish people themselves. Zionism is an *ideology* based on bigoted supremacy, it's not a race or a religion and must be open to criticism like any other political philosophy.

None of this is to deny that genuine anti-Semitism exists. And to be sure, there are individuals who will weaponise criticism of Israel as a smokescreen for their prejudices. But if we allow those individuals to define the boundaries of public debate, we surrender the entire field to the authoritarians and allow the Netanyahus of the world claim that every act of dissent is hatred, and that all criticism is an act of anti-Semitic violence. It's not just wrong—it's dangerous—it undermines the legitimacy of real work against racism, and allows actual hate to hide behind the very legal and rhetorical protections that are meant to oppose it.

What's happening in Gaza is not some kind of ethereal abstraction. It's not just about ideology. It is about people dying—massacred, starved, displaced—under the watch of the international community. And it's not a secret: every day we see the live-streamed massacres and daily reports of more killings in Gaza, and more settler violence in the West Bank. Israel has even publicly announced its intentions to create concentration camps in Rafah—as if Gaza hadn't already been an open-air concentration camp—yet, the world watches on, allowing this to happen with indifference and complicity.

Nearly every major scholar of genocide has declared that what Israel is doing in Gaza is a genocide. When that is the scale of the crime, we need to speak up more, not be silenced by the apparatus of the state. The way in which we hold power to account must be fearless—to protest against genocide is not an act of *hate*, it's an act of *humanity*. And in any just society, if that's what we really live in, that distinction should be absolutely obvious to everyone.

SEGAL IS TRYING TO SILENCE DISSENT AGAINST ISRAEL

The release of the federal government's anti-Semitism report—prepared by Jillian Segal, the Prime Minister Anthony Albanese's handpicked Special Envoy—didn't seem to be a coincidence. Its timing, dropped into a news cycle already inflamed by the Melbourne synagogue arson and the protest outside an Israeli-owned restaurant, was a nice little political calculation. These two incidents, exploited by political and media elites as examples of Australia's supposed descent into hate-fuelled chaos, provided the perfect emotional backdrop for a document that seems to be less about combating anti-Semitism and more about redefining dissent as hate speech.

Segal's report, heavily leaned upon by Australia's most powerful pro-Israel lobby groups, such as the conservative Executive Council of Australian Jewry—Segal being the Immediate Past President—and enthusiastically amplified by outlets like *The Australian* and *Sky News*, has reignited the public debate over the boundaries between anti-Jewish bigotry and political criticism of Israel. But there's a massive contradiction within this report: it claims to be a shield for vulnerable communities, but in practice—if any of Segal outrageous recommendations are implemented—it will become an instrument used to punish critics of state violence.

Segal is not a neutral figure. As a former head of a pro-Israel lobby organisation and the partner of John Roth, a man who donated $50,000 to Advance Australia—a far-right group that campaigned aggressively against the Voice to Parliament referendum in 2023—her appointment as a supposedly impartial envoy on antisemitism raises questions about conflicts of interest, and the intent behind the report were compromised from the outset.

The central part of Segal's report is its push for the formal adoption of the International Holocaust Remembrance Alliance definition of anti-Semitism, which has been used across multiple jurisdictions to blur the lines between anti-Jewish hate and legitimate political opposition to the Israeli state. The joining of criticisms of Israel and Zionism with anti-Semitism have made the IHRA definition a tool of repression in those jurisdictions—used not just against protestors and academics, but against the very idea of open public debate.

Segal's recommendations would roll in a new era of censorship: where questioning military occupation, apartheid policies, or genocide in Gaza would be treated as hate speech, and where institutions would face funding cuts or public censure for hosting controversial speakers or events or not doing enough to stop anti-Semitism in an undefined way—it's already happening on a *de facto* basis as we've seen in recent months, but to enshrine this in law would be a disaster.

Once again, we have to point out that genuine anti-Semitic abuse and violence must be condemned and combatted. But if we are constantly forced to condemn Hamas, we must also be forced to condemn Israel for its actions in Gaza and West Bank. What the Segal report proposes, however, is a shutdown of public debate where publicly condemning Israel would be considered a crime.

In the Australian context, this concern is heightened by the reality that recent tensions have not emerged in a vacuum.

They are linked to Israel's relentless assault and genocide on Gaza—attacks that have killed well over 55,000 and more than likely, a significantly higher number, displaced millions, and shocked much of the world. To release an anti-Semitism strategy that ignores this context is not only dishonest—it's politically dangerous.

There are so many blind spots in Segal's report. There's no mention of Gaza or Palestine. There is no space for solidarity with the suffering of *all* peoples, no room for justified outrage. Instead, the Segal report channels the conversation through a single, ideologically loaded perspective: protecting one community by silencing many others.

This approach won't create harmony, and why Albanese has allowed this process to go this far is difficult to comprehend. Sure, he only had a slim majority in Parliament and with an election to win, offered as much support as possible to appease the Israel lobby groups—and got nothing in return politically—but what's the excuse now? Labor now has ninety-four seats in Parliament after its crushing win at the 2025 federal election, and is facing a feckless Coalition as the opposition.

Albanese should take this report and, as diplomatically as possible, tell Segal that it represents an outrageous overreach and an implausible, excessive demand—and clearly let her know that all it will do is deepen suspicion, polarise debate, and undermine faith in democratic institutions. That's what Albanese *should* do but we know that he won't: his previous support for the cause of Palestine—as recently as 2019 but before he became the leader of the Labor Party—has been shown to be a charade and a convenient façade. Albanese now exists in the space of power and privilege, and he's unprepared to cede any of this power to support truth, justice, and the right to speak out against oppression, even when supporting one particular group of privilege might be detrimental to his political standing. He's become the Keir Starmer of the South.

But he does need to understand that if we are to live in a truly pluralist society, we must reject anything that weaponises one group's plan to erase the existence of another. And we must insist that the fight against hate includes *everyone*—or it will end up protecting no one.

***

THE IRRATIONAL FEAR OF CHINA AND THE IMAGINARY CRISIS

21 July 2025

In what should have been recognised as a sign of maturity for Australian foreign policy, Prime Minister Anthony Albanese's meeting with Chinese President Xi Jinping—their fourth meeting so far—has resulted in a predictable response of conservative hysteria, empty rhetoric and a hyperbole that's verging on racism. This meeting wasn't just another round of pleasantries, banquets, visits to the Great Wall or, that tired old cliché the media loves to rev up during state visits to China—"Panda diplomacy"—it was an important step in repositioning Australia's role in a quickly changing geopolitical landscape.

The Asia–Pacific region is becoming more complicated by the day, with the increasing power of China, a change in allegiances, and the unreliability of a more insular United States to act as a global stabiliser. Within this context, Albanese's efforts to strengthen ties with China are not acts of "submission" or "appeasement", as some reactionary commentators have claimed—these are steps toward promoting and protecting Australia's national interest. And, so far, he's succeeding.

The Coalition and its media proxies are trapped in a rusted-on Cold War mentality where, just like the Hollywood's post-war anti-German propaganda movies, China is *always* to be cast as the villain that can never be trusted or rehabilitated. Within this mindset, every diplomatic act from Xi Jinping is twisted into a narrative of capitulation and suspicion, and every improvement in bilateral relations is somehow narrated as a betrayal of Australian values. From their perspective, China is either perpetually on the verge of internal collapse under the inherent contradictions of communism, or preparing to invade Taiwan, dragging Australia into a catastrophic conflict through its association with the U.S. Meanwhile, the government's efforts—just getting on with expanding export markets, stabilising university partnerships, and supporting Australian jobs—are downplayed or ignored entirely. Why run with the positive news when there's free and readily available anti-China propaganda to propagate?

Albanese is engaging in the difficult but necessary task of foreign policy realism. He's not indulging China, but negotiating with it. He is not abandoning the United States, but refusing to be blindly linked to it in the same way the Coalition was during its time in office: it's an outcome the Coalition had years to develop but failed to deliver. During its decade in office, the Coalition government allowed Australia's most important trading relationship to stagnate to the point of near collapse, especially after 2020, during the early stages of COVID, and made little effort to diversify exports or protect economic sovereignty. Instead, they relied on inflammatory rhetoric, leaning heavily on fear of the "China threat" as a blunt political instrument. Their mishandling of the AUKUS agreement in 2021 is probably the pinnacle of their incompetence: a nuclear submarine deal with unclear terms, a lack of strategic objectives that could be in Australia's national interest—all because the U.S. told us that we were "underprepared" in case of war with China—and a public left largely in the dark (and still is).

Now that the Labor government is restoring relationships with Beijing, the same conservative commentators who cheered on the diplomatic attacks on China by the Coalition, are claiming that this progress is a sign of weakness. They want China as both an enemy and an economic benefit to Australia—something that defies logic, yet persists because of a deeper discomfort within Australia's political psyche and the white-man colonialist's outlook of south-east Asia. There's a strong undertone of racial anxiety and cultural insecurity as a part of this discomfort: a preference for the familiar white, Western ally over the rise of a confident, non-Western superpower.

And yet, despite this tension, there is no coherent strategy behind the right-wing bluff and bluster. It's just the usual fear and suspicion, as well as that recycled myth that Australia can only ever be safe and successful if it defers unconditionally to the United States. This isn't diplomacy: it's the classic colonial dependency that appears publicly as foolish and self-defeating patriotism.

Of course, China's government is not without flaws or human rights concerns, but the double standards are always on show when it comes to these concerns. Albanese is expected to confront Xi on these issues or otherwise face accusations of cowardice and "not standing up to China". But, when it comes to U.S. leaders—especially someone like Donald Trump—there are no such demands. Few in the media ever question whether Albanese should challenge human rights abuses in the United States or the immigration policies brutally implemented by their Immigration and Customs Enforcement. Xi must *always* be challenged on the treatment of Uyghurs and other Turkic Islamic minorities in Xinjiang—and rightly so—but the U.S. is never asked to be held to account over its treatment of Indigenous Americans,

Afro-American and Hispanic communities. Or the human rights violations at the Guantánamo Bay detention camp.

The United States is now a nation where citizens have been deported despite their birthrights, or detained in facilities that resemble open-air prisons, such as "Alligator Alcatraz". These are violations which are just as severe, if not more so, than the many that are attributed to Beijing. But, for conservatives, China is the only one that needs to be singled out, because the United States is *always* in the right.

Albanese's engagement with China is not perfect, but it is grounded in diplomatic pragmatism where he's trying to navigate a path between old alliances and the emerging *realpolitik*. Unlike the ideological stubbornness of his critics, Albanese's approach is a genuine effort to maintain a balance in an increasingly unbalanced world. This isn't weakness: this is how diplomacy is meant to work and to be used strategically—for Australia's future—and it might end up being the most important foreign policy decision of the post-Cold War era.

A DIPLOMATIC RESET BUT THE COLONIAL MINDSET PERSISTS

This visit to Beijing was a lot more than just a symbolic photo opportunity, or an "indulgence", as the Liberal Senator, James Paterson claimed during the week.

It's a clear break from the belligerence and mismanagement that defined the Morrison era and, for the first time in years, an Australian prime minister has arrived not with conditions and accusations, but with the intent to listen, negotiate, and rework the Australia–China relationship. And the results are already visible.

All of the punitive trade barriers China had placed on Australian exports—wine, barley, timber, coal, lobster and many others—have now been removed. These weren't abstract economic disputes or debates at the World Trade Organisation;

they had real consequences for Australian producers and regional communities. Albanese's re-engagement has helped restore access to key markets, creating economic certainty and reversing the damage that never should have occurred in the first place.

This is positive news for Australia, as it is for China. So why is Australia's conservative media and political class so quick to portray this as a *negative*? Why is the right's instinct always to view China not as a country with whom we can work with, but as a looming threat that has to be contained, even to the point of engaging in a war?

This paranoia, unfortunately, is not new. It is the echo of a long and ugly tradition in Australian public life since colonisation in 1788—a mix of racial anxiety, Anglophile nostalgia, and an enduring sense that our place in the world must always be etched into an imagined Western superiority. The Coalition's worldview, while not as overtly reactionary as One Nation or the far-right fringe, still clings to a mythic past: a simpler time, supposedly safer, whiter, wealthier. But, as former Prime Minister Paul Keating once observed, these visions of an idealised past are fantasy, and are fabrications that were never grounded in any real sense of history.

It's a yearning based on a parochialism that refuses to accept that Australia *is* a part of Asia, and believes that China—like other countries in the south-east Asia region—is a threat to be feared. But have a look at a map: yes, Australia *is* in Asia, and far far away from either the United States, or from Britain. Keating was right—Australia always has been and it always will be in Asia.

Australia is not in a position to dictate terms to the world's largest economies. We don't possess the economic clout to punish Beijing, nor do we have the military capacity to confront Washington. But what we do have is a voice: Australia can offer principled, measured criticism—privately and respectfully—where necessary. That's what mature diplomacy looks like. And if we are to have any credibility on human rights, we must apply our standards universally—including to our closest allies.

This is why Albanese's stance is sensible and successful: he's not grandstanding, nor is he promoting the tough-guy image that Scott Morrison or Tony Abbott wanted to portray when they were engaging with China. Instead, he's promoting the economic, strategic and cultural ties that are important for Australia's long-term interests—and for this, he's being punished by a media class that just refuses to grow up.

Each and every week, we see the same cycle of cynicism: we see outrage instead of nuance, a search for scandal over substance, and if there is no scandal, an invented one. Australia deserves better from its mainstream media. And if we are to meet the challenges of this new century—climate, economic realignment, technological disruption, shifting global alliances—we will need a media that is capable of reporting on the world as it is, not the conservative fantasy that they all want to be a part of.

AUSTRALIA'S PATHWAY BETWEEN THE WORLD POWERS

Beyond the diplomacy, there are hard economic realities that highlight Australia's relationship with China—and these are the realities that are often ignored by sensationalist media through their outdated Cold War mentality.

China is by far Australia's largest trading partner, accounting for 27 per cent of total exports, valued at around $180 billion annually. In contrast, the United States is just 4.6 per cent of our export market, worth around $30 billion. And sure—$30 billion is still a substantial amount, but it's small when compared to the size and value of the trade with China. Yet, too often, these facts are ignored.

Instead, the Australian conservatives are obsessed with hypothetical war scenarios: a Chinese invasion of Taiwan, or even more absurdly, of Australia itself, and what is even more absurd is that these fantasies are peddled as an *inevitability* rather than just a remote possibility. Journalists harass the Prime Minister with gotcha-style hypotheticals, egged on by defence analysts and hawkish think tanks. Their aim isn't to inform the public, but to manufacture consent for this supposedly impending confrontation, and to continue conditioning the Australian public to fear China as a looming, existential threat.

Meanwhile, U.S. military officials continue to float the idea that conflict with China could erupt by 2027. No evidence is provided, no rationale is outlined and, of course, *it's never needed*. But it's hard to escape the conclusion that 2027 is politically convenient—a stage for destabilisation just before the 2028 U.S. presidential election—but it's a strategy that assumes that nations like Australia will obediently play along, just because the U.S. says so.

The reality is that Australia doesn't need to choose sides in a new cold war—or an unlikely hot war—that hasn't yet begun. In fact, the entire point of diplomacy is to avoid being forced into these kinds of decisions. Australia can maintain its longstanding alliance with the United States while also deepening economic and diplomatic ties with China. That is the essence of modern diplomacy—getting the best out of all relationships, rather than collapsing into subservience to just one, and acting as an independent regional power with its own voice and interests, rather a U.S. "deputy sheriff".

And these interests are clear. Australia is a middle power, but it is also a major force in the Asia-Pacific region. The fantasy of a permanent Atlantic allegiance—culturally Anglo, militarily American, and economically self-sufficient—is outdated and unsustainable. Gough Whitlam recognised this in 1971, visiting China even before he became Prime Minister. While he was mocked and ridiculed by the conservatives and the media at the time—U.S. President Richard Nixon made the same move months later and was lauded for doing so.

Nixon's visit to China is now regarded by many historians as his most significant achievement. And yet, it was Whitlam who beat him to it. Whitlam understood that a future without China at the table would be a poorer, more dangerous one, and Keating's urge for Australians to recognise that they are part of Asia, is a part of this thinking. That assertion still unsettles those who cling to the illusion of empire and the imagined safety of a bygone Commonwealth.

But the truth is, Australia can't rely on nostalgia to navigate its place in the modern world of diplomacy. It has to deal with the reality of its geography, its dependencies, and its role as an economic player. And when we antagonise China—as the Abbott, Turnbull and Morrison governments did with their mindless posturing and unproductive provocation—we discovered quickly who benefits the most from this relationship. When China implemented sanctions and tariffs on Australian goods in 2020, it wasn't Beijing that suffered.

We're no longer in the 1950s and the world doesn't bend to the will of the "free world" as once imagined. This is the new reality: Australia must grow up and *is* growing up, and is looking to its own region, and its own future, not hanging on to the myths of its past. Albanese's path forward—diplomatic, methodical and based on Australia's national interest—isn't "appeasement" or "indulgent", as claimed by his critics. It's all about becoming an adult in international affairs. And the sooner Australia embraces and understands this, the better equipped we'll be to shape our own future, rather than having it shaped for us.

***

ALBANESE AND WONG ARE ON THE WRONG SIDE OF HISTORY

28 July 2025

The first day of a new parliamentary term always contains the ceremonial pantomime of speeches, pageantry, and the carefully staged managed political of *business as usual*. But outside the walls of Parliament, there is a façade that is starting to break—ever so slowly—but *it is* starting to break. Thousands of protestors converged on Canberra not to celebrate the opening of the Parliamentary term but to demand that Australia end its silence and complicity—in the face of what many consider to be a genocide inflicted by the state of Israel upon the people of Gaza, and to take substantial action against the Israel government's systematic and obvious destruction of Palestine.

The Australian government's position on the conflict in Gaza has been untenable for some time, with Israel continuing to blockade Gaza's borders, preventing adequate food and medical aid from reaching the population, and enforcing mass starvation. International agencies have been forced out of Gaza and replaced with much-criticised Israeli-controlled entity—the so-called Gaza Humanitarian Foundation—the Orwellian name that has become a symbol of the obscene and brutal failure to meet even the most basic humanitarian standards: over a thousand Palestinians have been killed since May, either gunned down at food distribution points or crushed in stampedes after being corralled into cages, just like cattle in a slaughterhouse. And yet, the international response still remains weak and putrid, unable to respond to the stench of Israel's acts of genocide. The Australian government, while it did join a list of twenty-eight countries condemning Israel's actions, has offered little else besides sterile diplomatic language.

Foreign Minister Penny Wong still continues with this sterilisation—delivering statements stifled by caution, and carefully crafted to avoid upsetting Australia's domestic Israel lobby or distort the broader Zionist narrative. Her performative concern is *less* directed at the lives being lost in Gaza and *more* at the political optics of dissent within the Parliament itself. If it wasn't evident before, it was made pretty obvious when Wong moved a rare and severe censure motion against the Australian Greens Senator Mehreen Faruqi, for the grand offence of holding up a sign that said "Gaza is starving. Words won't feed them. Sanction Israel" during the Governor-General's address in the joint parliamentary sitting.

Rather than engage with the message and the uncomfortable truth it represents, Senator Wong punished the messenger, describing Faruqi's actions as a breach of "decorum," accusing her of disrespecting Parliament and denigrating those who disagree with her. The Senate's censure went far beyond a symbolic reprimand; it includes an extraordinary punishment that strips Faruqi of any right to represent the Senate on delegations for the remainder of the term—effectively sidelining her for next three years.

A Senator censured and silenced, not for inciting violence or spreading disinformation, but for calling for sanctions against a foreign government accused of war crimes. It was a clear indication of how far Australia's political establishment is willing to go to preserve its diplomatic and ideological alliances—supporting a genocide even at the cost of democratic dissent. Again, this was a performative and over-the-top action that ultimately wasn't even directed towards Faruqi, or even the Australian electorate: it was directed towards the Israel lobby in Australia, to make it clear which side of the genocide Senator Wong is siding with.

Senator Faruqi, in her response, drew on Martin Luther King's 'Letter from a Birmingham Jail', and criticised the "white moderates", more concerned about procedures and protocols, rather than justice, setting their standards to cover over the truth and not wanting to do anything about the genocide in Gaza. And as the bombs continue to fall on Gaza, as children continue to starve, as neighbourhoods are reduced to rubble, the Australian government will find that the most enduring legacy won't be anything else it does this term, but its silence and failure to act on a genocide that everyone else in the world can see in plain sight.

SILENCE IS COMPLIANCE

The speed at which this censure motion against Senator Faruqi was introduced, debated, and passed was also a sign of how desperate the Labor government is to appease the Israel lobby and Zionists in Australia. Within just an hour of the Senate's commencement, Senator Wong negotiated a censure—not against the state of Israel, whose military actions, according to independent reports, have led to the deaths of well over 80,000 Palestinians—but against a fellow Senator who was simply protesting in silence. All over a cardboard sign—and on a type of cardboard that Palestinians are currently eating, just to fill their stomachs and force away the pangs of hunger, because they have *nothing else* to eat—there were no threats, no incitement, just a plea to acknowledge the starvation of a people under siege.

It wasn't wearing a burqa into the Senate—as Pauline Hanson did in 2017 to make a racist point—or turning the back on a Welcome to Country event—Hanson, again to make a racist point, this time in front of the Governor-General—or wearing a fluro vest, brandishing a large salmon, or wearing a wig—all of these events have taken place in Parliament, yet only Faruqi's actions have received a censure.

Faruqi's act was moral statement, and the nature of her punishment—above and beyond anyone else—reveals the deep capture of Australia's political establishment by the Israel lobby and aligned Zionist organisations, and provides the clearest example of how lopsided the political landscape has become and how pathetically weak our governments are.

Faruqi didn't call for violence or deny Israel's right to exist; she just demanded that Israel be held accountable for its actions and crimes against humanity—had the same sign expressed solidarity with Israel, there's little doubt that it would have gone unnoticed, and even applauded by Wong. And this is the grand act of hypocrisy: the rules of so-called "decorum" are only enforced when they challenge the dominant narrative from vested and racist interests, and the dominant narrative within this Labor government remains solidly pro-Israel, no matter how severe the atrocities become. Senator Faruqi was punished not for disrupting Parliament—she didn't do any disruption anyway—but for daring to tell the truth and speaking out against Israel.

But things are shifting—slowly but surely and, as usual, the political class is lagging far behind public sentiment. The barbarity of Israel's actions is now too obvious, too public and too cruel to ignore. What once existed in the shadows—carpet bombing and "lawn mowing" of refugee camps, deliberate starvation of children, shooting at aid queues—now floods social media feeds, news broadcasts, and diplomatic circles. Protests are growing. The Australian public is beginning to understand what's being done in its name, and many are rejecting it. Eventually, the political class will get it, despite its psychopathic desires to ignore it.

The language used by Prime Minister Anthony Albanese over the weekend has become *marginally* more critical of Israel, where at least he acknowledged that the actions in Gaza breach international law, before self-censoring himself and adding that he's not a lawyer and couldn't be too sure about that. But these sterner words have been said before, yet never matched up with action. The Albanese government refuses to take the next obvious steps—recalling the Israeli ambassador, cutting military co-operation, halting arms exports, suspending trade, or issuing meaningful diplomatic condemnation.

If the Australian government does not change course soon—if it continues to mumble platitudes while Gaza is turned to rubble and its population is massacred—it won't be remembered very kindly at all on this issue, irrespective of how large its parliamentary majority is at the moment. History won't be looking back and admiring Albanese's caution; it will remember the silence and the moral cowardice. It will remember a government that had a choice but chose not to offend a lobby group and stood idly by as tens of thousands of people were slaughtered.

This should be a turning point—not just for Palestine, but for Australia. A nation that claims to champion democracy, human rights, and a rules-based international order can't stand by while those very principles are obliterated in the same way that the Palestinian tent cities have been. To avoid acting isn't neutrality, it's cowardly complicity. And complicity, no matter how softly spoken or politely phrased, will always be on the wrong side of history.

WHAT AUSTRALIA CAN DO TO END THE GENOCIDE

Many Australians claim that the geographic distance from the Middle East limits our ability to intervene, and that includes Senator Wong, who claimed it was "always very difficult from over here to make judgements". But it's a weak and pathetic argument that makes no sense at all. We made a judgement to sanction Russia, which is even further away—there are many other sanctions in place on countries such as Syria, Libya, Yemen, South Sudan, North Korea, Lebanon, Iran—and a quick look at a map will show that all of these countries are far away and not within Australia's usual sphere of influence.

In contrast, Australia actively opposed the apartheid regime in South Africa in the 1980s—another country half a world away with white supremacy beliefs and policies at the time that are not too dissimilar to Israel—and used a great deal of pressure to bring about change, a change that finally arrived in 1990 with the release of Nelson Mandela. And, at the time, there was bipartisan support within Australia to act against South Africa, despite the efforts of the U.S. and British governments to cease and desist.

Many of the same actions could be taken today against Israel to help bring an end to its occupation of Palestinian territories and the genocide it has inflicted on Gaza. Australia could formally recognise the state of Palestine—as France has promised to do in September—and a move already made by over 140 United Nations member states. It could expel Israeli diplomats, suspend military co-operation, and more forcefully condemn Israel's violations of international law. The government could support Palestinian efforts to join global institutions such as the International Criminal Court and the International Court of Justice, and it could endorse South Africa's genocide case against Israel.

Trade restriction is another option. Australia could ban imports produced in illegal Israeli settlements in the West Bank and impose targeted Magnitsky-style sanctions on Israeli military leaders involved in the bombing campaigns and siege of Gaza. It could stop exporting weapons components to Israel's defence industry and cut defence co-operation agreements. Public funds could be divested from companies that support or profit from the occupation and war.

Cultural and academic boycotts would also have impact. During the apartheid era, Australia refused to host South African athletes and artists, and encouraged international bodies to boycott South Africa from global events. What Australia did then, can be applied to Israel today, alongside an increase in humanitarian aid and support for Palestine.

But the reality is that Australia has done almost none of this. Despite the growing body of evidence of human rights abuses and collective punishment in Gaza—and the evidence can be seen almost every single moment on social media and international news broadcasts—the Albanese government has behaved in morally bankrupt way and supported the oppressors.

Within federal Parliament, there seems to be very little appetite for change. While the Greens have consistently called for sanctions and recognition of Palestine, and some Labor MPs have expressed concern—this week, Victoria Labor Party members have pushed for the immediate recognition of Palestine, as has the federal Labor member Ed Husic—the leadership has opted for cautious, ambiguous language. Statements from Senator Wong and Prime Minister Albanese have largely reflected those from the United States, reflexively condemning Hamas because they haven't got anything else to say, and going out of their way to avoid any direct critique of Israel's military campaign or its decades-long occupation of Palestinian territories. And while they actively condemn

Hamas, they fail to explain the ongoing terrorism and settler violence in the West Bank, where Hamas doesn't even exist.

Today's pro-Palestine campaign in Australia is still gaining traction—it's frustratingly slow, but it's moving at a pace that might soon be impossible to stop, and that's what the government fears the most. The trade unions, churches, and student groups were instrumental in the 1980s in building the political momentum needed for action against South Africa are going through a similar mobilisation now and will ultimately force the government to abandon its passive stance.

Public opinion is shifting in Australia, with the continuing mass protests in many cities, more pressure from human rights organisations, and a greater awareness of these issues within the electorate, especially among younger people. But without bold political leadership, Australia risks remaining on the sidelines of history—condemning atrocities in words, but not in deeds.

Australia didn't let distance stop it from acting against apartheid in South Africa. It shouldn't let it be an excuse now. Palestine can't wait, and it really time for Australia to act right now.

***

KILLING JOURNALISTS WON'T STOP PALESTINIAN STATEHOOD

11 August 2025

The conflict in Gaza has continued to bring of death and destruction to the people of Palestine, with more than 60,000 people killed and 145,000 injured, including a disproportionate number of women and children. It's very clear now—if there was ever *any doubt*—that this is an act of genocide—and there's a heavy weight of evidence, coming in from UN experts, human rights groups all around the world, including from within Israel. The deaths, the ethnic cleansing, lack of medical care, a lack of food, forced and continuous displacement, the destruction of homes, businesses, schools and hospitals—these are the internationally agreed conditions of genocide, whether Israel accepts this or not.

And in the midst of this genocide, the very voices that are documenting the suffering—journalists—are being deliberately murdered and silenced by the state of Israel. Gaza has become the deadliest place for media workers, where fatalities among journalists and media personnel ranges from at least 178 confirmed by Committee to Protect Journalists to well over 237, according to the local Gaza Media Office.

The most recent murders were of Al Jazeera's Anas al-Sharif and four of his colleagues—Mohammed Qreiqeh, Ibrahim Zaher, Mohammed Noufal and Moamen Aliwa—

in a co-ordinated strike on their press tent outside al-Shifa Hospital in Gaza City, where the Israeli Defense Forces allege alSharif was a "Hamas cell leader", despite the lack of any evidence at all to support their claim.

And this is the *modus operandi* of the state of Israel— besmirch the reputation of a journalist through a total fabrication, and then use that fabrication to justify the killing—Hossam Shabat was killed in the same manner in March, with a wave of unverified accusations followed up with an Israeli airstrike. Reporters Without Borders, the CPJ, and other press freedom advocates have denounced these acts as "intentional" and "unprecedented", warning that the systematic murder of journalists in Gaza is an assault on global press freedoms and humanity. However, there is usually a comradery amongst international journalists when one of their own is killed in a conflict zone, but nearly every journalist in the mainstream media in Australia has been quiet over the past two years, even though there have been at least 178 occasions when they could have raised their voices. So why the silence?

GAZA'S JOURNALISTS ARE BEING KILLED TWICE

Israel's consistent practice of branding journalists as *militants*, without presenting any evidence that could be independently verified, is a debasement of international law, the key tenets of press freedom and the free flow of information. Journalists are protected civilians under the Geneva Conventions, yet in Gaza they've become routine target practice for the IDF. This continuous blurring of that distinction between combatant and correspondent—even though most of the people that Israel has killed in Gaza have been civilians—not only endangers journalists but undermines the key element of independent reporting in a conflict zone.

The killing of these five journalists came after weeks of public vilification by Israel, making claim after claim about a supposed relationship with Hamas—again, no evidence was provided—to build up a narrative that would justify these killings in retrospect. It's clearly a tactic used by Israel to kill journalists and, just before their deaths, Al Jazeera Media, the United Nations, and the CPJ each issued separate statements calling for the protection of these journalists. These appeals, however, did nothing to stop these killings by Israel.

The death toll in Gaza exceeds the number of journalists killed in any other conflict over the past century—150 journalists were killed during the Iraq War, over an eight-year period, and eighty-one during the first four years of the war in Syria, and now, 237 journalists in Palestine in less than two years. Despite this, the reaction from Australia's mainstream journalists has been close to invisible. The Media, Entertainment and Arts Alliance—the union representing journalists—has issued sporadic statements, condemning the Australian government's support for Israel's "genocide assault on Gaza", a handful of media releases calling for the safety of journalists, and the creation of a solidarity fund in 2024. But that's it.

From within the ABC—the *unpublic* public broadcaster—there has been some level of *concern*, with News Director Justin Stevens publicly *urging* Israel to allow international journalists—especially the Palestinian freelancers the ABC relies upon—to move freely in and out of Gaza. The ABC's Middle East correspondent, Matthew Doran, recently described the physical toll on these freelancers, including one who lost 34 kilograms and was too weak to hold a camera or even speak. Yet even within these acknowledgements, there was the obvious omission: no explicit reference to the killings of journalists, and no attribution to Israel for being responsible for this. Whether this silence stems from editorial disinterest, fear of political backlash, or direct pressure from media executives, the result is pretty much the same—the most dangerous campaign against journalists in living memory—possibly ever—and Australia's mainstream media journalists, for most part, just want to pretend that it's *just not happening.*

THE LAST WORD WILL BELONG TO PALESTINE

The history of modern war reporting shows a slow but steady tightening of state control over the media. For many journalists, the Vietnam War was the high-water mark for reporting from a conflict zone—reporters moved freely between sides, spoke directly with civilians and soldiers alike, and were rarely targeted—although, clearly, journalists did die while reporting on the conflict.

Of course, this openness proved to be catastrophe for the public image of the United States, as the uncensored coverage eroded domestic support for the war in the U.S. and, ultimately, helped to end the presidency of Lyndon Johnson, who decided not to run again for office in the 1968 U.S. election campaign. In the decades since, governments have learned from those experiences of the Vietnam War that information and soft power can be more destructive than the *actual* firepower. Since that time, media access to conflict zones has been increasingly restricted, from the Pentagon's "embedding" program during the 1991 Gulf War to more recent policies warning that the safety of journalists could not "be guaranteed", effectively excluding them from these zones.

Israel has taken these measures to an extreme. Since October 2023, all foreign journalists have been banned from entering Gaza, leaving coverage to the internal Palestinian reporters already on the inside—journalists who then became direct targets for the Israeli military. At the same time, Israel maintains some of the most restrictive media control laws in the world; its High Court upheld the government's right to limit press activity in Gaza on the grounds of "operational security" and broader "strategic goals"—provisions so broad they allow for the removal of any outlet that Israel chooses, and for any reason, whether it be a factual or fabricated reason. These legal frameworks reinforce near-total control of the narrative: preventing coverage of their war crimes, enforcing pre-approved footage, and silencing dissenting voices.

The killing of journalists in Gaza is more than a tragic by-product of war—it's a direct attack on the important principle of bearing witness. The leaders of the wars in Bosnia in the early 1990s—Slobodan Milošević, Ratko Mladić and Radovan Karadžić—were found guilty of crimes against humanity largely because of the massive weight of evidence that was documented by the actions of many brave independent journalists who upheld those key principles of journalism: *speak truth to power* and make people in positions of this power accountable for their actions.

It's unacceptable conduct for any state, let alone one that presents itself as the "sole" democracy in the Middle East (even though it's not) with a supposedly free press. If Israel considers its actions in Gaza to be defensible, why not allow unrestricted media access and then we can see for ourselves? If its accusations linking reporters such as al-Sharif to Hamas leadership are true, why not present credible evidence? For a state celebrated for its intelligence capabilities and surveillance reach, especially the draconian control over the Palestinian people in Gaza and West Bank, the absence of any proof at all is quite telling.

These repeated claims, unsupported by verifiable evidence, function as propaganda designed to justify otherwise indefensible actions. But despite the suppression, the intimidation and the killings, Israel's control over the narrative is fraying and falling apart quite quickly, with Israeli

Prime Minister Benjamin Netanyahu now facing a global shift in political will.

The Prime Minister, Anthony Albanese, recently announced that Australia will recognise the state of Palestine at the United Nations meeting of the General Assembly in September and said that it's a step towards a long-overdue recognition that is needed to end the violence in Gaza and the West Bank.

Predictably, Netanyahu has condemned such moves from Australia and European nations as "shameful", insisting they won't alter Israel's stance in Gaza. But that's what he always says, and we've come to expect this from a leader who shouldn't be speaking as the Prime Minister of Israel but speaking at the dock at the International Criminal Court in The Hague, and taking up his place in the hall of infamy, alongside all the other war criminals who have been indicted by the Court.

Palestine has been disappointed by the international community many times before, ever since the disaster of the Balfour Declaration was released in 1917, the document that gave rise to the misguided colonialist Zionist project of Israel and set itself on a path of continuous genocide. There's no guarantee that this disappointment won't continue.

But the point is that the symbolism of Albanese's announcement can't be ignored: the weight of numbers is there, and Australia will join the other 147 countries around the world that have decided to be on the right side of history, even if it has taken some of these countries some time to work this out. It also indicates that despite Israel continuing to silence and kill many Palestinian journalists who have been reporting from Gaza, the truth will find a way to come to the surface, as it always does. Their efforts haven't been in vain.

***

WHEN JOURNALISM BECOMES PUBLIC RELATIONS

18 August 2025

The Australian mainstream media continues its descent into irrelevancy and complete compromise, especially when it comes to its coverage of Israel and Palestine. Once seen as important check on the excesses of political and corporate power, much of media press is now less concerned about the truth and more about siding up with and protecting those vested interests. The *Sydney Morning Herald*, for example, has been running many stories that align almost perfectly with the messaging from pro-Israel lobby groups, and when the inaccuracies or distortions are exposed—as occurred last week—they've been quick to retreat or quietly amend these articles without any accountability at all. This pattern isn't just a bit of casual sloppiness: it's an insidious link between media organisations, powerful lobby groups, and the political class.

Journalists who report in a way that expresses even the smallest and tokenistic support for Palestine, are punished, sidelined or sacked, as journalist Antoinette Lattouf found out in 2023, when she lost her job for social media comments that were made *outside of her actual job* that were deemed to be too sympathetic towards Palestine. In a similar incident, cricket journalist Peter Lalor was sacked for offering comments about the acts of genocide committed by Israel, even though—again—his comments were made far away from the confines of a broadcast studio. These experiences show how, in Australia, press freedom is conditional and transactional: a robust interrogation and discussion of almost every other issue that we can think of, but non-existent when the subject of Palestine is brought up.

This selective application raises a deeper question about the industry itself. Journalism is meant to be *fearless*, reporting *without favour* and prepared to *confront* the powerful—speaking *truth to power*; that's the main game. When reporters are forced out for telling uncomfortable truths, even when they're speaking these truths in some distant parts of social media, the profession risks collapsing into little more than a public relations scheme for those in authority—Orwell's suggestion that "journalism is printing what someone else does not want printed" still remains relevant: when journalists fail in that duty, they are no longer journalists at all, but *propagandists*, and we're seeing a lot of that within Australia's mainstream media.

The contrast with the experience of Palestinian journalists could not be more different. In Australia, those who speak up risk losing their careers. That's bad enough but in Palestine, they risk *losing their lives*. Hundreds of reporters, photographers, and media workers have been killed in Gaza and the West Bank while performing the craft of journalism.

Conversely, any unwavering support for Israel carries no professional penalty in Australian newsrooms—in fact, it's actually encouraged—while the slightest micromillimetre of deviation away from Israel and in support of Palestinian rights is career-ending. If such standards were applied evenly, there would be very few journalists left in mainstream Australian media at all—while that might be a good thing, it just means that at the moment, there's not much difference between a journalist and a propagandist.

MANUFACTURED LIES AND COMMERCIAL CONSIDERATIONS

The tension between the ethics of journalism and commercial reality has always shaped the media landscape—we did see a lot this after Indonesia annexed East Timor in 1975, where reports by the Fairfax journalist David Jenkins were frequently filed but rarely published—but nowhere is it more extreme than the reporting on Israel and Palestine.

News executives know that advertisers can be quick to withdraw their campaigns if their coverage begins to question Israel's actions or show sympathy for Palestinian civilians—or be dealing with yet another Zionist lobbyist from the wealth class screaming down the barrel of the phone to demand the sacking of a journalist who might have written something mildly critical of the state of Israel.

This commercial pressure shouldn't override the fundamental obligation to truth, yet too often it does. For most news executives and journalists, *it's just a job*: just do as you're told, reduce the paths of resistance, and everyone can just go home at the end of the day, safe in the knowledge that the entire editorial team will still be on the invitation list for Christmas drinks in Bellevue Hill. The result is a media culture where maintaining relationships with powerful lobby groups and protecting advertising revenue takes precedence over accuracy, fairness, and integrity.

This pressure sometimes manifests itself in subtle editorial choices, but at other times it crosses into outright fabrication. The episode involving the *Herald*'s recent report on Hamas is an excellent example of how propaganda becomes the news. The outlet published a story claiming that Sheik Hassan Yousef, a founding member of Hamas, had praised Prime Minister Anthony Albanese for recognising the state of Palestine. The problem was that the claim was obviously false: Yousef has been imprisoned in Israel for many years, with no ability to communicate freely with the media, let alone deliver their commentary to a gormless and compromised journalist in Australia, chewing their lunch looking out over the splendid views of Sydney's Pyrmont Harbour. Yet the story ran in the *Herald* in loud headlines and was soon amplified across the country by News Corporation (of course), the ABC, *The Guardian* and SBS.

It took little more than a basic search to establish that the story was fabricated—no Arabic or English source material existed, and no credible journalist had made such contact. Yet the piece was framed as though direct contact had been made with the journalist in question, Matthew Knott. When the fabrication was exposed, primarily through independent commentators on social media and independent journalists who know how to use basic search engines on the internet, the *Herald* quietly rewrote the article without acknowledgement of the error. Instead of a transparent correction, the story doubled down and was reshaped to obscure their failures.

This continued on the ABC's Insiders, where Nine Media's James Massola—a colleague of Knott's—attempted to smooth over the debacle by suggesting it was a "cock-up" rather than deliberate propaganda, just reworked as a minor mistake and *no big deal*: it was better to offer lame excuses than admit to an obvious failure. In contrast to this feckless behaviour, journalists in Gaza and conflict zones all around the world put their lives on the line to hold power to account.

What do Australian journalists do? Too many are in the role of stenographers for state power, presenting propaganda as fact and happy to be part of the very structures they should be interrogating ruthlessly. The cost of their inaction isn't only to individual careers and reputations—there won't be any problems for these mainstream journalists; they'll be able to retire in a life of comfort and be able to regale to each other about all the times they managed to trick the public—but the true cost is to public trust in journalism itself.

If it wasn't for independent media, these falsehoods and fabrications would have gone unnoticed, and recorded as fact. And many Australians still rely on mainstream media as a record of fact at face value, even though it's a reputation that is totally undeserved. This grip on the so-called "truth" means that propaganda—if repeated often enough—becomes indistinguishable from reality and an accepted part of the truth, even though it's not.

A story about Hamas allegedly praising Albanese just fell apart after a simple inspection by social media and citizen journalists, but the damage had already been done: the *Herald*'s actions left an impression that the recognition of Palestine is linked to terrorism, and that supporting Palestinian statehood is also supporting extremists. That was the goal of the *Sydney Morning Herald*, and they achieved this in spades.

It's not just misleading but it's also destructive of the body politic—even if Hamas were to welcome international recognition of Palestine, it shouldn't invalidate the decision of the Albanese government. But the story was framed to discredit Albanese's move by association with terrorism, and not to inform the public: it was propaganda, pure and simple, dressed in journalism.

By stripping away any subtlety, the mainstream media ensures that audiences are offered little more than binary choices between black and white, or of *good* versus *evil*: there are no shades of grey in this discussion—to quote George W. Bush, "you are with us, or you are with the terrorists". This is not journalism, but the construction of a narrative that serves political power. And unless independent voices continue to question and contest these distortions, Australia will be left with little more than manufactured lies masquerading as the truth.

SILENCING PALESTINE BEYOND THE NEWSROOM

As we have seen many times, the reach of the conservative pro-Israel lobby in Australia reaches far beyond the newsroom and, because control over media narratives is never going to be enough, cultural spaces have to become the battleground. Universities, writer's festivals, and literary gatherings—institutions traditionally dedicated to free expression and a contest of ideas—are increasingly being pressured into silence, with the aim of not just stifling criticism of Israel, but to erase Palestine from the public conversation altogether.

The Bendigo Writers Festival was established in 2012 and celebrates writing and storytelling by "bringing together writers, readers, and creative thinkers from diverse backgrounds and genres". It's a successful regional event and over the past thirteen years, it has invited many authors and intellectuals from Australia and all around the globe to discuss the contemporary cultural issues in this complex world we live in. But no event is too small or too far away for the belligerent and chauvinist Israel lobby to shut down any discussion about Palestine.

Perhaps thinking that they were in the back streets of Gaza City and ready to launch yet another rocket attack on innocent civilians, a pro-Israel academic group known as "the 5A" mounted an aggressive campaign against the participation of Palestinian–Australian author Randa Abdel-Fattah. Just days before the festival, 5A accused her of antisemitism and extremism, branding her "a racist" and "a direct threat to the Jewish community in Australia". 5A has long lobbied universities to suppress pro-Palestinian activism, and after their pressure in Bendigo was successful, Abdel-Fattah withdrew from the event in protest—how could she not?—and more than fifty other writers followed suit, objecting to a new code of conduct that banned "inflammatory" or "divisive" topics.

The boycott left the festival in ruins due to the last-minute intervention by 5A, and the cowardly acceptance of this pressure from La Trobe University. What should have been three days of debate and celebration of ideas, descended into chaos, with panels removed and programs cancelled.

Universities should be a place of intellectual inquiry, not rolling over at the first sign of external pressure. Worse still, many Australian institutions have become complicit in their quest to save face with these Zionist tyrants, sacrificing their own principles to avoid controversy. And while conservative groups dominate the discourse, the voices of progressive Jewish Australians—many of whom oppose the occupation and support Palestinian rights—are routinely ignored.

But a democracy that silences writers, punishes journalists, and rewrites news to appease lobbyists is a democracy that has lost confidence in its own values. The 5A group claimed that the Bendigo Writers Festival was not "a safe space" for Jewish people, but where was the safety for everyone else who was subjected to this imperious and bigoted assault on their freedoms to listen to perspectives from Palestinian people? Why is their safety—or the safety of Palestinian people—never up for consideration?

This intellectual dishonesty breeds resentment, mistrust, and fear, while wiping out the possibility of honest engagement. It's a disturbing development in Australian public life: one where power dictates what can be said, who can speak, and what stories can be told, whether it's within the mainstream media, or a literary festival in a regional city.

If there is to be any hope of reversing this development, Australians needs courage from their institutions and honesty from their media; that universities foster debate rather than suppress it, and that journalism return to its core duty of holding power to account. Otherwise, what is the point? For too long, these Zionist lobbyists have dictated the limits of acceptable conversation. To defend free expression is not to endorse every idea, but to protect the space in which ideas can be contested in. The alternative is *silence*—preferred, of course, by the Zionist lobby—but as history has always shown us, silence is the ally of the oppressor.

***

NETANYAHU'S INSTABILITY AS AUSTRALIA STARTS TO ACT

25 August 2025

The endless devastation and genocide in Gaza has finally started to cause unrest within Israel—sure, it's not a popular movement yet but they're belatedly seeing what the rest of the world has been seeing for almost two years—and the alarm bells are ringing all across the world, leaving the Prime Minister of Israel Benjamin Netanyahu increasingly isolated.

For two years, Netanyahu has aggressively sought international support for his actions in Gaza and has fended off most criticisms, but it's reached a point now where it's impossible for any country to defend the actions of Israel, especially after the Integrated Food Security Phase Classification was made by the United Nations that Israel is causing a famine in Gaza, "a man-made disaster" according to UN Secretary-General António Guterres, and "a failure of humanity itself".

Allies who had long stood firmly behind Israel are stepping away—bar the United States and a few other compromised nations—and Australia has become one of the more visible examples of this shift. Prime Minister Anthony Albanese recently announced that Australia will formally recognise Palestine at the UN general assembly meeting in September, and this marked a significant departure from decades of cautious diplomacy—very predictably—Netanyahu reacted with fury, lashing out at Albanese by calling him a "weak politician" who had "betrayed Israel" and abandoned Australia's Jewish community. This outburst came after Australia also refused entry to Simcha Rothman, a member of Israel's far right and ultranationalist political party Mafdal-Religious Zionism—surely, Australia has the right to refuse entry to unacceptable miscreants, especially if their sole purpose to create mischief and promote Netanyahu's political agenda overseas.

For Netanyahu, his reaction wasn't just about Australia's decision but about domestic politics back home. Facing escalating protests, corruption charges, and an increasingly fragile grip on power, he has sought to paint Albanese as an enemy of Israel so he can rally his own supporters—as well as some Australian citizens who are eligible to vote in Israeli elections. It's a familiar right-wing tactic: amplify external threats to shore up fragile authority at home, and while that might work in Israel, the strategy has backfired locally and encouraged even more people to support Australia's actions.

On the weekend, an estimated 350,000 people participated in nationwide marches demanding Palestinian recognition and accountability for Israel's actions in Gaza, one of the largest co-ordinated protests in recent Australian history, and a major shift in public sentiment that can't be ignored by the political establishment. Certainly, Australia has been highly and mysteriously uncritical of the Israel government over the past two years, but surely that has its limits—governments that ignore these types of national actions ignore them at their own peril. And far from isolating Albanese, Netanyahu's attacks seemed only to strengthen the resolve of the government.

Home Affairs Minister Tony Burke captured the mood last week, when he said that "strength is not measured by how many people you can blow up or how many children you can leave hungry", but in the courage to take principled decisions even when they are unpopular with powerful allies—and he went on to offer a clear message to Palestinians: "you are not invisible, we see you"—an odd comment, considering it's almost been two years of the Australian government mostly ignoring the suffering of the people of Gaza and *not* seeing them, and doing everything possible to overlook the crimes against humanity and genocide being carried out by the state of Israel.

The nation-wide marches—as well as the recent Sydney Harbour Bridge March for Humanity, where around 300,000 people attended—shows that protest and public pressure do matter. The massive marches, disturbing images of starving children in Gaza, and the increasingly unreasonable and authoritative demands from the defenders of Zionism—such as the special envoy on anti-Semitism, Jillian Segal—have sent a clear signal to the Albanese government that the public wants more decisive action against Israel and more moral clarity on what everyone else can see with their own eyes.

The irony is that Netanyahu's attempt to cast Albanese as weak has only highlighted his own weaknesses. It's too early to claim that Australia will now act more decisively on Palestine but, at least where it might have previously offered stubborn hesitation, it is now starting to take on more tangible actions, instead of the bluff and blustering, or claiming that it's all too 'difficult to see from afar to judge'—as Foreign Minister Penny Wong suggested in 2023—or mindlessly suggesting Israel has a 'right to defend itself' while implementing starvation as a weapon of war and a genocide against the people of Palestine.

A DISCREDITED LEADER AND THE QUESTION OF SANCTIONS

Albanese now has the political cover to act more stridently on Palestine and against Israel. Netanyahu's political fortunes are in freefall: his authority is crumbling, with waves of mass protests across Tel Aviv and other Israeli cities reflecting deep public anger at his leadership. Internationally, his standing is even weaker. His reputation among European leaders has become toxic, and the International Criminal Court has issued an arrest warrant against him for alleged war crimes—hardly the type of international leader that Albanese would want to be supportive of.

If it wasn't half obvious before, every act by Netanyahu is designed to deflect attention away from Israel's domestic and economic turmoil, from his own charges of corruption, and the genocide in Gaza. Even in Australia, he's become so toxic that conservative Jewish lobby groups are distancing themselves from him, because they've realised that supporting such a discredited leader will damage their own credibility.

Labor backbencher Ed Husic has been one of the most consistent and outspoken advocates for stronger measures—at least since he became a backbencher—that Australia mustn't just "express concern" but needs to hold Israel to account and implement sanctions. This week, he repeated this call, referring directly at the suffering in Gaza.

"We need to work with our trusted friends and allies internationally in terms of sanctions," Husic said. "A lot of our sanctions so far are focused on activity in the West Bank but looking at what's happening in Gaza, we do need to hold decision makers to account. We should remain open minded about sanctions ... people are still suffering from starvation and the Netanyahu government doesn't seem to want to take a change of approach."

This momentum around sanctions is significant. For years, they were dismissed as unrealistic, a fringe suggestion from a radical Greens–BDS movement, and too extreme for an Australian government to consider against Israel. Yet with little sign of a policy change from Netanyahu, sanctions are increasingly being seen as the only international instrument that will influence his behaviour, because it seems that nothing else is working. Certainly, sanctions are a slow-moving instrument, but they do work eventually—and at the least, the discussion itself shows how a fringe idea from just a few years ago has moved into mainstream thinking.

While Netanyahu is the classic and stubborn right-wing 'do-whatever-it-takes' survivor of Israeli politics, there is a realisation that he's not going to survive politically for too much longer. Observers who have tracked his career since the 1990s, and who long warned of his authoritarian tendencies and overreach, can now see his demise quickly approaching. And within politics, when the end arrives, it arrives *very quickly*.

Whether his departure comes through legal prosecution, political overthrow, or internal party revolt, it's uncertain how much longer Netanyahu will remain as Israel's leader, with a splintering and fragmented coalition, and elections due before October 2026. His carefully constructed image as a strongman has crumbled to the point where even long-standing supporters no longer see him as an asset.

PUBLIC OPINION IS SURGING AHEAD OF POLITICAL LEADERS

Australia's shift—albeit a slow shift—is symbolic of a wider reassessment of the politics in the Arab World and a better understanding of the toxicity of Netanyahu's leadership and policies, and the recognition of Palestine is part of a broader shift where many longstanding allies of Israel are beginning to question their unequivocal support.

Some of this reflects the slow but unmistakable movement of a changing international order, where incompetent leaders who thrive on conflict are no longer given a free pass. Australia has been good at moving on these types of leaders—Tony Abbott, Scott Morrison and, more recently, Peter Dutton—Brazil too—but other political systems such as the United States, who reinstalled a clearly incompetent, unstable and divisive President Trump, have not yet worked this out.

While diplomatic processes move slowly—often frustratingly so—the cultural and political undercurrents are moving quickly. People in many countries, including Australia, are just refusing to accept the narratives that have been dished out in the past: they're demanding accountability, justice and a different way of solving problems, not the top-down practices of the past where governments take on the 'here are our policies, sit down, shut up, and just accept them' approach. Those days are over.

The Nationwide March for Palestine was one of these moments. While the media downplayed the numbers as "tens of thousands" (the *Herald Sun* in Melbourne suggested even less, reporting just "hundreds" of protesters), the reality was undeniable: hundreds of thousands of Australians from diverse backgrounds, took to the streets to support the recognition of Palestine, immediate sanctions on Israel, and an end to the famine and destruction in Gaza. *The public has had enough.*

This mobilisation also suggests a deeper frustration within the Australian community: that successive governments—Liberal-National and Labor—have too often acceded to the demands of small but powerful right-wing lobby groups who are determined to shield Israel from criticism, primarily because any critique of Israel undermines their belief that Palestine doesn't exist, and undermines the ethos of Israel as *a land without a people for a people without a land*, surely the most extreme definition of *terra nullius* ever, and the underlying logic that's created the pathway for the genocide currently underway in Gaza.

The public has also had enough of the continuous calls for new laws to silence dissent on behalf of Israel, of equating criticism of Israel with anti-Semitism, and the suppression of any discussion of war crimes and apartheid, which they can clearly see occurring on a daily basis. In a democratic country, the public sees such attempts as unacceptable, and these mass protests are a result of this. If Australia claims to uphold universal human rights, then it cannot apply them selectively at the behest of powerful interests. Palestinians, too, must be entitled to those rights: *that's what the Australia public is saying*.

The public can also see the footage of famine and starving children, cities blown to smithereens, the double and triple standards of international diplomacy. They want action; that much is clear. For Albanese and his government, the decision to recognise Palestine might just be the first step in a much broader process of matching up policy with principle but governments acting without principle, even if they do have a massive majority—won't hold public support for too much longer, as we are seeing with Keir Starmer's Labour government in the UK, who are now lagging behind in opinion polls to a tinpot Reform UK and an unnamed and a not-yet-formed political party that could be led by Jeremy Corbyn and Zarah Sultana. And this is after the Labour Party secured their largest ever victory in the 2024 general election, just over a year ago.

While there are many other factors in Starmer's diabolical drop in opinion ratings—there are lessons for the Albanese government. Denying a just cause that has popular support and siding with the oppressor does have political ramifications, especially when the leadership of that oppressive and genocidal force has become so toxic.

Netanyahu's political collapse, both here and internationally, shows the limits of politics built on fear and manipulation: it might take a while for that limit to be reached, but it always gets there. As his influence wanes, the responsibility will shift to those who can shape what comes next. The pressure from the public—in Australia, in Europe, in the United States, and in Israel itself—has to be the constant reminder that leaders can no longer afford to ignore the demands for justice. History is moving quickly, and those who hold on to the politics of the past will be left far behind and will pay the political price.

***

THE SINKING CREDIBILITY OF ASIO

1 September 2025

Australia's decision to expel Iran's ambassador is the most dramatic diplomatic incident in over eighty years, with Prime Minister Anthony Albanese using ASIO assessments—announced by the Director-General of Security, Mike Burgess—to make a link that Iran was behind the arson attacks on the Jewish community in Sydney and Melbourne in late 2024. In Albanese's words, these were "extraordinary and dangerous acts of aggression orchestrated by a foreign nation on Australian soil," claiming that Tehran sought to undermine social cohesion and spread fear among Australian Jews.

On the surface, these allegations are serious, of course they are. The attacks—one at the Adass Israel Synagogue in Melbourne, the other at the Lewis Continental Kitchen in Bondi—were described as part of a broader pattern of hostility directed by Iran. Yet beyond the Prime Minister's carefully chosen words about "credible intelligence", there's many areas that need to be resolved, and much material that just doesn't make any sense. No evidence has been publicly presented to substantiate the broad claims from ASIO and, unlike the usual diplomatic processes, the ambassador was not summoned for consultation or given an opportunity to respond. Instead, Albanese moved directly to remove the ambassador, a rare and provocative action.

THE SINKING CREDIBILITY OF ASIO

There are so many obvious contradictions: Albanese has consistently downplayed Australia's role in Middle Eastern affairs—as recently as last week—often defending his muted response to mass pro-Palestine marches and Israel's genocide in Gaza by insisting that "Australia is not a major player in the region", or in the case of Foreign Minister Penny Wong, her comments that it's difficult to "judge from afar" the grotesque actions of Israel. If that's the case, why suddenly elevate Australia's position by making it the first Western government in decades to expel an Iranian ambassador? And on such flimsy material presented to the public?

There is also the question of just how plausible it would be for Iran to be involved, which would gain nothing at all except for international opprobrium. Of course, Iran, like many authoritarian states, runs surveillance operations on its diaspora communities, including on the 85,000 Iranian Australians, many being dissidents who are hostile to the government of Tehran. But orchestrating crude arson attacks on local synagogues in Australia doesn't have any strategic relevance or importance.

Not only is there no precedent for Iran directing such attacks in Australia, but the incidents themselves were amateurish and clownish—fires that caused limited damage, allegedly carried out by hired bikies whose own text messages reveal incompetence rather than professional co-ordination. As notorious as Iran's Revolutionary Guard is, it's established methods involve large-scale, high-impact operations abroad—lighting fires at minor community sites is not its *modus operandi*, and would probably be insulted at being accused of such an incompetent act.

This narrative coming from ASIO is even more questionable when considering the nature of the targets—at least one synagogue affected was known for its anti-Zionist stance, making it an unlikely target for a regime that is vehemently *opposed to Israel*, rather than the Jewish religion itself.

The attack on the Lewis Continental Kitchen, a small kosher restaurant in Bondi, also raised further doubts—why choose a modest food business when larger, more symbolic Jewish institutions are nearby? The inconsistencies feed a belief that the Australian government is either overreacting, or—more likely—that there are other motives are at play.

Complicating these issues is the credibility of ASIO itself. This is the same intelligence agency that supported the false claims of weapons of mass destruction in Iraq in 2003, a "credible assessment" that justified an invasion and a war which killed over 200,000 people. Over twenty years later, Australians are being asked to "just trust the intelligence" once again, and it's understandable that they might be sceptical, especially when it involves an escalation with Iran, and possible another invasion and a war. Without transparency, ASIO's role looks less like a credible and analytical assessment and more like political theatre, where intelligence is being politicised to fit in with the policy objectives, either of Australia, or other international players.

Against this background, the timing of this expulsion also needs to be taken into account, coming just a week after Israeli Prime Minister Benjamin Netanyahu publicly berated Albanese for his intention to recognise Palestine at the upcoming meeting of the General Assembly at the United Nations. These events suggest the expulsion might be more about appeasing international relationships and managing domestic political pressure that any genuine national security threats.

INTELLIGENCE AND THE PALESTINE CONNECTION

While governments occasionally expel lower-ranking diplomats and declare them *persona non grata*, forcing an ambassador to leave is an extreme measure. Iran has already indicated that it will expel Australia's ambassador from Tehran in retaliation—perhaps a moot point, considering Australia already evacuated the diplomats before the announcement was made—and it has firmly rejected the allegations levelled by Australia.

The timing of this move also opens up more speculation. Albanese's decision to recognise Palestine at the United Nations drew condemnations from Israel and the United States but, in contrast, Iran strongly welcomed the move, as did its ambassador in Canberra. Was his expulsion a convenient way to silence his voice? Or could the situation provide Prime Minister Anthony Albanese with an excuse to backtrack from his promise to recognise Palestine? Albanese had already hedged his position by insisting recognition should proceed only in co-ordination with other states in the region and the acceptance of Israel's right to exist. Iran, of course, refuses to recognise Israel at all, making it an easy scapegoat if Albanese decides to delay or dilute his commitment, providing the Prime Minister with the political cover where he could argue that Iranian "aggression" makes it impossible to advance Palestinian statehood while maintaining Australia's credibility on security matters, however weak that might be.

There's also other inherent contradictions within Iran. Iran has the largest Jewish population in the Middle East outside of Israel, a population of around 10,000 people. While Jewish life within Iran is not free of restrictions, it is worth remembering that after the 1979 Revolution, Ayatollah Khomeini issued a *fatwa* to protect the Jewish communities who live inside Iran. Tehran's hostility has always been directed at Zionism as a political ideology and the Israeli state, not at Judaism as a religion, and this situation makes the claim that Iran would target a non-Zionist synagogue in Melbourne even more illogical.

The deeper concern is the way intelligence is being used here. Professional intelligence work requires solid sourcing, verifiable evidence, and rigorous analysis. But intelligence agencies also exist in a clouded political space—funded through secretive channels, operating through cut-outs and plausibly deniability, sometimes venturing into activities that governments always seem to deny. The record of agencies such as MI6 and the CIA shows how often intelligence has been politicised, manipulated, or simply wrong. But it hasn't stopped that intelligence from being used to justify nefarious ends, as shown through the "weapons of mass destruction" debacle in Iraq.

If this is the basis for expelling the ambassador, then Australia has moved once again into dangerous territory—using intelligence as a political weapon. Whether the target is Iran and a war that Israel and the United States have longed for over many years, or obstructing Palestinian statehood—or both—the consequences will be profound.

THE DOUBLE STANDARDS AND THE POLITICS OF BELIEF

There is also a severe diplomatic imbalance at play that many people in Australia have called out. Iran, accused without clear evidence of sponsoring two arson attacks that caused minimal damage—certainly no damage to human life—has faced the most serious diplomatic sanction Australia can impose, short of severing these relationships altogether. Meanwhile, Israel—accused of war crimes by the International Criminal Court, practicing a brutal form of apartheid, and accused of genocide by many reputable international bodies—faces nothing at all, never faces any condemnation or red lines that cannot be crossed and, if anything, is encouraged to continue its crimes against humanity, supported through yet another shipment of arms from Germany and United States, and F-35 parts provided by Australia.

Israel's bombing campaigns have killed more than 64,000 Palestinians—at the very least—including civilians, doctors, and journalists. The Australian aid worker, Zomi Frankcom, was killed by a deliberately targeted Israeli drone strike in Gaza in 2024, yet the Israeli ambassador is still there in Canberra, rescued by Albanese's infamous political caution, diplomatic inertia and a few words of "concern" from Foreign Minister Wong. In this context, the expulsion of Iran's ambassador is selective, and breathtakingly cynical.

The mainstream media, too, has largely fallen into line, amplifying ASIO's claims with hardly any scrutiny at all. Hard questions about the credibility of the evidence have been rare, and what little scepticism exists has been drowned out by the government's framing of events. This blind acceptance has a familiar ring to it and Australians have been here before: the Hilton Hotel bombing in 1978, where bungled intelligence led to wrongful arrests; the 2003 Iraq war, where false intelligence about weapons of mass destruction paved the way for invasion and mass slaughter; the debacle of Man Haron Monis, the terrorist behind the Lindt Café siege in 2014, who was also an ASIO operative.

Security services, like all human institutions, are imperfect, and there's no question that they will make mistakes. But when their judgments carry consequences as profound as unjustified wars, mass casualties, a siege in the heart of Sydney, or the unprecedented expulsion of an ambassador, there can't be any margin for error.

In practical terms, the fallout from this affair within itself, will be limited. Australia has doesn't have a significant trade with Iran, and the embassy's primary functions concern air travel, tourism, and consular assistance for dual citizens. The closing of the embassy might complicate the lives of the few Australians visiting family or touring Iran, and Iranian Australians dealing with paperwork or cultural exchanges.

But strategically, the expulsion achieves little. It doesn't weaken Iran's regional position, nor does it advance Australian security in any meaningful way. What it does achieve though is symbolic theatre: a show of resolve directed not so much at Tehran, but at domestic audiences and international allies.

The Australian government will claim that it has acted out of security necessity, but in reality it has exposed itself to accusations of hypocrisy, politicisation, and subservience to allies. Expelling an ambassador on the flimsiest of grounds, while excusing far graver offences by Israel, undermines the credibility of both the government and its intelligence services. This is a decision that won't be remembered as a principled defence of Australia's sovereignty, but as another moment when intelligence was used as a political weapon, and the truth was left far behind.

***

FROM KNESSET TO COUNCIL: THINK GLOBAL, INFLUENCE LOCAL

8 September 2025

The recent Australian Mayors Summit Against Antisemitism was presented as a "community safety initiative" but its agenda was far more political than that. Over several days on the Gold Coast, local mayors and councillors from across the country were given all-expenses-paid trips to hear from speakers carefully chosen by the U.S.-based Combat Antisemitism Movement to push their particular agenda. While the event advertised the idea that it was address antisemitism within Australia, in reality, it was a platform designed to discourage criticism of Israel and its ongoing genocide in Gaza.

The Movement, which organised and financed the Summit, is heavily funded by Republican-aligned donors in the United States and has a history of targeting pro-Palestinian academics, attacking human rights organisations, and amplifying political rhetoric and attacks against the United Nations.

Its ultimate goal is to universally implement the International Holocaust Remembrance Alliance's definition of antisemitism—a definition that many legal experts and civil liberties groups warn is being used to link critiques of Israel with antisemitic hate speech, which would then be used to legally sanction anyone who makes any kind of criticism of Zionism or Israel's genocidal actions in Gaza.

Australia's Special Envoy for Antisemitism, Jillian Segal—who incidentally has been very quiet about the recent spate of neo-Nazi fascist attacks throughout Australia—was a keynote speaker at the event and has been one of the most vocal advocates for embedding this definition into public policy. Former neo-Nazi leader Jeff Schoep also appeared on the program, while one of the conference co-chairs, businessman and political donor Stan Roth—the brother-in-law of Segal—contributed $50,000 to the far-right lobbying group Advance Australia, which has run campaigns against "mass migration", and advocated for the recent right-wing March For Australia event.

The presence of these types of figures just shows how ideological this Summit was, and far from it being a neutral or inclusive forum on community safety, it just reflected the agenda of a narrow, hard-right movement, exporting U.S.-style Zionist culture wars and violence into Australian politics.

What makes the Summit particularly concerning is the expectation that will now be placed on the attendees. As we know, nothing is free in politics: when councillors accept funded trips to glossy conferences and propaganda talk-fests—*all expenses paid*—there is a strong chance that they will return to their councils and communities carrying the ideological baggage of their hosts, with the expectation that they will deliver on their agenda. The message delivered at the Summit was clear—advocacy for Palestinian rights and criticism of Israeli government actions are to be stigmatised and silenced, even at the local council level of Australian politics.

And it has now reached the point of *pure ridicule*. Among the items officially deemed "antisemitic" are watermelons displayed in solidarity with Palestinians; the simple slogan "Free Palestine" (of course); wearing a *keffiyeh*; the phrase "All

Eyes on Rafah"; or referring to Israel as a "settler colonial state" and Gaza as an "open-air prison". It's the politics of the preschool playground and it's as absurd as the Bundestag in the 1930s outlawing pretzels or accordions as symbols of resistance and foreign influence—although, given the mindset of that era, it's quite possible that it would have been considered.

But we have already arrived at—or even surpassed—that point where the absurdity or extremity of these measures no longer matters. The image of the innocuous watermelon is now treated as a *threat*, all because this stubborn fruit—through the process of evolution—landed on the colours of green and red, and dotted itself with black seeds: *antisemitic, guilty as charged* and to be *hanged from the neck until dead*.

And yet, despite their ridiculous and infantile demands, there is no shortage of local councillors and politicians eager to enforce the dictates of the Zionist agenda and accept their political proctology, fearful of jeopardising funding or support from the Israel lobby. As we have seen with the proscription of Palestine Action in Britain—where pensioners and even people in wheelchairs have been arrested for simply holding up a sign—political leaders of all persuasions are increasingly choosing to make *themselves* the object of ridicule rather than risk the opprobrium of the Israel lobby. That's how bad this has all become.

None of this should distract from the fact that antisemitism itself is abhorrent and must always be condemned. We always need to point this out as a ballast of any commentary about Palestine, because it always opens the unreasonable "what-about-ism" and accusations of antisemitism. Of course, *we will condemn antisemitism*, but we will also condemn the actions of Israel and Zionist supremacy.

The Holocaust revealed the consequences of state-sanctioned antisemitic hatred. Yet, matching up legitimate criticism of the political project of Zionism with that same hatred does a disservice both to Jewish communities and to democratic freedoms in Australia. Zionism, after all, is a political ideology—one shaped as much by English evangelical Christianity and European colonial interests as by Jewish nationalism, and historically influenced by currents of antisemitism that sought to remove Jewish populations from Europe rather than embrace them as equal citizens.

By aligning with organisations that push for this conflation, political leaders in Australia continue to narrow the space that exists for open and democratic debate. Councillors who attended the summit should now be pressed to explain not only what they learned, but whose interests they now serve and allow voters to decide at the next election whether a practice that prioritises excusing Israel from its genocidal actions over addressing the genuine threats posed by rising far-right extremism is acceptable or not.

COMMUNITIES ARE REJECTING THE AGENDA OF THIS SUMMIT

Many unions, grassroots community organisations, and even Jewish groups themselves, have called out this Summit—the Jewish Council of Australia, for example, was one of the most prominent voices urging councillors to boycott the event. Their position was clear and unambiguous: this was not a summit to combat antisemitism, but rather a carefully packaged exercise in pro-Israel propaganda, advancing the right-wing political ideology of Zionism under the guise of community safety.

And the criticisms have gone far beyond "the fringe" which usually the terminology used to dismiss these voices. The Australian Services Union, Democracy in Colour, Jewish Voices for Peace, councillors from the Inner Sydney Greens, and a range of other civil society groups have all warned that these events compromise accountability. The message is clear:

antisemitism is real and must be condemned, but political junkets financed by foreign-linked organisations with explicit ideological agendas must also be condemned and have no place in Australian public life.

Transparency International and other governance watchdogs have long argued that while accepting travel and hospitality from lobby groups might not technically breach the law, it erodes public trust in local decision-making, irrespective of which level of government it occurs. Ratepayers don't elect local representatives so that they can accept paid trips from overseas interest groups and return with a pre-packaged political program, ready to be foisted upon them. Councillors are meant to be accountable to *their* communities, not to donors in Washington or Tel Aviv.

At the heart of this is also a deeper philosophical point: to suggest that opposing Zionism—or Israel—is inherently antisemitic is not only intellectually dishonest but actively harmful to democratic institutions. Zionism is not synonymous with Judaism, nor is it universally embraced by Jewish people. Indeed, some of the loudest critics of Zionism today are Jewish organisations and individuals—as we saw on the weekend in Bondi at the event organised by Jews Against the Occupation '48 to show their support for Gaza and the Sumud flotilla—and includes conservative religious communities who reject the idea of a nation-state on theological grounds.

To label these critics as "not real Jews" or the offensive "Kapos" and dismiss their arguments as *antisemitism*, is to deny the diversity of Jewish voices and to reduce centuries of debate into a single, state-sanctioned right-wing extremist narrative. This process punishes pro-Palestine advocacy, it stifles dissent and silences people. It's also a process that undermines democratic principles and restricts what people in Australia can say about foreign governments and their actions.

There's no question that the work against antisemitism needs to continue—but it can't be hijacked by bad ideas requested by small minority of ideologically-driven zealots. Zionism, as an ideology, should be open to the same scrutiny and criticism as any other political project. To shut down that conversation is to confuse faith with politics, and to make the mistake of blind allegiance to a state, over solidarity against racism.

THE SUMMIT WILL FUEL THE ANTISEMITISM IT CLAIMS TO FIGHT

The 250 local council representatives who attended the Summit will now have to return to their communities and justify why they were there. One councillor in particular—the mayor of Sydney's Inner West Council, Darcy Byrne—took part despite opposition from his fellow councillors. The Council had been on the verge of adopting a Boycott, Divestment and Sanctions resolution against Israel, but this was blocked after Byrne's intervention—a move that left many people in the Inner West community bewildered and disillusioned.

The astroturf Better Council group, backed by the Zionist movement to campaign against pro-Palestine initiatives at the local government level, threw its weight behind Byrne and the Labor Party during the 2024 council elections, rewarding his role in shutting down the BDS resolution. His prize was a junket to the Gold Coast and the promise of political support in future elections, provided he continues to *do the right thing*. This is how the process works. Why support action against the state of Israel—even if that's what fellow councillors and the local community are demanding—when there's an election to be won?

However, this issue goes far beyond the one mayor. This Summit was bankrolled by some of Australia's wealthiest pro-Zionist organisations and corporations, including entities in heavy industry and peak Jewish lobby groups. Their ability to provide unlimited funding for such events is precisely what should raise many red flags about influence and integrity but all it's doing is raising the flags for more political interference and opening up the gates for more donations.

When elected representatives accept hospitality and travel from lobbyists with clear political agendas, the line between independent governance and corporate capture becomes dangerously blurred. This is a problem that has long been associated with the federal and state levels of politics and needs to be stamped out. But to now see it more obviously entrenched at the local government level—where transparency and accountability should be at their strongest—is really concerning.

If the stated aim was to counter antisemitism, it has already failed. In the week leading up to the Summit, neo-Nazi groups marched openly through Australian streets, presenting—at least on the surface—the most immediate threat to Jewish communities. Yet the Summit gave no meaningful reaction to these movements: not a single word against the neo-Nazis and fascists visible in our cities, as though it went out of its way to accommodate ideological bedfellows, a trilogy of Nazism, fascism, and Zionism.

Instead, the Summit focused almost entirely on redefining antisemitism to shield Israel from criticism, targeting symbols such as watermelons and *keffiyehs*. *The important parts of antisemitism*. Paradoxically, this approach will probably add to antisemitism rather than diminish it. When people witness elected officials attending lavish junkets—bankrolled by foreign-linked lobby groups—to defend the policies of a corrupt, hard-right genocidal Israeli government, resentment and cynicism will only get worse.

At its core, the Summit was not about protecting Jewish Australians from harm—if it was, Jillian Segal would have condemned the shameful actions of the Zionists against the Jews Against the Occupation '48 at Bondi Beach on the weekend. Instead, the Summit was about shielding Israel's current government from accountability, exporting American-style lobby politics into Australia, and embedding a culture of silence around one of the most pressing human rights crises of our time. When this ugly edifice eventually crumbles—and it inevitably will—local political leaders who attended will have to explain why they sided with influence peddlers and propaganda merchants instead of defending free speech, democratic principles, and the fight against genuine antisemitism.

***

MANUFACTURING THE FEAR OF CHINA

15 September 2025

Last week marked the 80th anniversary of the defeat of fascism in World War II, an event that should have been an occasion for reflection on sacrifice, alliance and peace, and a defeat of one of the most insidious and repulsive ideologies that has ever afflicted the world. In Beijing, President Xi Jinping delivered his speech declaring that China is "a great nation that does not *commit* violence." Yet in much of the Western media, this was mistranslated as "China does not *fear* violence"—it's a subtle but big shift in meaning, and it was enough to transform a commemoration of peace into headlines portraying China as a belligerent threat.

In Australia, the reaction followed a familiar and *all-so-tiresome* script. This mistranslation was used to frame China once again as a looming menace, supposedly preparing to invade Taiwan and destabilise global security. It's not new, but for decades, Australia's mainstream media and conservative commentators have depicted China as an enemy, irrespective of the context. Each occasion becomes another opportunity to recycle Cold War rhetoric, exaggerate the threats and present a pantomime of paranoia as serious analysis. Instead of sober debate about diplomacy, trade or regional security, the Australian public is fed a steady diet of fearmongering that reduces China to a simple caricature.

Of course, it will always be legitimate to criticise China's government and its policies—just as one might criticise the United States, Britain or Australia itself. Certainly, the issue of Tibet is unresolved, there is the treatment of groups such as Falong Gong and Uyghur Muslims that breaches human rights, and China's record on these matters is far from perfect. But there's an imbalance how the records of different countries are perceived.

America—*the good guy*—always has its wars, military bases, invasions and bombings downplayed or rationalised, while something as simple as the diplomatic events of China—*the bad guy*—are reframed as sinister and always bring discussions about an immanent invasion of Taiwan. But if China truly intended to take Taiwan by force, it would have found time over the past eighty years to do this yet, so far, it has not—and anyway, it's more advantageous for China if the rest of world believes an invasion is imminent, even if the chances of that are quite remote.

The anti-China rhetoric in Australia also carries unspoken racist undertones. No one comes out to say outright that the "Anglo-European powers" are better suited to global leadership, but that's exactly what the implication is. The selective outrage, the mistranslations, and the constant suspicion reveal more about Australia's insecurity than what they do about China's intentions. What comes out of this is not policy analysis but a cultural knee-jerk reaction: to cast China as the perpetual *other*, incapable of being trusted, always a threat to *our way of life* if we drop our guard, even if it is for just a moment.

This dynamic is intensified, of course, whenever it can intersect with domestic politics, and that's exactly what happened when former Victorian Premier Daniel Andrews appeared at the Beijing commemorations, where his presence was treated by sections of the media as proof of Chinese infiltration into Australian politics. Such portrayals verge on the absurd, but they resonate with a media ecosystem primed to turn any Australian engagement with China into evidence of treachery.

Rather than acknowledging China's role as a wartime ally against fascism in 1945, or considering how stability in the Asia–Pacific region might be better served through diplomacy, Australia's media and conservatives prefers fear and suspicion. The outcome is an endless cycle: commemorations of peace recast as threats of war, cooperation reframed as infiltration, and mistranslations weaponised into menacing headlines of aggression.

THE DOUBLE BONUS OF DANIEL ANDREWS

For Australia's conservative media, the Beijing commemoration developed into a double bonus—not only could China once again be depicted as the global menace, but the presence of Andrews provided another target: the chance to vilify Beijing and Victoria's former premier at the same time.

Andrews' presence was framed as proof of disloyalty, as though a single photograph with Xi Jinping or Vladimir Putin confirmed years of the media's suspicion about "Dictator Dan". The coverage ignored his electoral record of popularity within Victoria—three decisive victories, despite the full weight of the media campaigning against him in 2018 and 2022. It overlooked the fact that Andrews had long survived the conservative "Get Dan" strategy: a relentless media campaign to destroy his leadership that repeatedly failed. And, of course, this bitterness *lingers*: the media still resents that fact that Andrews outplayed them and left office undefeated—as well as having his statue erected in Treasury Place to commemorate his longevity—so any opportunity to revive the "Get Dan" strategy will be taken.

The irony is, however, that conservatives who despise Andrews for his supposed disloyalty to the West also share many of his positions on Israel. Andrews has long been an uncritical supporter of Israel, even as evidence of war crimes and the mounting death toll in Gaza grew. In a political climate where Australian politicians—Labor, Liberal and conservative independents alike—line up for free trips to Israel and come back to parrot its propaganda, this stance would normally be enough to shield him from these conservative attacks. Yet the media's vendetta against Andrews was never really about foreign policy, or whether he supports Israel or not: it was about his success in defying the media, and for that, he will always remain their enemy.

But there were also some glaring and convenient omissions by the media: alongside Andrews at the Beijing event were a wide range of political figures, including former New South Wales premier Bob Carr, and two former New Zealand prime ministers, John Key and Helen Clark, representing opposite sides of politics. They too were present, yet only Andrews became the story.

Even more conveniently forgotten were the images of former prime minister Tony Abbott with Xi Jinping, when Abbott himself invited the Chinese president to address the Australian Parliament in 2014. Or the photographs of Abbott with Russian President Vladimir Putin cuddling koalas at the G20 meeting, just a few months after Russia annexed Crimea and began its war in Ukraine. Malcolm Turnbull too was photographed with Xi and Putin. None of this generated the monikers of "Dictator Tony" or "Dictator Malcolm": the selective outrage was always going to be reserved for Andrews.

The broader question has to be: what does this strategy achieve? In opposing China at every opportunity, in reducing diplomacy to basic fearmongering and in tearing down domestic political figures for even attending commemorations,

Australia just confirms its reputation for immaturity on the world stage. If China does become the world's leading superpower within the next fifteen years—a scenario that is highly likely rather than a vaguely plausible theory—will Australia just pretend that these years of infantile hostility just never happened?

WHY AUSTRALIA SHOULD BE THANKING CHINA

Ultimately, constructive engagement with China is in Australia's national interest. The trade relationship supports hundreds of thousands of jobs and economic wellbeing in both countries. China is not just Australia's largest trading partner but also the single most important market for the state of Victoria. Andrews, who spent more than a decade as premier, understands this clearly, as does his successor, Jacinta Allan, who is travelling to Beijing to secure further deals with China.

Rather than demonising China, the media should be recognising the role these relationships have in advancing Australian economic interests, but nuance is rarely rewarded in today's media landscape. For conservative commentators, it's far easier to reduce any engagement with China to a betrayal than to acknowledge the clear reality: Australia's economic health depends on strong relations with Beijing, and this was evident when trade sanctions were applied by China after the Morrison government irresponsibly almost destroyed the relationship in 2020.

China, for its part, seems to take Australia's media and political theatre in its stride. While the conservative press delights in portraying Beijing as a ghoul to be feared on the world stage, Chinese officials view this as little more than petty domestic posturing—a mixture of historical xenophobia and cheap point-scoring. From their perspective, the spectacle of Australian media railing against China while relying on it for iron ore, coal, and agricultural markets is not a mark of strength, but of immaturity and gross stupidity.

Australia is, by any standard, an advanced economy, despite the recent issues that have been caused by the pandemic, global instability and the effects of inflation. But to maintain this standard requires good solid diplomacy with our trading partners, not reckless posturing. The choice in this case is very clear: do we want a strong economy structured around constructive ties with its biggest partner, or one that's hamstrung and weakened by outdated Cold War reflexes?

What is also interesting is how Australia responded to the 80th anniversary of the defeat of fascism. Rather than sending a strong delegation to Beijing to acknowledge China's wartime sacrifices—millions of lives lost in a struggle that tied down Japan's military and helped secure victory for the Allies—Australia largely ignored the event. This was an opportunity to show gratitude and recognition, but instead it became an occasion for ridicule, mistranslation, and hostility.

The problem is not criticism itself but the way it is weaponised, and a political culture that can't distinguish between constructive criticism and cheap attack lines. Until that changes, Australia will continue to behave like a country trapped in adolescence, unable to see that the very partner it fears is also the one most essential to its future.

If there is a lesson in this whipped-up frenzy controversy, it's that Australia just needs *to grow up*. Engagement with China shouldn't be treated as treachery. And if the media hopes to have any credibility at all, it must do more than repackage paranoia as patriotism. Until that shift occurs, Australia risks being trapped in a cycle of self-defeating hostility, blind to history and blind to its own long-term interests.

***

THE CASCADING DANGER OF CLIMATE CHANGE

22 September 2025

Cascading, compounding, concurrent. That's how the Australian Climate Service has described the way climate change will affect *every* community across the country. *Cascading*, because the impacts will intensify over time; *compounding*, because each new impact will amplify all the others that preceded it; and *concurrent*, because no part of Australia will experience these effects in isolation—communities across the nation will need to deal with multiple crises at the same time.

Australia's first national climate risk assessment, finally released by the minister for Climate Change and Energy Chris Bowen after a long delay, is the most comprehensive analysis of its kind. It's a disturbing picture of what Australia is confronting, even in the best-case scenarios. This report was expected before the 2025 federal election but was delayed—a decision that now seems unsurprising given the severity of its findings and a government not wanting to be distracted during an election campaign, after suggesting they would definitely be doing a lot more to address climate change issues than their counterparts, the Coalition.

According to the report, by mid-century—just twenty-five years away—1.5 million people in Australia will be at risk from rising sea levels; if global warming can be contained to 1.5 degrees, sea levels are projected to rise by around 0.15 metres; if temperatures rise three degrees, the increase could be closer to half a metre. Eighteen of the twenty most exposed regions are in Queensland, with northern New South Wales also among the danger zones, where flooding that was once thought to be a *once in a century* event is already occurring far more frequently, and by 2030 nearly 600,000 people could be living in areas vulnerable to inundation.

Northern Australia is also at a much higher risk: health, infrastructure, and ecosystems will be under intense strain, but the assessment makes clear that no part of the country will escape consequences. Heat-related deaths are projected to skyrocket: fatalities in Sydney could increase by more than 400 per cent, while Melbourne could see an increase of around 250 per cent.

These figures are not just abstract numbers—Sydney's hotter summers will claim thousands of lives if adaptation and actions to mitigate climate change fail—and other cities such as Melbourne, Brisbane, Perth and Adelaide will face similar numbers.

Australia's ecosystems also face dire consequences. Between 40–70 per cent of species will be forced to migrate, adapt—or perish altogether—if global warming increases by three degrees. Eucalyptus forests will be under threat, while coral reefs—already under severe threat from bleaching—are projected to suffer catastrophic collapse. There's not much doubt in this report: biodiversity loss isn't some distant concern that can be kicked down the road for future generations to deal with, but an immediate reality that's going to affect many people who are alive today.

Of course, the political response has been polarised and the climate wars are never too far away. Climate sceptics have dismissed the findings as alarmist or a deliberate attempt to undermine the fossil fuel industry but for many others, there has been a shock at the sheer scale of the crisis outlined. The reports highlights all the climate change issues that has been known about for decades, yet consistently downplayed and ignored: Australia has had over fifty years of repeated warnings, but weak responses and action has followed. The longer deep emissions cuts are delayed, the harder and more costly the task of remediation will be, as well a smaller window for effective action, with some scientists now suggesting that the opportunity to avoid catastrophic damage has already passed.

What is clear, however, is that piecemeal measures will never be enough and the report makes it impossible to ignore the urgency. It is not enough to just plan for 2050: Australia needs aggressive policies for the *here* and the *now*. Heatwaves cannot be solved with more air conditioning and hope the problems just go away; rising seas cannot be held back with token seawalls. Fossil fuel dependence must be wound down, fuel usage drastically reduced, and renewable energy scaled up—decisively and immediately.

POLITICS AND THE LIMITS OF AMBITION

When Prime Minister Anthony Albanese announced Australia's new 2035 emissions reduction target, he framed it as a balanced and responsible decision, saying that the government had "accepted... that Australia's 2035 emissions target be 62–70 per cent," presenting the figure as science-based, practical and backed by proven technology and insisting this is the right target to safeguard the environment, protect jobs and the economy, and acting in the national interest for both current and future generations.

Of course, the timing of this announcement wasn't by accident. Just days after the devastating release of the national climate risk assessment, the government sought to move from *catastrophe* to *solution* and prepare the public for new emissions target, something that will shape Australia's climate policy for the next decade. But the big question still remains: is a target of between 62–70 per cent ambitious enough?

Currently, Australia is on track for a 42.6 per cent emissions reduction by 2030 (based on 2005 levels)—if we are to believe the data provided by National Greenhouse and Energy Reporting scheme—just short of the legislated 43 per cent target. Meeting *that* goal is already a challenge. To then accelerate cuts toward a 62–70 per cent reduction by 2035 represents a massive leap, one that demands transformation across every sector of the economy. The Climate Change Authority has recommended an even higher range—65–75 per cent—but the government chose a middle ground. In the politics of climate change—certainly in Australia—the "middle ground" often means a delay, and delays means more warming, more damage, and less options later on. There might be different rules in play, but it's the same of game of kicking the problem further down the road, yet again.

Ambitious targets have to be *non-negotiable*—they are absolutely essential. To reach net zero emissions by 2050, Australia—and the rest of the world—will need sweeping reforms: rapid electrification of transport systems and urban travel, the phasing-out of coal and gas, large-scale investment in renewable energy, and a national adaptation strategy capable of addressing everything from urban heat to coastal erosion. There needs to be an overhaul of policy, markets and infrastructure at a scale unseen since the post-war industrial boom in the 1950s.

Politics, inevitably, will complicate the process, irrespective of how large a majority the Labor government has at the moment. The Coalition continues to resist ambitious climate policy—in their continuing mindless and unambitious quest to destroy everything in sight—but even they might end up have little choice.

By the time the Coalition next returns to government, these targets and the technologies implemented to achieve them will likely be so embedded within the economy that dismantling them would carry large political and economic consequences. If a Liberal Party in the future wants to return to power, it will have to embrace the very measures it's now resisting, otherwise it's going to be in opposition for a long period of time—and in any case, based on its current performance and parliamentary status, 2050 might be the time the Coalition *does* return to office, well after all the debates about climate change have been settled.

This climate challenge isn't just confined to domestic politics. The climate doesn't recognise borders or wait for anyone, and Australia's actions—or inactions—will be linked into other global efforts. For developing nations, reliance on older, cheaper fossil-fuel technologies will always remain a temptation, while wealthier countries must move decisively toward renewables—and support these developing nations in their own transitions. Although the renewable infrastructure is costly to establish, once it's embedded, energy prices start to fall. And this is precisely why entrenched fossil fuel interests fight so hard to slow the transition: it threatens their revenue streams.

In theory, capitalism should be thriving on innovation. Companies such as Apple, Amazon, Google and Tesla have reinvented technologies and developed new markets. But modern crony capitalism—the type favoured by Trump's America—generally tends to resist innovation, and focuses on short-term profits rather than looking at the longer-term benefits and future sustainability. And this is the issue that works against climate action: a system that supports vested interests rather than fully rewarding true innovation.

And it's also an issue for the federal government: challenging these vested interests. Australia's 2035 target is a step forward—*a small step*—but whether it's enough, is doubtful.

THE GLOBAL CLIMATE CHANGE DAY OF RECKONING

As things stand at the moment—with all the current legislative and practical mechanisms in place—the world is on track for an average temperature rise of around 2.9 degrees this century—a catastrophic outcome by any standard.

A modest increase in the global average temperature will trigger extreme weather events—as we've been seeing over the past decade—and there will be human and environmental displacement on a scale that we've never seen before. What might seem like a simple difference between 24 and 27 degrees on a thermometer or phone app—a pleasant afternoon that's just is a little bit warmer but *still pleasant*—is in practice, the difference between a liveable planet that we have now and one that's a dystopian mess that will be unrecognisable.

The United Kingdom is aiming for a 78 per cent reduction by 2035, with the European Union working towards similarly levels. The United States, mired in political backsliding under the influence of Donald Trump's extremist administration, has stalled. China, paradoxically, is both the world's largest emitter at the moment and the largest investor in renewable energy—its emissions are expected to fall sharply once investments start to replace fossil fuel industries and energy. Against this backdrop, Australia's target of 62–70 per cent is too cautious, and the risk is that if Australia adopts half-measures, other countries—especially developing nations—will feel emboldened to do the same. If other countries have had the benefits of the industrial revolution over the past 200 years or so, why should they miss out?

COP30 will be held in Brazil later this year, and Australia arriving with half-hearted commitments and political compromises while simultaneously approving new coal mines and gas fields will send a mixed message to the international community. It's difficult to claim climate leadership while digging up the materials from the earth that are driving the crisis in the first place. Labor's internal balancing act—protecting mining union jobs while professing climate ambition—is an inherent contradiction. Transitioning workers from coal and gas into sustainable industries is essential, but resistance to retraining and moving to new practices and other industries is real, and political will has too often been blunted by electoral calculations.

But his is not just about the *loss* of jobs; it is about the *transformation* of jobs. A genuine transition requires *honesty*: acknowledging the value of past contributions by old industries while making it clear that clinging on to these old industries will condemn future generations to an environmental dystopia, far worse than anything seen in *Soylent Green* or *Blade Runner*. Those movies are classic science fiction, but they'll soon become the reality if the world fails to act.

Australia's credibility on climate change will also be in tatters unless it acts in a far more comprehensive way, including greater emission reduction targets, boosting foreign aid to its Pacific neighbours to adopt cleaner technologies, and accepting environmental refugees who essentially will be displaced by the many years in which the West has been polluting and destroying the planet.

Like all nations, Australia must decide which side of history it wants to occupy: to make a contribute to the solution, or be remembered as a country that chose short-term expedience over long-term survival.

***

SIGNS OF THE AMERICAN EMPIRE IN DECAY

29 September 2025

It says it all really. United States President Donald Trump took out his frustrations with the United Nations by mocking a broken escalator and a faulty teleprompter, a performance that encapsulates much of his approach to international diplomacy: reducing serious global forums to personal grievances, insults and theatrical soundbites. From that podium at the UN, he spoke in apocalyptic tones about Europe being "devastated by energy and immigration," urging nations to clamp down on what he called "the unmitigated immigration disaster" and a "fake energy catastrophe". It's rhetoric designed to appeal to nationalist and MAGA sentiment within the U.S., but it did little to reassure allies or uphold America's reputation as a steady global leader.

Trump's second term has been marked by an accelerated erosion of democratic norms, where institutions are being hollowed out and experienced officials are being replaced by loyalists chosen for political obedience rather than their competence. Conspiracy theories are elevated to fact, while expert advice is routinely ignored and dismissed. The result is a U.S. government that functions more like a personal fiefdom and continuing whingefest, rather than a professional administration, and it's starting to groan under the weight of its own ineptitude.

On the international stage—or any stage—Trump's speeches are littered with lies and mistruths. He boasts of having "ended seven wars," halting immigration and talks about climate change as a hoax, *the big con*. None of these claims are true, of course, but they resonate with the far right MAGA base, and feed into a culture of complaint and paranoia. Trump relentlessly attacks immigrants, independent media and any critic who refuses to bow to his wishes. The result is a deeper polarisation in the United States, and a rapidly declining international credibility.

America's decline, however, can't just be pinned solely on Trump: this would give him *too much* credit. He's less the cause than a catalyst—a symptom of deeper structural weaknesses within U.S. society. For decades, the country has neglected the infrastructure and social foundations that once underpinned its global leadership. With an estimated $3.7 trillion backlog in essential repairs, according to the Information Technology and Innovation Foundation—roads, hospitals, schools and public services—the U.S. has consistently chosen to funnel resources into foreign wars and alliances with corrupt regimes, rather than investing in its own people. Even under leaders widely seen as competent, such as Barack Obama, foreign policy often prioritised military action over domestic renewal.

Trump's actions have simply brought these flaws into the open, so the world community can more readily see them. His chaotic leadership has exposed what happens when an advanced society elects a figure who thrives on spectacle, grievance and division. The fact that his election was even possible—whether narrowly won outright or nudged over the line by interference and manipulation—it reveals a country willing to gamble its democratic tradition for the promise of far-right disruption. Trump's 2024 presidential election was not a landslide victory, but it was enough to reshape the trajectory of the United States. Since Ronald Reagan and the onset of neoliberalism in the 1980s, America has been drifting toward this cliff; and Trump is the accelerant on this path.

But the rest of the world isn't waiting: as the United States retreats towards its new phase of isolationism, other nations are stepping into the vacuum. The choice remains America's to make: to embrace isolation and authoritarianism, or to adapt and renew its place in the world. Countries will always have the right to choose their own national direction but one thing is very clear—no nation can withdraw from global responsibility and still expect to be a leader.

THE SELF-INFLICTED WOUND OF ISOLATIONISM

The suggestions of American decline are not new, and nor did they begin with Donald Trump's second presidency, or even his first in 2017. The roots stretch back decades, through Reagan's almost maniacal embrace of neoliberal economics across all aspects of American society. The dismantling of regulatory safeguards, the neglect of public infrastructure, and the elevation of markets over social cohesion have all chipped away at the foundations of American power. Under Trump, the hollowing-out of institutions has continued: it's no longer unusual to find government departments led by conspiracy theorists or opportunists whose qualifications are measured only by how low their genuflection to the President stoops.

Nowhere is this more dangerous than in health and science policy. With figures such as Robert Kennedy Jr.—an anti-vax crusader inexplicably elevated to Secretary of Health—policy has been shaped not by *science* but by *paranoia*, where spurious claims, such as links between paracetamol and autism, have made it into official pronouncements. This weaponisation of mindless conspiracy theories not only undermines trust in medicine but it endangers public health. They're not harmless theatrics; they corrode America's standing and hasten its retreat from global leadership.

And while Trump is feeding his own paranoias and those of the far right, other powers—China, Russia, India, Brazil—are creating new alliances, experimenting with trading currencies and financial networks outside of the U.S. dollar, and deepening their regional influence. Far from weakening China—Trump's biggest agenda—his policies are bolstering its role as a counterweight to American hegemony. An isolationist United States is not a stronger one: it's a wounded power inflicting damage upon itself while others prepare to occupy the space it vacates. For allies such as Australia, the message should be obvious: the blind attachment to the United States carry many risks, and diversification of partnerships is becoming essential in a world that is being reorganised.

American isolationism isn't a new phenomenon: for much of the 20th century, the United States flirted with disengagement, cushioned by its abundant resources and the capacity for self-sufficiency. But globalisation, especially this third wave, has removed the possibility of true isolation. In a connected world, withdrawal means *irrelevance*. Nations will not follow the lead of a power that turns inward and rubbishes and ignores international agreements. The perception of the United States as a stabilising force—whether that was warranted or not—created the foundation of its global role. But this perception is disappearing very quickly.

And this is where the paradox lies: Trump claims to be strengthening America by isolating it, but this process makes it weaker. What has always provided the United States with leverage is not just its military power, but the *perception* that it could be a global stabiliser. Of course, we always knew the perception was a façade—the U.S. has been a leader of global *instability*, but has used soft power and bullying tactics to keep up this appearance. And once that perception goes, it's difficult to get it back: the vacuum is now starting to be filled, not just by the chaos alone, but by rising powers eager to reshape the international order on their own terms.

AUTHORITARIANISM AND THE FRAGILE RESISTANCE

Trump's latest performance at the United Nations was a showcase of bluff and bluster—a bizarre kind of Dunning–Kruger diplomacy in which ignorance is presented as strength. To many outside the United States, Trump's speech was comedic, even clownish, yet its impact was deadly serious. This is the public face of American leadership for at least the next three and a half years and, for much of the world, the sight of an American president railing against allies and institutions has become normalised. The United Nations—already a favourite target of conspiracy theorists and Trump's MAGA base—was mocked as "useless" and reduced to a punchline about a body that only prepares "strongly worded letters"—and malfunctioning escalators, even though the break in the escalator that Trump railed against so much, was caused by once of his own social media managers who triggered a safety mechanism while trying video record Trump gliding up the escalator.

In reality, the UN's record is far more complex. While it certainly failed in areas such as Bosnia and Rwanda—largely because the Security Council's veto system paralysed action that could have been taken—it has also helped end or prevent conflicts: Namibia, El Salvador, Mozambique, Cambodia, even mediating an end to the brutal Iran–Iraq war in the 1980s. Trump's cartoonish portrayals ignore this history, reinforcing his narrative of American victimhood while undermining a unique global institution which actually is capable of multilateral problem-solving.

And then his allies in the media, such as Fox News host Jesse Watters, take up the attacks with violent fantasies—"bomb the UN," "gas it," and "demolish the building"—rhetoric that would once have been unthinkable on mainstream television. That such calls now pass without consequence, while comedians like Jimmy Kimmel are "cancelled" for virtually no reason at all, reveals how degraded and diminished American public discourse has become.

Yet even amid this increasingly polarisation and the normalisation of authoritarianism, there is resistance, as there always will be. California Governor Gavin Newsom—widely seen as the leading Democratic candidate for the 2028 U.S. Presidential election—has been blunt about the recent failures of due process in the United States, and its descent towards an authoritarian state, rather than being the supposed leader of the free world.

Of course, every country around the world is polarised to some extent: if we look at election results, the gap between voting patterns on the progressive and conservative side of politics is not great, irrespective of which party is in government. However, progressive governments—and we can certainly look at the Albanese and Starmer governments in Australia and Britain—tend to be cautious, slow and reactive—whereas conservative governments arrive with a wrecking ball and wreak havoc that takes many years to repair, and then move towards an ugly brand of authoritarianism.

Trump and his inner circle are symbolic of this descent into authoritarianism. Former adviser Stephen Miller has branded the Democratic Party "a terrorist organisation" and promises to "go after enemies" and Trump himself posted on Truth Social calling for political opponents to be "taken out". These aren't just momentary lapses, they are signals to supporters and threats to institutions, and intended to desensitise the public to intimidation and violence.

The appointment of Robert Kennedy Jr. was disastrous; the naming of Kash Patel as head of the FBI was arguably worse. Under Patel, high-profile investigations—such as the shooting of conservative activist Charlie Kirk—have been mired in confusion, conspiracy theories and questionable evidence. Even the FBI's eventual arrest in that case reportedly relied on a family member turning in the accused, not on federal investigative work.

All of this highlights a deep fragility with the United States. Checks and balances are only as strong as the willingness of officials to uphold them. As Australians learned during the Morrison years, when oversight is ignored or weakened, it effectively disappears. In the U.S., that fragility has become more obvious. The question now is not whether resistance exists—it does—but how much damage can be inflicted before institutions are so degraded that recovery becomes almost impossible. The next three and a half years will test not only American democracy but the world's tolerance for a superpower behaving like a rogue state.

THE SEARCH FOR A NEW GLOBAL STRUCTURE

Despite the continuing political chaos and descent towards authoritarianism, many are arguing that the performance of the American economy is evidence that the country is still in a strong position. These numbers might seem reassuring, but the headline figures of rising GDP growth, low unemployment and higher corporate profits hide the economic instability that's bubbling under the surface.

By the end of the June quarter—essentially the first quarter of Trump's second presidency—growth had already begun to slow, personal consumption had fallen to its lowest level in two years, and businesses are hesitating to expand in the face of policy uncertainty. Inflation is rising again and the prospect of long-term stagflation—an affliction that has neutered Japan's economy for many decades—is now looming over the United States.

America might appear prosperous in the short term—which has reached this point through four-years of hard economic work in during the early stages of the COVID era—but much of this work is now starting to fall away, and very vulnerable to Trump's self-inflicted shocks and inconsistent policy. His tariffs and erratic trade wars are unsettling businesses at home and abroad, while the broader structural weaknesses of American society—crumbling infrastructure, political dysfunction, deep inequality—remains unresolved and will be unresolved for some time to come. These vulnerabilities will extend far beyond America's borders: Australia, for instance, will not be insulated from the ripple effects of U.S. economic turbulence, whether through trade, wanton tariffs, capital flows or shifting diplomatic alignments.

And these vulnerabilities and self-inflicted wounds are creating opportunities for others. The BRICS grouping—Brazil, Russia, India, China, and South Africa—is still in its infancy, but this growing momentum shows that an American-led system is increasingly unjust and unreliable. Just as the League of Nations gave way to the United Nations after the second world war, a new global alliance is not as far-fetched as it might have seemed even just a few years ago. Whether Australia plays a role in shaping such an alliance—as it did with the UN in 1945—remains to be seen, but failing to engage would be a dereliction of duty to its own citizens.

Globalisation itself—or at least this current third wave of globalisation—is fragmenting. The old empires have collapsed, and the U.S.-dominated order that followed is no longer viable. China is often described as building its own "empire" but it functions differently: through trade, investment, and influence rather than direct colonial control, although the Tibetan and Uyghur populations within China would like to differ on that prospect. For middle powers such as Australia, this shift will require more maturity and shift away from empire and going through its own process of "decolonising the mind". The days of comfortably attaching ourselves to one great power—the British Empire, then the American empire—are over.

This doesn't mean abandoning allies or throwing away strategic relationships. But it does mean recognising that clinging to the old myths of Western supremacy is futile.

The empires of the nineteenth and twentieth centuries have long dissipated, the imperial attitudes that seem to still be influencing Australia's diplomacy. To advance its interests, Australia needs to adapt and become far more sophisticated: cutting the ties where interests are no longer relevant, strengthening partnerships when the new opportunities arise, and maintaining relationships when these serve Australia's national interest.

In a world that is becoming less defined by empires and circulating around networks of influence, the test will be whether we can embrace independence without isolation, and have a level maturity that doesn't resort to the nostalgia of empire.

***

THE NATIONAL PRESS CLUB SHOOTS THE MESSENGER

6 October 2025

The National Press Club has cancelled an upcoming address by Pulitzer Prize-winning journalist Chris Hedges, who had been tentatively scheduled to speak in Canberra on October 20. "The Betrayal of Palestinian Journalists" was to examine how the mainstream media has failed in the ethical duty to report truth and ignored solidarity with colleagues working and dying in Gaza.

Hedges' lecture was to highlight how Western media outlets, including many in Australia, have repeated Israeli disinformation despite clear evidence of atrocities, censorship and the routine targeting of Palestinian journalists, with over 278 killed since the start of Israel's assault on Gaza in 2023. The proposed lecture was removed from the schedule, and CEO Maurice Reilly relayed to Hedges that "in the interest of balancing out our program, we will withdraw our offer," despite the Club's public commitment to being a "vigorous champion of media freedom".

Of course, Reilly's explanation has provoked widespread criticism from journalists, academics and supporters of free speech in Australia, who have accused the Club of hypocrisy and political cowardice. Reilly later justified the cancellation by noting that the Club was hosting several speakers on the issue Palestine, including Chris Sidoti, Ben Saul, UNICEF spokesperson James Elder, and Judge Navi Pillay, who had served on the UN inquiry that found Israel is committing genocide, arguing that the Club needs to "balance" its speaker lineup.

But this is disingenuous: Hedges' address concerned journalistic ethics and accountability, not geopolitics, and cancelling such a figure undermined the very principles the Club claims to uphold. And surely, a club that purports to be an organisation representing the intellectual interests of journalists *should* be presenting the type of address Hedges was going to provide.

Reilly has denied any external pressure, insisting that the decision was made solely by the Press Club's board. Yet, there's many questions about the relationships between some Australian journalists and pro-Israel advocacy groups, many of whom have attended "Journalists' Mission to Israel"—a media "study tour" sponsored by the NSW Jewish Board of Deputies. The program, according to its organisers, is designed to "demonstrate the complexity of the situation in the Middle East," but such trips often serve to frame narratives in Israel's favour and shape sympathetic media coverage back home.

The cancellation of Hedges is a direct affront to press freedoms in Australia—and shows that one of the nation's elite media institutions has become more concerned with political optics and donor sensitivities when it comes to Gaza—like so many other institutions—rather than with defending the right to speak truth to power.

A MORAL WITNESS

Chris Hedges is an acclaimed war correspondent who built his reputation by reporting from the world's most brutal conflicts for well over thirty years, including from Central America, the Balkans and the Middle East/Western Asia. He was the Middle East and Balkans bureau chief for the *New York Times*, and was a member of the team that received the Pulitzer Price in 2002.

Hedges' approach to journalism is based on what he refers to as the "moral witness"—the belief that a reporter's duty is not just to relay information but to confront power and expose injustice, even at personal risk, and suggests a clear delineation between two types of war correspondents: the few who risk their lives to document the realities of war—such as the ones in Gaza—and the many who "play at war," relying on official briefings and producing narratives shaped by military and political handlers.

It's a distinction that has never been more important than in the coverage of Gaza, where "official" accounts from Israel are routinely presented as fact while the testimony of Palestinian journalists and civilians is marginalised or dismissed. By their actions, it's clear which side of this ledger the National Press Club stands on.

During his years reporting from Gaza, Hedges witnessed first-hand the destruction and terror inflicted on its population. He's seen children shot by Israeli soldiers, families buried under bombed homes and entire neighbourhoods reduced to rubble under what Israel claimed were "surgical strikes". For Hedges, the language of state-sanctioned reporting—"collateral damage," "security operations," or "being caught in crossfire"—is an example of the moral blind spot within modern journalism.

Since the Israeli assault on Gaza in late 2023, Hedges has turned his attention to the "betrayal of journalism" itself, suggesting that Israel's military campaign amounts to genocide and ethnic cleansing—now confirmed by many reputable human rights organisations—carried out with the backing of the United States and Europe and justified through a compliant global media that reproduces official lies. According to Hedges, this is not just a political failure but an ethical one—a symptom of a profession that has surrendered its moral authority to the interests of power, profit and propaganda. The action of the National Press Club is symptomatic of that.

The highest obligation for a journalist in the field of war should be to veer towards truth, not neutrality, and Hedges said that we "cannot stand by while one people is exterminated and call it balance". His address at the National Press Club was expected to explore this collapse of journalistic integrity—how the media's complicity in Gaza reflects a broader decay in Western journalism, driven by corporate consolidation, political fear, the loss of moral courage, and a failure to hold power to account.

The silencing of Hedges isn't just about the one event—it's about the crisis he has spent his career warning about: a media culture so compromised by power that it no longer tolerates those who insist on telling the inconvenient truth.

THE HYPOCRISY AT THE HEART OF THIS DECISION

This decision by the National Press Club has tarnished its credibility, as well as raising many questions about its commitment to media freedom, as it's now engaging in the kind of censorship that it has frequently challenged in the past.

In 2019, the Club hosted "Press Freedom: On the Line," a forum that was held after a spate of police raids on journalists' homes, unions and news organisations during the time of Morrison government. That event became a key part of the #YourRightToKnow campaign—a co-ordinated effort by Australian media to push back against government secrecy and defend the public's right to information. The Club's own publicity at the time offered a direct question: *When government keeps the truth from you, what are they covering up?*

While the Club wasn't officially a part of that campaign, it was a strong supporter of the notion that journalism's core duty is to confront the powerful, not to appease them.

Six years later, it's apparent that for the Club, there are certain issues that *can* indeed be swept away. By cancelling Hedges—a lecture that was to be dedicated to the betrayal of journalists in Gaza—the Club has answered its own question about *your right to know*. The Club has aligned itself with the same forces of suppression it claims to oppose, trading moral conviction for comfort and conformity, and engaging in its own betrayal of the principles of journalism.

The Club was a signatory to the International Association of Press Clubs statement in September 2024 that condemned Israel's killing of journalists in Gaza, and called for independent investigations into the deaths of reporters, denounced attacks on hospitals and medical staff, and reaffirmed the protection of journalists as an essential part of international law. But that was just lip service: when the opportunity arose for a journalist of the calibre of Hedges to discuss these crimes from firsthand experience, the National Press Club chose silence.

Reilly has also claimed that "when the details of the address were made available, we made a decision to pursue other speakers on the matter". What exactly were those details? It's not as though Chris Hedges is an unknown journalist who just appeared out of nowhere: the National Press Club would have known exactly who they were working with. Who were the details of the address made available to? What were these deliberations? Who made the decision?

The claims of "no external pressure"—as far as we can tell—might be plausible, but what about pressure from within the National Press Club or from the other eighty-six journalists who have been on the Israel-sponsored "study missions" designed to shape media narratives that are favourable to the policies of Israel? How many of these are also members of the National Press Club? Of course, a claim of "no external pressure" can always be made when compromised club members know exactly what needs to be done *internally*, when the moment arises.

These connections explain why an event that exposed media complicity in Gaza and those sailing too close to the government of Israel was deemed to be too uncomfortable to host. And, of course, who would want to be reminded of their complicity and failures to act or listening to Hedges' talk about a blood-soaked Gaza while enjoying Merimbula rock oysters, Daintree barramundi, Chantilly crème or the many other fine dining choices available for members during these addresses? It's hard to enjoy the Four Pillars gin or Drambuie—or Hawke's Legend Ale—in the after-lunch bar when reminded of the many journalists in Gaza who died in their choice to tell the truth, when the main choice Club members need to make is whether they can fork out the $165 for their annual membership, and whether it will be a valid tax deduction or not.

This incident has shown the National Press Club—supposedly a forum for fearless journalism—is just another weak symbol of timidity, a gatekeeper of acceptable speech rather than a defender of free expression. The institution that once championed the public's "right to know" now appears to be deciding what Australians are allowed to hear.

The question that now confronts Australia's media community is much bigger than one cancelled talk: if the National Press Club can't find the courage to host a veteran Pulitzer-prize winning war correspondent speaking about the killing of journalists, what remains of press freedom in a country that once prided itself on it?

***

PEACE MIRAGE: WILL ISRAEL FOOL THE WORLD YET AGAIN?

13 October 2025

U.S. President Donald Trump's proclamation that this Gaza ceasefire marks "a great day for the Muslim and Arab world" is typical of his bombastic style of diplomacy: a grand announcement made to create a headline—and a last-gasp effort to gain the Nobel Peace Prize (which turned out to be unsuccessful)—rather than a genuine attempt at ending the conflict and holding Israel to account for its war crimes and acts of genocide.

Trump's plan is a one-sided act where Hamas has been handed a 20-point ultimatum, and a choice between compliance or annihilation. The agreement is based on short-term issues—the exchange of captives and hostages, limited Israeli withdrawal and the delivery of humanitarian aid—while leaving the many questions of reconstruction, future governance and sovereignty mainly unresolved.

Certainly, any agreement that results in a ceasefire has to be welcomed, but what's the cost to a just and lasting peace in the region? The deal seems to be more about the spectacle of negotiation and political convenience: the fact that Israel Prime Minister Benjamin Netanyahu so readily accepted the plan and gained approval in Knesset within days, suggests that it's not really a framework for peace—which effectively would signing his own political death warrant—but more a strategy for him to buy some time and prepare for the upcoming Israeli general elections, due before the end of October 2026.

Looking at Trump, his instincts are based around the "transaction", ego and self-promotion, and his record over two terms shows a pattern of timed announcements that maximise media exposure or opportunities for personal gain and self-promotion. His approach to the Middle East/Western Asia is more about foreign policy stunts engineered for the media, rather than serious reform—from the Abraham Accords to the impromptu recognition of Jerusalem as Israel's capital in 2017—and implementing simple solutions in a region built on historical and political complexity that requires difficult negotiations and clever diplomacy, none of which Trump has the stamina for.

This Gaza deal—and, of course, we'll have to let this latest action play out to see what the exact outcome is—might end up being another act in a long-running political performance played out by Israel and the United States over the past eight decades. Trump's preference for the spectacle, combined with Netanyahu's endless habit of scuppering agreements at whim whenever it suits him politically, suggests this ceasefire is built on self-interest rather than sincerity—a mirage that might collapse and end up continuing the occupation, just like all the other ones that have preceded it.

ANOTHER NETANYAHU GAMBIT FOR POWER AND CONTROL

For Netanyahu, the Gaza ceasefire isn't a peace accord but a *new strategy*—a quickly-agreed-to plan that allows him to recalibrate his campaign for political survival. His leadership over the decades has never been guided by goodwill or the pursuit of reconciliation, but by a relentless focus on his authority and perpetual conflict, irrespective of the cost to Israeli society—Netanyahu would sell out Israel in a heartbeat, if it could be used to save his political skin—and it's becoming more apparent that the electorate is not going to provide him another opportunity to sell them out, irrespective of when the next election is held.

Throughout this war, humanitarian aid was obstructed, ceasefires agreements were broken, and hostage negotiations delayed until the constant public demonstrations made them politically unavoidable. Every decision that Netanyahu has made over the past two years—in fact, during his entire career—has been shaped by his instinct for *preservation* rather than *principle*.

In reality, war is Netanyahu's *only* remaining instrument of governing and a leader in this situation doesn't have too much time remaining in their political career. Each escalation in Gaza and the blaming of Hamas reinforces his narrative of Israel's perpetual victimhood—a state surrounded by enemies and in constant need of his leadership. This is not sustainable. The siege mentality he cultivates legitimises repression at home and aggression abroad but the political costs of this latest war have mounted: international condemnation has intensified, the International Criminal Court is closing in on him, and Israel's once-supportive allies have had enough and their support is falling apart at the edges.

In the aftermath of this ceasefire, Netanyahu is now trying to position himself as the diplomat who ended the war and brought the hostages home, even though he did everything possible to prolong the war and soiled every offer from Hamas to return the hostages. This is the standard process for Netanyahu—continue with the circus act, use every catastrophe as a political opportunity, and somehow claim a victory, even though it's obvious that his strategies over the past two years have failed.

But Netanyahu is shallow and predictable: this is all a calculated move toward the next election—rebranding himself as a pragmatic peacemaker, while quietly maintaining the occupation of Palestine—and this could allow him to distance himself enough from the extremists in his coalition like Itamar Ben-Gvir and Bezalel Smotrich, whose maniacal and barbaric rhetoric is offensive to many foreign governments, and is increasingly alienating the Israeli public.

While we always should remain hopeful, none of this suggests a genuine move toward peace. Netanyahu's ceasefires in the past have always been tactical or non-existent: a pause to deflect criticism, absorb international and domestic pressure, and consolidate control before resuming his approach of *business as usual*. The ambiguity surrounding Gaza's postwar governance in this plan is deliberate: as long as Gaza remains broken, aid-starved, and politically fragmented, Israel can continue to exercise *de facto* control without the burdens of occupation. The reconstruction of Gaza will be delayed or undefined, Palestinian leadership will be divided, and the dependency of Palestine on their erstwhile oppressors will be entrenched, which gives Netanyahu exactly what he wants.

This is at the heart of Netanyahu's "two-option" strategy, where he gets the best of both worlds: either resume military action under the guise of security or tie up the Palestinian leadership in another endless cycle of negotiations—a modern-day extension of the Oslo "agreements", designed to keep onside with international opinion while ensuring nothing changes at all in Palestine. And in either case, Netanyahu wins: Israel retains dominance as an occupying colonialist-settler, settlements in the West Bank continue to expand, and Israel's brand of apartheid becomes further entrenched.

A DISSONANT WORLD BUT ARE THERE ANY GROUNDS FOR HOPE?

While this might seem like an overly pessimistic outlook—and why shouldn't there be a high level of pessimism after the litany of broken promises over the past eight decades—

are there any grounds on which this Gaza plan *could work*? Absolutely nothing has changed since 1948 when Israel was created on the stolen lands of Palestine—*a land without a people for a people without a land*—mainly due to the intransigence led by the United States. Could this plan succeed after all the previous failures? Why would this one be any different?

The key issue *at this point of time* is that the geopolitical world is reacting in a different way in 2025, primarily because of Israel's genocidal overreach. The moral, diplomatic and strategic force shield that protected it for decades—a combination of American immunity, European indulgence and Arab disunity—is no longer as strong as it used to be. A global change seems to be underway and, for the first time in generations, Israel's dominant narrative and *hasbara* is collapsing under the weight of its own contradictions and sheer inhumane brutality. Put simply, *Israel has gone too far*.

The devastation in Gaza—almost 70,000 civilian deaths (although according to UN Special Rapporteur on the Occupied Palestinian Territories, Francesca Albanese, the figure might be closer to 680,000), razed neighbourhoods and systematic targeting of hospitals and infrastructure—has triggered an unprecedented collapse in Israel's international credibility. The imagery of human suffering, transmitted across the world, has pierced through Israel's simplistic propaganda that no-one believes any more, and forced a moral awakening across the world, similar to how the United States war in Vietnam piqued international consciences during the 1960s.

The legal pursuit of Israel at the International Court of Justice and the ICC has stripped away the old rhetoric of "acting in self-defence," reframing Israel's actions as one of deliberate cruelty and oppression. The recognition of Palestine by France, the United Kingdom, Canada and Australia—long seen as Israel's most dependable Western allies—has marked a symbolic but profound shift within the world community, where over 150 countries now formally acknowledge Palestinian statehood, a clear sign that the era of Israeli impunity might be finally coming to an end.

This transformation isn't just confined to international institutions; it is also reshaping the domestic politics of Israel's allies. In the United States, what was once a bipartisan act of faith for Republicans and Democrats is now beginning fracturing—and we can look at the commentary of Marjorie Taylor Greene in the U.S. Congress as an example of this—while these are only small fissures at this stage, the fractures are certainly starting to get bigger.

Even within Trump's populist base, elements of the MAGA movement now view Israel as a liability, its actions morally indefensible and politically toxic—it's hard to be pro-life when Israel is killing a classroom of babies and children every single day of the week—and younger generations of Americans, exposed to unfiltered realities through social media, are rejecting the old Cold War binaries of *democracy versus terrorism*, or to use the words of George W. Bush, " you are with us, or you are with the terrorists". Across Europe, governments are having to deal with the growing public opinion that's opposed to the genocide and the ongoing sale of military equipment to Israel.

In the Arab world, the political deliberations are shifting just as dramatically. States that sought regional stability through quiet normalisation—Saudi Arabia, Egypt, Jordan, Qatar and the UAE—can't ignore the outrage that's appearing on their own streets, where they see the Gaza war not as a regional dispute but as an existential affront to their dignity. Even rival such as Turkey and Saudi Arabia are finding a common cause in the need to contain Israel's extremism and create a different regional balance to deter this expansionist behaviour. What had once been a fragmented bloc of Arab states is now forming partnerships based around the shared goal of ending the war, even if this is more about their own respective political survival than any form of altruism.

Coming into this shifting political dynamic is President Trump, not as a visionary peacemaker but as a manager of a decline, whether he likes it or not. His intervention reflects the reality that even Washington's most transactional leaders now view Israel as a burden. The Gaza war has also exposed the limits of American credibility: a superpower preaching human rights while enabling atrocities and the moral cost of complicity has begun to outweigh the strategic benefits of alliance. For the first time in decades, exhaustion—diplomatic, economic and psychological—has achieved what diplomacy couldn't: a fragile consensus that the war must end, and that some form of Palestinian sovereignty must take shape.

AFTER THE FIRE: GAZA'S STRUGGLE FOR JUSTICE

The early stages of the ceasefire—deals for prisoner exchanges, the influx of humanitarian aid and Israel's limited troop withdrawal—appears to be holding but beneath the surface, there's a long list of unanswered questions. Who will govern Gaza? Certainly not Tony Blair, that is *totally unacceptable*. What happens to Hamas—will it disarm, dissolve or reconstitute itself under another a new name? How can reconstruction proceed under the blockade that has defined Gaza's as an open-air prison for nearly two decades? Will Israel finally release its iron-gripped control over Palestinian borders and resources or just rework the occupation under a new legal entity?

The proposed roadmap—a four-phase plan resulting in a new authority, Hamas's disarmament and a theoretical pathway towards a two-state solution—all sounds familiar because we've heard it so many times before: variations of this theme have been announced, celebrated and then discarded for well over thirty years. And each variation has failed because of the same reason: Israel seeks to continue the subjugation of Palestinians rather than end it. The architecture of these plans have always been based on a denial—a denial of sovereignty, denial of justice and the denial of the right for Palestinians to resist an occupation.

Meanwhile, the displaced people of Gaza are currently walking north through the scorched remains of their cities, and this, despite all the devastation and despair, represents an act of *profound defiance*. It mirrors the cyclical tragedy of Palestinian history—from the Nakba of 1948 through the displacements of every subsequent war—and highlights the truth about Palestine: despite the attempts to erase them, Palestinians continue to return, and *will continue to return*. Their movement back to their homes—even if they are just rubble—is a moral declaration that Palestine exists, and will continue to exist, despite the genocidal intentions of Israel.

This resilience continues despite the cynicism of international diplomacy. For decades, "peace" has been a performative lip-service act, rather than something that has been genuinely pursued—conferences, accords and commitments have recycled the same hollow words of reconciliation without meaning, insisting on more negotiations instead of the pursuit of justice and support for Palestinian rights.

Genuine peace cannot emerge from this endless cycle of violence, especially if the perpetrators of the genocide—the state of Israel and Benjamin Netanyahu—escape punishment for their crimes. It will also require the dismantling of Israel's systems of apartheid, and the recognition of Palestinian nationhood as an inalienable right—not some concession to be negotiated away that wasn't even mentioned in the Trump-Netanyahu 20-point plan.

This ceasefire does present the world with a *big opportunity*—not to impose another formulaic "peace process," but to choose accountability over their collective amnesia. If the international community enforces *real consequences*—sanctions, legal action and political isolation for Israel—it might end up being the beginning of transformation for the region. If it doesn't, the ceasefire will just become a brief stop-gap measure in Netanyahu's forevers wars which, in themselves, have been one long continuum of war against Palestine which commenced in 1948, if not before.

The fate of Gaza, and of Palestine itself, doesn't depend just on American diplomacy or the restraint of Israel but depends on the global conscience forcing political leaders to listen and act, just as they did in the 1960s on Vietnam; just as they did in the 1980s to force an end to apartheid in South Africa. For the first time in decades, the illusion of Israel as the "good-guy" in the region has cracked: peace without justice for Palestine is not peace at all. The world needs to act: otherwise, it will just a brief silence in between the dropping of the bombs, before history repeats itself again.

***

LABOR'S FEAR OF ITS OWN SHADOW

20 October 2025

The Labor government's decision to water down its own superannuation reforms is yet another retreat from meaningful reform of the taxation system. The original plan—taxing superannuation earnings above $3 million at 30 per cent instead of 15 per cent—was hardly radical, and it would have affected less than 90,000 of the wealthiest people in the country, but at least it was a small step towards a fairer tax system that has long favoured high-income earners. Despite this, the changes have been watered down and long-term reform has been put onto the backburner.

Treasurer Jim Chalmers has defended the amendments, claiming that the amended plan will still meets the same objectives and ensures a fairer system "from top to bottom". The numbers tell a different story though: the government has chosen to index the $3 million threshold and introduce a 40 per cent tax rate on balances above $10 million, the plan has been delayed by a year and will now raise only $2 billion instead of the originally forecast $2.7 billion. Once again, the most well-heeled Australians—those who need support from the government *the least*—have successfully lobbied for a change will result in them paying less tax.

The original plan itself wasn't *that* radical and was just a small step that would barely address the structural inequities that exist in superannuation. Yet even this small plan proved to be too much for a government that seems terrified of its own shadow. The message is clear: when powerful people make enough noise, Labor will back down, *always*. And if a government with the largest parliamentary majority in modern history can't make such a minor amendment, what chance is there for implementing the sweeping reforms Australia so desperately needs?

The broader concern is what this says about the Albanese government: we've known about this government's infamous caution for some time but after almost four years in office, it remains cautious to the point of paralysis—a government that prefers a muddied and undefined consensus rather than follow its convictions. While Chalmers insists the changes were made after "considered and methodical" consultation, the optics suggest something completely different: a Treasurer overruled by his ever-so-cautious Prime Minister, a Cabinet spooked by getting negative headlines, and a reform agenda that's been thrown away even before it begins.

What makes the government's backdown even more unacceptable is the contrast with previous Labor governments: Whitlam's sweeping social reforms and Hawke and Keating's economic restructuring were often accused of being *too* bold but this government is guilty of the opposite. It has the numbers, the political capital, and the public goodwill, but lacks the will to use it. When even the most modest policy changes are discarded after pressure from the usual suspects, the idea of tackling the far bigger challenges—housing affordability, tax reform, climate transition—becomes increasingly remote.

Labor claims to be the party of reform, and that's certainly what's contained within the Labor National Platform. But reform requires *courage*—the willingness to take risks, to confront the vested interests that have traditionally opposed the labour movement, and to stand firm when the predictable backlash arrives. By backing down on this minor superannuation measure, the government has let everyone know where it stands: the appetite for reform ends as soon as the conversation becomes uncomfortable for these vested interests.

HOW LABOR GOVERNS: LET THE POWERFUL SET THE AGENDA

The opposition to Labor's proposed superannuation changes came from the same players that always come equipped with their megaphones—wealthy individuals, industry lobbyists and business groups with something to lose, irrespective of how small that loss might be. Their responses were predictable: yet another fear campaign based on a litany of stories about "cash-poor farmers" and retirees supposedly being forced to sell their homes to pay the tax. But in reality, the change would have affected fewer than half a percent of Australians and, even still, the increase represented only a modest and affordable change to their tax obligations.

Instead of holding its ground and explaining that these changes are about fairness and equity—which most people would accept—the Albanese government backed away at the first sign of pressure. There's also the question of what exactly these "struggling farmers" are doing with multimillion-dollar farms held within their superannuation accounts. That, in itself, suggests using the system in a way that it wasn't designed for—superannuation being used as a tax shelter, not as a mechanism to ensure a dignified retirement.

It's now a very familiar pattern, and suggests that Labor is still spooked by the mining and carbon tax campaigns that were run against it by the mining industry in 2010, which helped end the prime ministership of Kevin Rudd and, ultimately, caused it to lose office in 2013. When pressure comes from powerful business interests—the banking sector, the property lobby or the mining industry—Labor's default position is to cave in—and the wealthiest 1 per cent of Australians, and the industries that serve them, have now learned that even a modest protest is enough to send this government scrambling for cover.

Meanwhile, the media has played its usual supporting role. Instead of challenging the absurdities of the scare campaign—the notion that multimillionaires were somehow the victims of government overreach and the Treasurer was "after your super"—most outlets either echoed the fear or stood back in silence. The result is a public debate where misinformation thrives, and governments feel justified in backing down.

Week after week, the same cycle repeats: powerful interests protest, the media amplifies their grievances, and Labor loses its nerve. A party that once prided itself on standing up for ordinary Australians now seems more comfortable managing the stakeholders of society, through cautious, fear and constantly looking over its shoulder for the next issue that needs to be avoided at all cost.

POLITICAL CAPITAL AND WASTED OPPORTUNITY

Former Prime Minister Paul Keating's frequent message to Anthony Albanese has always been simple but effective: use your political capital *while you have it*. History's great reformers understand that power is ephemeral, and that the purpose of political capital is not to bank it up, but to spend it on the long-term wellbeing of the nation. Yet the current Labor government doesn't seem to understand this: instead of leveraging its massive majority to drive meaningful reform, Albanese keeps his political capital for the rainy day that's never going to arrive, certainly not for the foreseeable future, given the current political landscape.

This approach has become hyper-cautious—a political strategy built on avoiding offence; to avoid upsetting the markets, the donors, the conservative media, and the business community that will never ever, *under any circumstances*, support Labor when it comes to elections, and this fear of a backlash has become a defining feature of Albanese's leadership.

The Hawke–Keating government of the 1980s didn't waste its time in office: they rebuilt Medicare, restructured the economy and modernised the nation's industrial base. And sure, this wasn't to everyone's liking—many of those reforms were controversial and more suited to the style of a neoliberalist government—but they did transform Australia. Keating's point is that political capital *only matters* if it's spent on transformative change.

And there is no shortage of issues calling out for transformation: the entrenched inequities of negative gearing and capital gains tax; the continuing housing crisis that treats a home as an investment rather than a human right; the need for a fairer tax system; genuine social security reform; a rethinking of higher education funding; and the long-overdue cancellation of the deeply flawed AUKUS deal. Addressing each of these areas requires courage, not caution—yet Labor's instinct is to postpone, to consult endlessly, or to water down ideas until they become meaningless.

The irony is that the Labor government—either with Albanese or his successor at the helm—could end up being in office for another two terms, or close to a decade. What would it have to show for it? At this pace, the risk is that it becomes a government defined by its *longevity* rather than its *legacy*, a government of caretakers, rather than reformers. What's the point of being in government if a timeline is all you achieve, rather than substantive stage?

By their fourth year in office—2000—the Howard government had already introduced the GST, privatised key public services, reshaped industrial relations and embedded the neoliberal framework started off by Hawke–Keating that still dominates Australian society today. Much of that agenda was damaging and according to ideological right-wing orthodoxy, but at least it was ambitious and coherent. Howard used his political capital to reshape the nation—albeit negatively—and Labor, instead of reversing those changes when it regained power, has slowed down the pace of this neoliberal path. This has become a bipartisan holding pattern: the Coalition drives radical right-wing reform; but Labor inherits it and manages the aftermath with restraint and timidity, instead of reversing this trend according to a labour-based and progressive values-based agenda.

When the best that can be expected from a progressive government is that it won't make things more right-wing as quickly as the conservatives, the idea of reform becomes a new form of inertia. Albanese's stated goal of making Labor the "natural party of government" encapsulates this problem: it's an ambition of duration and longevity, not direction. The objective should be to make Labor once again the *great reforming party*—the party of Fisher, Curtin, Chifley, Whitlam, Hawke and Keating—not just the keepers of a political compromise defined by the other side of politics.

History offers the big lessons in political courage: the Fisher government in the 1910s created the foundations of modern welfare; Curtin's leadership during wartime redefined Australia's national identity; Chifley's post-war reconstruction built the economy for a new era. Even Menzies in the 1950s, their conservative successor, didn't undo their reforms—he simply managed them in a different way. It was only after Labor's ambitions receded and its caution grew that Australian politics began to calcify.

John Howard, hardly a hero to Labor voters, understood the benefit of political timing. He made his most controversial reforms up to the midway point of each term—spending eighteen months implementing them and another eighteen months helping the public forget about them, just in time for an election. It's a cynical but effective model for durable change. By contrast, Albanese's government seems to be waiting for a moment that never arrives—he usually responds by saying there's no mandate for change now, so it will be presented at the *next* election, if anyone cares to remember what was actually promised.

Great leaders use their moment: they understand that reform is not about being universally liked—it's about being *effective*. Whitlam, Keating, Curtin and Chifley all faced bitter opposition, yet they changed the nation in ways that could never be fully undone. Albanese risks being remembered not as a reformer in the mould of these leaders, but the one who slipped into the political comfort zone and was too afraid of change—a leader who had the power to act, the opportunity to change Australia, but chose to put his finger up to the wind, sniff the breeze and wait for *that* something to arrive but never did.

LABOR RISKS BECOMING A GOVERNMENT OF LOST OPPORTUNITIES

This Labor government has a massive majority from the 2025 landslide, and should be operating from a position of strength. Yet Albanese himself remains a curiously unpopular prime minister. That, in itself, is not fatal—many great reformers were divisive figures in their time—but the problem lies in what he chooses to do with that power. Instead of governing with confidence, Labor has become hesitant, cautious and oddly quiet about its own achievements.

It's true that the Albanese government has made progress across a range of areas—wages, manufacturing, renewables and international relations—but it's not enough. Labor seems afraid to articulate a vision, as though promoting its record might somehow be seen as boastful or politically arrogant. This self-effacing approach has left the public uncertain about what the government stands for—or what it intends to do next.

Winning an election by a landslide is not an end in itself. It's a mandate to *lead*—not so much on the minutia of policy details—but to use power with purpose. If Labor continues to govern with timidity, it will be brought back to earth very quickly, despite all the problems that currently exist within the Coalition. The public's patience will always wear thin if the much-needed changes are avoided—and voters will never forgive political inertia and politicians just wasting their time in office.

For now, the opposition remains weak and divided, offering little credible alternative—which is exactly the time when a government needs to act. Figures like Andrew Hastie and James Paterson from the hard right of the Liberal Party, continue to alienate mainstream voters and undermine their own side's chances of recovery. And why should Albanese care too much about what the Liberal Party thinks about *anything*? Let them wither away and sort themselves out; as Napoleon Bonaparte said, "never interrupt your enemy when they are making a mistake". This dynamic gives Albanese some breathing space—but it won't last forever. Governments that rely on the dysfunction of their opponents to stay afloat usually find that time runs out when they least expect it, and they're left with little room to move, as Paul Keating found out when John Howard became the leader of the Liberal Party in 1995 after years of internal battles and leadership struggles.

If Labor continues to play it safe, history may judge it as the government that governed for years but changed very little. A government that sought stability over vision, consensus over conviction. And that might be great for Labor politicians: it's far better to be in government than it is to be in opposition, with the higher salaries, privileges and the opportunity to make decisions, but what's in it for the public when nothing changes for the better?

This would be the greatest tragedy of all—a government too busy with entrenching its power, but eventually defeated by its own fear of power. That's something that needs to change, and change quickly.

***

JOURNALISM, FEAR AND THE PRICE OF OBEDIENCE

27 October 2025

The recent treatment of Pulitzer Prize-winning journalist Chris Hedges in Australia has exposed a deep moral and professional failure within the mainstream media. After his scheduled address at the National Press Club was cancelled a few weeks ago—a cowardly and politically compromised decision—the speech he was due to deliver was hosted at independent venues in Sydney and Melbourne. Listening to that speech, it's clear why the Press Club cancelled the event—it wasn't convenient, polite or politically safe—they were going to being held to account and, generally, powerful players in Australia's mainstream media *do not* like being held to account.

In his speech, Hedges criticised Western media for its reporting on the events in Palestine, and called out the journalists who have largely ignored the genocide in Gaza, and defaulted to a recycling of Israeli government talking points instead of trying to verify the truth. His argument was simple and clear: Western journalism has abandoned its true purpose and has lost its integrity.

If we needed a reminder of this collapse of integrity in journalism, it was on full display when Hedges had a follow up appearance on the ABC's *Late Night Live*, and was interviewed by David Marr. What should have been an important exchange between two experienced journalists instead became an act of defence in protecting the narratives of power and establishment. Marr insisted that journalists have an obligation to report the "excuses" or explanations offered by the Israel Defense Forces and, in a rebuttal that should be evident to everyone, Hedges replied with a simple statement: "no... our job is to report the *truth*".

This small exchange revealed everything that's wrong with the response of mainstream journalism to Israel's war on Gaza. Rather than interrogating power, many journalists act as an echo chamber for it. Marr's suggesting that this idea of "balance" needs to repeat official propaganda—is exactly the type of moral relativism that Hedges has spent decades railing against. The ABC, once regarded as the pinnacle of independent journalism—not just in Australia but internationally—has increasingly become a platform for rehearsing the official lines of Western governments and their allies. While there might have been strong resistance in the past—such as when Prime Minister Bob Hawke pressured the ABC to give less coverage to anti-war perspectives and more prominence to the government's pro-war position during the 1991 Gulf War—today, it seems to be a case of *just tell us you want us to say, and we'll say it*.

Meanwhile, journalists continue to die in Gaza—not as incidental casualties of war but as deliberate targets. Israel has bombed homes and offices known to house reporters and, in some cases, the bodies of journalists were found to have been mutilated, in an obvious act to stop the documentation of the genocidal actions of the Israel Defense Forces. This is like no other conflict: more journalists have been killed in Gaza than in both world wars, the Vietnam War, the wars in Yugoslavia, Iraq and Afghanistan combined, according to the Watson Institute for International and Public Affairs'

Costs of War project. In Gaza, the targeting of journalists and aid workers has become a routine hobby of the IDF, and always met with Western indifference and excuses when it happens, as demonstrated by Marr in the safety of his studio environment.

This is what Hedges was trying to expose: a moral corruption so deep that even the murder of journalists provokes barely more than bureaucratic shrugs and a few media releases from foreign ministers wanting to *show concern*. His message is a call for courage and reflection—qualities now largely absent from the institutions that once defined the Australian media, at least at the ABC.

Hedges's insistence that "our job is to report the truth" might sound like an old-fashioned or even a naïve ideal, during an age of managed narratives and ideological posturing, but it's that single statement that cuts through the evasions and reveals the crisis of journalism today: when telling the truth becomes a radically subversive act, it's not the failure of the journalist—it's the failure of the media establishment itself.

THE COLLAPSE OF CREDIBILITY

This confrontation between Hedges and Marr might not make front-page news—and certainly not within Australia's mainstream media—but it says a lot about a deeper and more corrosive problem within Australian journalism: the willingness of respected figures and institutions to *protect* power rather than challenge it. This is not just a professional failure, but a moral one—the kind that defines the boundaries of acceptable speech in a country that supposedly sees itself as a protector of freedom of expression.

Others in the field have faced the same pressure and chosen a different path. The journalist Antoinette Lattouf—one of the journalists who remembered that *our job is to report the truth*—was dismissed by the ABC for posting factual information about Gaza, and refused to bow to the immense intimidation from the ABC. Her career suffered temporarily, but she kept her credibility—and, in the long run, that's what matters in journalism. She's now rebuilding her platform through independent media and podcasting, proving that holding onto that integrity is critical, even if it ends up taking the journalist to a different field. Marr, by contrast, traded his credibility for favour from the establishment, and this trade has cost him far more than he realises. And once credibility is thrown away so easily, it's very difficult to get it back.

Two of the clearest guiding principles in journalism are often quoted but rarely followed. The first, from the legendary BBC interviewer Jeremy Paxman, suggested that his first preparational thought before interviewing political leaders was *why is this lying bastard lying to me?*

The second one is more readily quoted and comes from the academic Jonathan Foster: "If someone tells you it's raining and another tells you it's dry, it's not your job to quote them both—it's your job to look out the fucking window and find out which is true". Journalism doesn't need to be overly complicated, and we should be able to narrow it down to these basic credos: seek the truth, verify it, and tell it without fear.

This moral inversion—where empathy becomes heresy and truth-telling becomes a risk to one's career—has destroyed more reputations than it has saved. From journalists to through to executives, many have chosen to sacrifice integrity to appease political and institutional power. As with Marr or the former ABC chair Ita Buttrose—who was the main instigator of the sacking of Lattouf from the ABC in 2023—the question lingers like a stale smell: was it worth destroying your reputation so comprehensively? Was the defence of the state of Israel and the preservation of corporate relationships associated with the Israel lobby, really worth destroying your own credibility and conscience?

Those who speak truth in times of suppression, like Hedges or Lattouf, will ultimately be remembered for their courage; those like Marr and Buttrose will be consigned to the dustbin of compromise, remembered for their fear of speaking out and holding up the white flag of surrender. This is their legacy.

THE GLOBAL SURRENDER TO ISRAEL'S NARRATIVE

This is part of a much larger pattern that we can see in many Western democracies. The same instinct to protect Israel from criticism has infected entire governments, political parties and public institutions, even when it's to their own cost. From London to Berlin, from Canberra to Washington, politicians and journalists are destroying their credibility to defend a state that's engaged in systematic violence against Palestinian people.

In the United Kingdom, the Metropolitan Police have humiliated themselves by arresting elderly peace protesters, people in wheelchairs and pensioners under vague pretexts linked to pro-Palestinian demonstrations and the proscription of Palestine Action as a terrorist organisation, and public resources are being wasted to criminalise people of conscience.

The British Prime Minister Keir Starmer, recently wanted to overrule Birmingham police after they decided to ban the supporters of Israel's Maccabi Tel Aviv club from attending a football game with Aston Villa, citing public safety concerns over violence by the club's fans, as demonstrated by their violent, destructive and offensive behaviour in Amsterdam during a game against Ajax in November 2024.

Starmer immediately condemned the decision as "antisemitic" and that "no one should be stopped from watching a football game simply because of who they are"— even if the Birmingham police described the Maccabi Tel Aviv supporters as a "toxic combination of hooliganism, and anger"—adding that he would do "doing everything in our power" to overturn the ban.

A few days later, Israeli police cancelled a domestic Maccabi match in Tel Aviv for the same reason: the violent behaviour of its supporters. The hypocrisy did the full circle, and the Labour government was made to look foolish: what was regarded as "antisemitic" in Britain was the same action taken by police in Israel. At least in this case, the calls by Starmer to do *everything in our power* calmed down: surely by now, he'd realised the stupidity of his actions but even still, we can't be too sure about that.

This willingness to sacrifice dignity and reason for the sake of political support and unison with Israel borders on the pathological, a kind of collective conditioning—like the *Manchurian Candidate* holding up the Queen of Hearts—a reflexive, panicked obedience that overrides any form of moral and political logic. Institutions that should stand for public accountability instead retreat into an absurdist clown show, protecting the Netanyahu government from even the mildest criticism. All throughout the media and within politics, public figures are throwing away their integrity—if they ever had it in the first place—ever so eager to look foolish and prostrate themselves to maintain favour with a malevolent foreign player in Israel, even if they are causing a genocide in Gaza.

These motivations are not a secret: money, influence and the racist imperial history that views Israel as the West's outpost in the Middle East/Western Asia: a friend who is doing the dirty work of the United States and other imperialist partners. But even acknowledging those obvious influences doesn't make the behaviour less disturbing. It's an abdication of moral agency on a mass scale—the surrender of conscience to propaganda. And the cancer has spread far beyond politics, culture and the media: even sport is not immune.

In Melbourne last week, the mascot "Captain Blue" was sacked by the Carlton Football Club after walking out of a Bar Mitzvah when he discovered it was raising money for Israeli soldiers. His comment—"I'm not doing this for fucking Zios"—was quickly framed as an act of antisemitism—apparently the term *Zios* is now deemed to be antisemitic and derogatory—and he was dismissed. In another case earlier this year, Fremantle Dockers captain Alex Pearce was forced into public contrition after reposting a pro-Palestine message from the Irish band Kneecap, and the usual suspects from the pro-Israel lobby came out to demand his suspension from the AFL.

In another issue, the cosmetics retailer Lush closed down its stores and website across Australia on Thursday and installed "Stop Starving Gaza" signage in its shop windows, only for shopping-centre managers at Westfield to issue a directive to cover over these signs—a simple humanitarian message that was deemed to be offensive to Israel. How have we arrived at this point in history, where the brutal, fascist and genocidal operations of the state of Israel, is so openly protected by corporate interests?

When athletes and business are punished for important moral gestures—even a sports mascot—it shows how deeply the fear and coercion from the Israel lobby has filtered through into public life. An Australian culture that once prided itself on fairness, debate, and dissent now polices and clamps down on empathy.

Australia—and every democracy that claims to value liberty—needs to stop criminalising truth and compassion. Free debate, religious equality and the right to dissent won't survive if public discourse is managed by intimidation and the worship of a foreign government, even when its committing genocide. The silence that's being enforced today in defence of Israel's war in Gaza is not neutrality—it's outrageous *complicity*.

No-one should ever need permission to speak the truth, and it's a question of whether we want to live in a society that's governed by fear from organised power, or one that offers a space for the moral courage to speak out, no matter how uncomfortable that might be.

***

A BIG BETRAYAL OF THE ENVIRONMENT

3 November 2025

The Albanese government has released what could be one of its most controversial backflips yet—amendments to the Environmental Protection and Biodiversity Conservation Act that will open up more new mining projects and erode environmental safeguards.

Environment Minister Murray Watt has outlined his plans to return decision-making powers for coal, gas and water-intensive developments back to the states and territories, supposedly in an attempt to "streamline" project approvals and "cut red tape"—the same language conservative governments have used in the past when reducing legislative protections that relate to the environment. But behind the rhetoric of efficiency is a totally different reality: the weakening of national standards that were implemented to protect fragile ecosystems, water systems and traditional lands.

One of the more concerning amendments is the neutering of the "water trigger", which was introduced in 2013 to safeguard Australia's groundwater from large-scale coal and gas extraction. Under Watt's proposals, these protections will be replaced by bilateral agreements with state and territory governments, the jurisdictions that are the most dependent on resource royalties. Queensland, Western Australia and the Northern Territory—governments that are heavily linked to mining revenues—will gain greater control over project approvals, and the risks of a conflict of interest are obvious—or, at the least, *should* be obvious.

Australian Greens Senator Sarah Hanson-Young has condemned the legislation as a capitulation to corporate influence, suggesting that "business has its fingerprints all over this draft—they get a fast track, cheaper and easier approvals for their projects". Environmental groups have also supported Hanson-Young's sentiments, arguing that these reforms are a "green light for destruction," undoing the years of progress that have been made in the federal sphere.

The Albanese government insists the amendments constitute "essential environmental reform," yet the evidence suggests otherwise: this is *not* environmental reform; it's environmental *regression*. The government, which holds one of the largest majorities in recent history—38 seats—could have used this majority to take Australia into a new era of ecological responsibility and protecting the future. Instead, it's using that power to entrench the same vested mining interests that have dominated Australian politics for far too long.

Labor's deep ties to the mining sector have long undermined its credibility on climate and environmental policy. The party that once championed its environmental credentials—going all the way back to the 1990 federal election, when they won the election on the back of state-based Greens preferences in key marginal seats—is now protecting the expansion and the profits of fossil fuel giants at the expense of both people and the environment. The "jobs" argument—that easing restrictions will support regional employment—rarely comes to fruition, with most mining operations trending toward automation and low-cost overseas labour. The wealth that's generated by these industries continues to flow mainly to multinational shareholders, while local communities see fewer benefits and face greater environmental risks.

If this legislation is passed through Parliament, it will not just be a betrayal of Labor's promises—which have been essentially made over the past two election campaigns—but a fundamental reshaping of Australia's environmental laws, and shift the balance of power from the federal government over to the states and territories. And once those protections are gone, they might be gone forever.

THE DANGERS OF THE "NATIONAL INTEREST"

There's also the bigger issue of the government's push for mining approvals vaguely deemed to be in the "national interest". Legislation created for the benefit of the national interest was once a wartime necessity—such as the *War Precautions Act* in 1914, or the *National Security Act* created at the onset of World War II—but today, it seems to have become a political catch-all—a justification for whatever benefits those in power.

At the moment, there is legislation that relates to foreign acquisitions and critical infrastructure that requires a national interest test, and these amendments will provide the Environment Minister with the discretionary power to approve projects that would otherwise breach Australia's environmental standards. It will create an open-ended loophole large enough for any major mining or gas project to slip through, no matter how damaging its impact might be to the environment.

The proposed legislation also fails to define what "national interest" actually means—and it's an ambiguity that appears to be deliberate. Without a precise definition, the term can be used to justify virtually anything: defence priorities, energy security, economic growth or even political advantage. In a country where resource industries wield vast economic and political power, this vagueness will guarantee many forms of exploitation, which will effectively become a legal *carte blanche* for environmental deregulation and destruction.

Environmental protection legislation was originally designed to establish a consistent national framework and independent oversight of decision-making, as it relates to the environment. Replacing this with ministerial discretion—a single individual provided with unchecked authority to decide which can projects proceed, based on a criteria that is undefined and unaccountable, is a brewing recipe for disaster and weakens transparency at the same time. The government can always claim that it's acting *in the national interest*, even as it approves developments that violate climate targets, damages Indigenous land, and erode Australia's global environmental standing, and this is a serious problem.

That other issue is that *vague law* is *bad law*—it's always the bad laws that give rise to corporate abuses and corruption. Without the clear boundaries, interpretations will always be viewed through the political prism of opportunism, shaped by the political mood rather than evidence or ethics. By constructing a legal framework that prioritises a half-baked and vague idea of the "national interest" over solid environmental protection, the government has created an instrument of political convenience and corporate benefit, not of clear and effective environmental management.

It also hands immense power to whichever minister occupies the portfolio—which will be managed by a minister from the National Party at some point in the future, a party that has been so hostile to the concerns of the environment—and in doing so, erodes public trust in the very institutions meant to protect Australia's land, water and biodiversity. The danger is not just in the projects that will be approved, but the precedent it sets: that the environment is negotiable, and

SILENCING COUNTRY: EXCLUDING INDIGENOUS VOICES

that the national interest is according to whatever those in power decide it to be.

Several Aboriginal land councils—Central, Tiwi, Northern and Anindilyakwa—have reacted with anger to these proposed reforms. There are communities that will be directly affect by mining and climate change issues, but the government decided they weren't worth consulting with, or even the worth receiving the courtesy of a briefing. For Indigenous people in these areas—areas that are already being affected by droughts, higher temperatures and diminishing water levels—the proposed reforms are not some kind of abstract policy; they're a matter of survival, something a minister based in urban Brisbane or Canberra might not be able to appreciate so well.

For Indigenous Australians, environmental protection is a critical part of cultural preservation. *Country* is not a commodity to be sold off cheaply to mining interests but a living system of connection to land, water, ancestors and community. Yet, this government's push to "streamline" environmental approvals essentially overrides Indigenous sovereignty and the principle of informed consent. A government claiming to position itself as the "sensible centre" between the Coalition and the Greens can't occupy that space credibly if it's excluding Indigenous peoples from the decisions that affect their own lands.

These amendments are also tied up with the recent Australia–United States critical minerals deal, which seeks to fast-track exploration and extraction of lithium, rare earths, and other strategic resources. Around 79 per cent of these deposits are located on land which is either under Indigenous control or subject to current native title claims, and to continue with this kind of exclusionary process is to repeat the actions from Australia's colonial past, where resources were extracted and profits were exported, without any consideration or consultation with the original custodians of the land.

It's an obvious double standard—a continuation of the colonial mindset that insists Indigenous people must be "helped" by having their lands taken and mined for their supposed benefit. The ideological basis of this clearly comes from the imperialist mindset: a modern, corporate version of Kipling's *The White Man's Burden*, which covers over exploitation using the language of economic opportunity, and offering peppercorn compensation while dismissing Indigenous authority and custodianship.

Always was, always will be Aboriginal land is more than just a slogan shouted at protest marches—it's a declaration of enduring sovereignty by Indigenous people. But under these new environmental reforms, that sovereignty will be eroded. The government's willingness to overlook Indigenous views, even as it claims to act in the national interest, exposes a moral contradiction at the heart of this agenda. Australia can't claim to protect its environment or act in good faith internationally while continuing to silence the voices of those who have cared for this land the longest.

A GOVERNMENT LOSING ITS WAY ON THE ENVIRONMENT

While there's always howls of outrage when it's suggested, the Albanese government is beginning to resemble the Morrison government that it once condemned—and nowhere is this clearer than in its handling of the environment. Certainly, the voices and personalities are different and it's evident that this Labor government is receiving far more favour from the electorate than its predecessor—which means that *it is* performing better, even if that is mainly at the political level.

But, ultimately, all governments start to look the same on key issues: the same deference to the mining sector, the same language of *jobs and growth*, and the same reluctance to confront corporate power which are becoming the defining features of Labor's second term. The rhetoric of transformation which promised so much, has given way to the politics of convenience and the management of stakeholders, rather than management of the *real* national interest on behalf of the public.

For many progressive voters who backed Labor in 2022 and reaffirmed that support in 2025, this change will feel like a betrayal. They expected leadership on climate action—to see a government willing to rise above the Coalition's short-termism of the past decade but, instead, they are getting *gung-ho* environmental policies that could just as easily have been drafted by former prime ministers Scott Morrison or Tony Abbott. The risk for Labor won't be an immediate collapse—the Liberal Party is in too much disarray for that to happen—but it's the slow erosion of trust which could have electoral consequences down the track. Large majorities do create an illusion of invincibility for politicians, but voters will eventually punish governments that drift too far away from their promises.

The Albanese government's overwhelming parliamentary dominance seems to have has emboldened it to behave with the confidence that it will be in office for a long period. And of course, there's good reason to think that this will be the case: if there's no viable alternative on the horizon and, because of this, poor and unpopular decisions can be made seemingly without consequence. But history suggests otherwise: Paul Keating after the 1993 election victory has an air of invincibility and an assumption that after Labor's decade in office, they had assumed the position of natural party of government. They were thrown out of office in 1996.

His successor John Howard also had this sense of arrogant invincibility after the 2004 federal election, gaining rare control of the Senate. But just like Keating, he went on to lose his next election campaign. Invincibility can breed complacency or arrogance—sometimes *both*—and this current action suggests the Albanese government is starting to reach this territory. Every government that starts to resemble its predecessor eventually meets the same fate, where the path from a massive majority to a minority position—or even a loss—can be surprisingly quick.

Labor's reliance on the "jobs and investment" argument, while politically safe, ignores the growing public anxiety about environmental collapse. Certainly, mining remains vital to the national economy, but the demand from the electorate—based on the results of the 2022 and 2025 federal elections—is to achieve *balance*: for a government to recognise ecological sustainability as a form of long-term economic security. Instead, we are seeing a repetition of old patterns: boosting the mining industry at the expense of environmental protection, while calling on the "national interest" to cover over these compromises.

Australia's environmental crisis isn't just a hypothetical issue. The "once-in-a-century" weather events now arrive every few years: catastrophic floods, as witnessed in northern New South Wales and Queensland; regular bushfires and unprecedented cyclones reaching further south. Cyclone Alfred's near miss early this year is a reminder that the global climate change is shifting far beyond anything that can be predicted. We're living in an age of politics where luck seems to have become a policy substitute—where governments rely on fortune to avoid catastrophe instead of resilience and good public policy to withstand it.

Clear-headed, courageous legislation won't stop every storm, but it can prevent political decay and produce a framework that at least reduces the chances of those events happening and, in the long run, national disasters. Unless Labor finds a way to improve environmental protection—and not *reduce* it—it might discover that no amount of political spin can protect a government that has lost its purpose on environmental issues.

***

THE PEOPLE'S VICTORY: WHAT MAMDANI'S WIN REALLY MEANS

10 November 2025

"For as long as we can remember, working people have been told by the wealthy and the well-connected that power does not belong in their hands; fingers bruised from lifting boxes on the warehouse floor, palms calloused from delivery by candle bars, knuckles scarred with kitchen burns—these are not hands that have been allowed to hold power. And yet, you have dared to reach for something greater. Tonight, against all odds, we have grasped it. The future is in our hands; we have toppled a political dynasty."

These are the powerful words from Zohran Mamdani, the 34-year old Democrat Socialist who, against all the odds, has become New York City's first Muslim, first African-born, and youngest mayor in over a century. After a grassroots campaign that lasted for over a year, his own hands reached for something greater and went on to succeed: a political landslide that has sent a strong message far beyond the city of New York.

Mamdani's win over Andrew Cuomo, the former Democratic governor and perhaps the most salient example of establishment politics at its worst, was a shock to America's political elite. Despite being outspent, lacking major endorsements from within the Democratic party, and facing a barrage of racist attacks and Islamophobic rhetoric—mainly from the Israel lobby and the capitalist billionaire class—Mamdani's campaign drew its support not from corporations but from ordinary people, from small donations, volunteers, and driven by a belief that politics should serve the many, not just the elite few, as it has done within New York City for some time.

What makes this victory resonate so strongly and makes it so relevant—especially in places like Australia—is that it demonstrates that the deeply entrenched political machines can be defeated, with the right candidate, the right messaging, and the right electoral techniques. Mamdani didn't just run on platitudes of *hope* or *change*: his program was based around the basic issues that affect the cost of living—rent freezes, free childcare, free public transport, cheaper groceries, and higher taxes on the wealthy to fund these initiatives.

In a political climate that's been largely dominated by cynicism, disinterest and distrust, voters have rewarded his conviction and with the highest voter turnout in New York since 1969, it suggests that if the electorate feels that a candidate is directly speaking to the issues that affect them the most, they will engage politically. Whether Mamdani can fulfil these initiatives will, of course, be the bigger test, but for the time being, his victory shows that establishment politics can be pushed aside with effective grassroots campaigning.

Mamdani also broke a powerful taboo in American politics, where he spoke openly about the genocide in Gaza, condemned Israel's actions, and questioned the influence of pro-Israel lobbying groups within U.S. politics. That such positions didn't destroy his campaign but instead helped to galvanise his support suggests that the once-unassailable power of the Israel lobby and the corporate media can be challenged—and may even be a paper tiger—and that political courage, combined with authenticity, can overcome the fear and smear that was prevalent in this campaign.

It's a moment that provides many lessons for Australian politics: when political parties become too safe, too corporate, and too removed from the people they claim to represent, disillusionment within the electorate continues to grow. The major parties—Labor and Liberal alike—have long relied on the assumption that the electorate has nowhere else to go, but Mamdani's victory shows that when the working classes finds a voice that speaks to its struggles and aspirations, that assumption can collapse quickly, but only if there are viable alternatives.

The establishment's reaction, especially from the Israel lobby, to Mamdani was predictable—before, during and after the campaign—and we've seen many times before. Jeremy Corbyn in the UK, was demonised into political oblivion and smeared with accusations of anti-Semitism, despite inspiring a generation of young activists; or, in the U.S., the early hope of Barack Obama, was tempered by the constraints of power and institutionalised behaviours. Yet Mamdani's position as mayor—outside the rigid machinery of Washington politics—might allow him more freedom to act on his principles.

For Australia, this raises a number of questions for the stultifying and stale brand of donor-style and stakeholder politics that exists in virtually every part of the country, and has done for some time. Could a similar political change emerge here? Could a new voice rise—one unbought by corporations, unafraid to challenge entrenched interests, and willing to call out the hypocrisy of the system?

Mamdani's triumph suggests that people everywhere may finally be reaching a breaking point with the late stages of neoliberalism; they're no longer willing to accept a political order that serves *vested* interests ahead of the *public interest*. It's not just a story about New York—it's virtually an invitation to the rest of the world to change the processes of politics: *this is how it can be done.*

THE LESSONS FOR AUSTRALIAN POLITICS

The true significance of Mamdani's victory lies in something much deeper than the numbers and statistics—it's the collapse in the authority of the political establishment itself. For decades, New York's power brokers have relied on fear, division and media-driven narratives to hang onto their power base. Yet, throughout Mamdani's campaign, every insult, smear, racist attack and inuendo thrown at him totally failed. *Totally*.

The conservative system's traditional weapons—branding a Muslim candidate as a *terrorist*, dismissing him as a *socialist*, or even worse—*a communist*—or accusing him of being an unhinged critic of Israel and anti-Semitic—just didn't work. The people stopped listening to the bullshit.

The moment that captured this factor the best occurred during the Democratic primaries debate in June, when each candidate was asked which country they would visit first as the new mayor of New York. Each contender offered the expected answer: Adrienne Adams said she would visit the Holy Land. Cuomo vowed to go to Israel "to combat anti-Semitism". Whitney Tilson promised multiple trips to Israel and Ukraine, framing them as allies "on the front lines of the global war on terror". It was the unthinking display of obedience to Israel and showed the orthodoxy of American foreign policy—an absurd moment for a municipal contest which was meant to be about housing, transport and crime. Sure, New York is a big city has a population of almost nine million people, but it's *not* an outpost of Tel Aviv.

Mamdani changed the script and said that he would "stay in New York City... I'll be standing up for Jewish New Yorkers, meeting them in their synagogues, homes, and on their subway platforms. Israel has the right to exist—as a state with equal rights—but my responsibility is here, to the people of this city."

In that one answer, he changed the conversation entirely, and sounded like *the* leader focused on the job, not a politician performing for lobbyists. The others in the primaries race looked rehearsed and *insincere*; Mamdani looked *authentic*. To many voters, it was a clear moment—a candidate calling out the bleeding obvious, but what no one else dared to say: that's the true sign of leadership.

Again, this has implications for Australia. The electorate here might ask: why do our own leaders feel compelled to follow these same scripts? Why do they make ritualised visits to Israel, or repeat the same talking points handed to them by lobbyists and Israeli government-funded "study tours"? Why can't they speak as plainly as Mamdani did—acknowledge Israel's right to exist, but also the right of Palestinians to live with dignity and equality?

This isn't just about foreign policy: it's about the entire political machinery of Australia a*s a captured state*—the fear of saying something unsanctioned, the instinct to avoid controversy even when truth needs to be stated. Mamdani's victory shows what happens when a politician breaks that cycle. He didn't win just because he rejected the pressure from the establishment; he won because he rejected it *completely*.

If the same courage existed here, perhaps Australian politics could look different. Have we ever heard the Prime Minister Anthony Albanese standing up for the people with bruised and calloused fingers hardened from lifting boxes? He mentions his *povo* upbringing in housing commission as a political identify, but when did he last speak the real words of hardship and affordability for working people? When did Albanese stand up to the Zionist lobby in Australia to let them know who's really in control? Or powerful gambling interests?

Maybe leaders would stop genuflecting to power and start serving the people who *did* elect them, not the people who *didn't* elect them. Maybe mainstream media journalists could start reporting the facts rather than regurgitating the handouts that support the establishment narrative. Maybe truth would start to matter again. *Just maybe.*

Of course, Mamdani could still disappoint, as most political leaders do. Even great reformers can falter under the weight of expectation—as Obama's presidency ultimately showed. But the point isn't to achieve some kind of utopian perfection: it's the willingness to try. Mamdani has shown that honesty engagement, empathy and conviction can still defeat cynicism. If it can happen in New York, considered to be the centre of global capitalism, then it can happen in Australia too. Change begins to happen when a leader stands up to call out the nakedness of the emperor, and decides to *tell the truth*.

CRUSHING THE MACHINE: HOPE, FAILURE AND VICTORY

The British conservative Enoch Powell said that all political careers end in failure; the political strategist Stan Greenberg suggested that "every great leader disappoints", due to the balance required between competing political interests, managing expectations, and failing to deliver what they promised—in most cases—because of the limitations of their power, or through their own inadequacies. It's almost a guaranteed rule of history.

The moment of victory in politics usually gives way to compromise, fatigue and the grinding machinery of governing. As the incoming mayor Tommy Carcetti is told in the television series *The Wire*, the job of politics is "eating shit all day long, year after year". Likewise, von Bismarck's analogy about laws being like sausages—best not seen while they're being made—captures the essence of politics: the daily grind of making a jurisdiction function as effectively as possible for its citizens. And it's *hard work*.

Even the most idealistic leaders are restricted by the system they seek to change. Australians have seen this pattern repeatedly—whether it's former Victoria Premier Dan Andrews retiring from politics and ruining his myth by revealing himself to be a full-on supporter of Zionism, or figures such as Albanese and Penny Wong constantly showing that moral conviction is often too difficult when it comes to standing up to vested interests, such as the Israel lobby or gambling interests. The lesson is not so much that these people are insincere, but that the harsh realities of politics float within a sea of imperfection.

Time can also make our memories more selective: we can forget the flaws of those political figures we may have once worshipped. John F. Kennedy, Clement Attlee, Gough Whitlam, Bob Hawke—each is remembered now as a visionary, even though their eras were also filled with disappointment and division. Winston Churchill, once the embodiment of British defiance, was quickly voted out after the war was won in 1945: people tend to forget that. Yet, there has to be a savoured moment before the disappointment sets in—that brief instant when the impossible becomes real.

The rapper Jay-Z suggested that when Obama's was inaugurated in 2008, even if his presidency turned out to be the worst possible administration in history, it was the victory that *still* mattered. It mattered because a man of colour had broken a barrier that was supposed to be unbreakable. That magic evaporated as soon as everyone realised that while he might have *looked* different, his presidency was not *that* different to all the ones who preceded him. But, even if was just for a short period, the hope itself was all that mattered.

Mamdani's election will probably be seen in the same light. Maybe he *will* falter. Maybe the pressures of city politics will force compromise, or the establishment he defeated will regroup and wear him down. Whenever there's the first sign of a problem—even if it's unseasonal or inclement weather that's out of his control—of course, it all be because of *socialism*. *Communism*. Or the fact that he's a *Muslim*. Or because of his *immigrant* background, or a combination of all of these factors. *See, we told you so*. The establishment *will* fight back, because they are some of the most grotesque psychopathic characters on the planet—the monsters of capitalism and the mobsters of digital disruption who will never give up.

But for the time being, none of this really matters. What matters is what Mamdani has done in crushing the machine. It's an issue that should be relevant for Australia, especially in a political environment where imagination seems to be short supply and barely scratches the surface. It shows that the electorate will respond to authenticity, courage and moral clarity, and will take a chance on someone who speaks to issues that matter in their lives rather, than to their donors and assorted vested interests. And, if they feel they have nothing to lose and the current forms of capitalism are not working in their favour, they will back a candidate who refuses to play by the rules set by those who already hold power.

Whether Mamdani ultimately becomes a reformer or a disappointment is almost beside the point. The main message is that the walls of the established political duopoly in Australian politics can be broken down; that the language of politics can change, and that ordinary people—as Mamdani said, those whose hands have never held power—can seize power for themselves. This brief, illuminating moment of the political victory might not last forever, but it will be enough to remind us that politics, at its best, still belongs to the people.

***

PROTECTING THE NEO-NAZIS OF SYDNEY

17 November 2025

Outside the New South Wales Parliament last week, almost seventy members of an openly neo-Nazi group assembled in black uniforms, carrying a large banner that read "Abolish the Jewish Lobby". They were also pushing their usual far-right agenda: white supremacy, anti-immigration, hostility to LGBTQI+ people, Islamophobia and explicit anti-Semitism. It's not as though this was a surreptitious and spontaneous gathering: the organisers of the rally lodged their application with NSW Police well in advance, clearly stating that the rally was directed against what they called "the Jewish lobby", and were granted approval around 10 days before the event.

On the day, police didn't move in to disperse the group; they didn't agitate and provoke them, pepper-spray them, punch or haul them off into police wagons. Instead, officers stood by while the rally went ahead directly in front of NSW Parliament House—a precinct that sits within easy walking distance of several major places of worship: a Presbyterian church across the road, an Anglican church in the same parliamentary square, St Mary's Cathedral a short distance away, and a synagogue not far from the parliamentary precinct. Under the "vicinity" provisions the government had recently tried to use to restrict protests near sensitive sites—although these provisions were recently ruled invalid by the Supreme Court—this should at least have triggered some serious concerns from police and ministers.

NSW Premier Chris Minns publicly described the rally as "shameful", condemning "despicable, hateful" demonstrations that spread division and racism on the streets of Sydney. Yet his outrage came after the fact, when it became clear the event had been approved and managed by his own police force. Both the NSW Police Commissioner and the Premier claimed to have been unaware of the authorisation—as is if it were some fun run event raising funds for charity and approved by a lower-level minion—despite senior police previously stating that these far-right networks were under active surveillance and "capable of extreme violence". So, why was this rally allowed to proceed?

The actions and objectives of the rally were not only ugly, but deliberately provocative. On any reasonable reading of the state's own hate-speech and public-order frameworks, this was exactly the type of gathering that should have attracted the attention of the NSW Police and the Premier. The group involved has been publicly identified by police and media as violent, extremist and committed to white supremacist politics, yet when these same activists assembled outside Parliament to denounce "the Jewish lobby" within sight of churches and a synagogue, the police approach was effectively hands-off. There were no arrests, no aggressive crowd control tactics, no sudden reinterpretation of "safety" or "security" that would justify shutting the event down.

Compare this with the treatment of pro-Palestine and climate activists over the past two years: supporters of the state of Palestine in Sydney have had their applications to protest frequently rejected by the NSW Police, usually ending up in the Supreme Court to essentially beg for their democratic right to protest. And then, when their protests have gone ahead, they've been meet with brute-force tactics and public denunciations by the Premier and senior police. Protesters at a recent pro-Palestine rally in Darling Harbour were also pepper-sprayed, shoved, beaten and arrested; climate activists have been targeted with new "anti-protest" laws designed specifically to make their actions as risky and punitive as possible.

It's an obvious contrast: neo-Nazis with their anti-immigration, anti-LGBTQI+, Islamophobic, anti-Semitic and explicitly white nationalist rhetoric are given the approval to protest right in front of the NSW Parliament. Meanwhile, the people protesting against war crimes, the genocide in Gaza, or against the government's refusal to act on climate change are regarded as a threat to public order, and subjected to aggressive policing.

It's a clear double standard and sends a message about whose actions are acceptable, and whose actions are not. The message to Muslim and Palestinian communities is that their grief and anger over mass killing in Gaza will be met not with empathy, but with riot squad brutality and legal roadblocks. And it tells the broader public that when it comes to protest in New South Wales, the real defining points aren't based around *violence* versus *non-violence*, or *lawful* versus *unlawful* assembly; it's a political choice made at the whim of the NSW Police: which side you are on, and whether your cause aligns with the interests and sensitivities of those in power.

HOW THE NSW POLICE TURN A BLIND EYE TO THE FAR RIGHT

The issue here is that the law is not being applied equally. It's a simple principle: the police shouldn't favour one political group over another. Yet when it comes to support for Palestine or demands for more action on climate change, the police response is quick, aggressive and usually brutal:

riot squads are always ready for the senior order to pounce after even the slightest provocation, and ministers take to the airwaves of the shock-jocks to denounce the protesters even before they arrive at their destination.

The behaviour is now so predictable that it's a well-rehearsed script. A rally is organised; the application is rejected by the police; the right-wing media stir up the outrage; Premier Minns appears on talkback radio—usually with Ben Fordham at 2GB—to reassure conservative listeners that the government is *in control*; and police then prepare for the confrontation, as though they're preparing for a weekend football game. Over and over and again, peaceful demonstrators are met not with dialogue but with provocations. The former Australian Greens candidate, Hannah Thomas, was left seriously injured at a Palestine rally at the SEC Plating workshop in Belmore— at least the officer responsible is now facing prosecution, but the police response should never have happened at all. These heavy-handed tactics are used so often now that they've come to define the policing of progressive action in the state.

Compare this with the treatment of neo-Nazis marching through Sydney with white supremacist banners. There's never a riot squad lurking in the shadows; there's no pepper spray and no tactical operations unit waiting to "circle the area". Nothing resembling the state's typical response to peaceful gatherings calling for an end to genocide or urgent action on climate change. If NSW Police can justify their aggressive approach to Palestine activists on the grounds of "safety" and "public order," they need to explain why none of that logic applies to a group whose ideology is rooted in violence and exclusion, which the police themselves have previously described as *capable of extremist harm*.

One explanation is the presence of far-right sympathies within influential parts of the police force. Not universally though—there are many honest, hardworking officers who perform their duties ethically and without prejudice (surely there'd be at least *some*)—but the institution has repeatedly demonstrated selective tolerance for the political issues that it disagrees with.

For example, the removal of Jeremy Smith's *Queer Sydney* mural outside the Surry Hills Police Station: the artwork, celebrating LGBTQIA+ history, was taken down after complaints from officers stationed there, and we can assume that it wasn't just about aesthetic preferences. This act suggests a police culture in which some forms of identity and protest are treated as illegitimate or unwelcome, while others—such as neo-Nazi rhetoric—are quietly accommodated. Officers shouldn't be allowed to choose whose rights they defend based on personal beliefs or cultural biases: once the law is applied unequally, it ceases to be law, and becomes a selective tool based on political preferences.

Minns doesn't need to be reminded of this but if he is willing to intervene against Palestine marches, to call for bridges to be cleared, or to support legislation designed to restrict climate activists, then he must also show the same approach when dealing with far-right extremism. Yet in this case, his government's reactions were muted, confused and defensive—there's a radical difference: neo-Nazis can march freely and are welcome here, while those opposing war, racism and environmental collapse are treated as enemies of the state.

MINNS IS OUT OF HIS DEPTH

Minns insists he was "outraged" by the neo-Nazi rally outside NSW Parliament, yet the explanation he offered for why his office failed to act—that it occurred on a weekend—doesn't hold any weight at all. Every major pro-Palestine and climate protest he has condemned, attempted to stop, or used as political theatre has *also* occurred on a weekend. The idea that the Premier wasn't aware of the neo-Nazi rally because it was held on a Sunday just doesn't add up, and it's even more bizarre that he offered up such a ridiculous excuse in the first place.

What is happening, in reality, is that Minns is using the neo-Nazi rally as political cover to argue for even more police powers, including a re-draft of the hastily introduced "places of worship" protest restrictions that were recently ruled unconstitutional by the Supreme Court. He is pushing for expanded law-and-order powers not because existing legislation is inadequate—in fact, NSW already has some of the toughest hate-speech provisions in Australia—but because the government and the police chose not to enforce those laws against the far right. You don't need new laws when you refuse to use the ones you already have. Demanding broader, more extreme powers in response to your own inaction isn't leadership; it's mini-dictator opportunism that covers over insecurity.

And insecurity might be the key issue here. Minns is only 46, politically young and naïve, and still untested in the pressure cooker of a minority government. It's entirely plausible that he's deferring to the most senior and most conservative elements of NSW Police—people who have spent decades shaping the internal culture of the organisation and who are, in practice, far more experienced in wielding state power than he is. If he feels uncertain about his standing within the Labor Party or his ability to control the Caucus, deferring to the police hierarchy would be a political shortcut. But it's a shortcut that has a big price: Minns looks like a *weak* Premier bossed around by the police, and not like a strong Premier who should be the one telling the police *what to do*.

And there's a sense within the NSW Labor Caucus that Minns is a reactive, law-and-order conservate more reminiscent of the Coalition years than anything that could be found within a Labor tradition, even though there have been some very right-wing Labor leaders in New South Wales.

It's telling that comparisons are now being made not with NSW Labor heroes such as Neville Wran or Bob Carr, but to the Liberal Party's former Premier, Dominic Perrottet. Perrottet's affiliation with the hardline Catholic right made him an ideologue of sorts, but at least he was a recognisable one. Minns is also a staunch Catholic but appears more like a political middle manager—one who avoids ideological clarity, masks uncertainty with calls for "stronger powers," and seems strangely comfortable enabling police overreach while claiming to stand for fairness. Where Wran kept his eye firmly on the needs of the working class, and where Carr—despite displaying the usual conservatism of the NSW Labor Right—maintained a coherent sense of what he stood for; Minns is drifting into something more erratic: law-and-order escalation without a clear Labor purpose behind it.

The result is a Premier who has now presided over the free passage of an anti-Semitic, white-supremacist rally in the parliamentary precinct while cracking down on those protesting genocide or climate collapse. Minns doesn't need to morph into a radical left-wing firebrand, but he needs to apply the law consistently.

Even the Special Envoy to Combat Antisemitism, Jillian Segal, has been silent. The rally wasn't too far from her residence in Darling Point, and while she would have been too far away to hear all the commotion, one would think that as soon as she knew about the appearance of nearly seventy neo-Nazis waving an anti-Semitic banner and hurling insults outside NSW Parliament, that would have been exactly the moment for her to speak out. Yet there's been a silence, mainly because raising a concern might be politically inconvenient when she's more focused on managing pro-Palestine criticism than confronting the far right.

Premier Minns has allowed a situation to develop where a neo-Nazi rally can take place on the steps of NSW Parliament without challenge—while progressive protesters face suppression, brutalisation, arrest and demonisation. In the process, he has alienated parts of his Caucus, emboldened the police hierarchy, and diminished Labor's identity in the state that he leads.

It's not the behaviour of a confident Premier, certainly not of a Premier from the Labor Party: it's the behaviour of a government losing its moral and political direction—and of a leader who may soon find that the strongest threats to his position are not coming from the streets, but from within his own party.

***

BLAMING THE MIGRANT: THE LIBERAL PARTY'S NEW STRATEGY

24 November 2025

The Liberal Party's lurch towards an anti-immigration campaign has come very quickly after its rejection of net-zero by 2050—a position that already alienated the business community, moderates and much of the electorate. As the party deals with chronic internal conflict, sliding opinion poll numbers, and the lingering stench of a humiliating defeat at the 2025 federal election, it has once again reached for the same emergency button conservatives all around the world push whenever they run out of ideas: *blame the immigrant*.

It's not a new tactic: when parties of the right feel cornered, they ignore policy and turn instead to an inane brand of retail politics—a shallow, transactional sense of pandering to prejudice, fear and misinformation. This strategy from the Liberal Party isn't about preparing for governing or solving *actual* problems, it's about scavenging for votes among the disaffected, especially those drifting toward One Nation and similar bottom feeders from the right. It's a very simple goal: inflame, distract and hope the scattergun tactic lands somewhere electorally useful.

The irony is that Australia's immigration program has been relatively stable for decades, regardless of which party is in power. Under the Coalition from 2013 to 2022, net migration consistently sat between roughly 180,000 and 250,000 per year—the spike in numbers up to 550,000 in 2023 under the Labor government wasn't an ideological push but a correction that reversed the collapse in migrant arrivals at the start of the COVID pandemic, when net migration plunged to minus 94,000.

For the current financial year, the government has returned the target to 185,000—the same figure former Prime Minister John Howard maintained across his final eight years in office up until 2007. Far from a radical "big Australia" program, immigration numbers today look almost exactly like they did twenty-to-thirty years ago.

Yet the Liberal Party now claims that immigration poses an existential threat to housing, services and cultural cohesion. This narrative isn't supported by data but by a selective, unspoken hierarchy about which migrants are "acceptable" to the right. This narrative will comfortably welcome arrivals from Britain, Europe, Canada or the United States—*these are the right countries*—but changes quickly when the origin shifts to Asia, the Middle East, or Africa; *the wrong countries*. It's the familiar and cynical sound of the dog-whistle: cut immigration not because of numbers, but because of who the numbers represent.

Of course, it's a narrative that's a political sleight of hand and clearly feeds into misinformation and disinformation. Migrants don't *steal jobs*; they actually create them. According to the Australian Bureau of Statistics, the Australian Institute of Criminology and research produced through the Parliament of Australia, crime rates among migrant communities are actually lower than among people born in Australia, and variations tend to reflect social context rather than cultural traits.

Many migrants come to Australia to contribute, either through meaningful employment, building communities and businesses, create their own families or reunite with existing families, or are escaping from turmoil in their home countries. In advanced economies such as Australia's, immigration is a *net gain*, supporting economic growth, fixing skills shortages, contributing to tax revenues and enriching the cultural wellbeing of the nation. When managed well, immigration is one of a country's strongest assets, although Indigenous people in Australia might care to differ about this, historically.

The Liberal Party's attempt to weaponise immigration is not about population pressures or economic management: it's a desperate search for relevance by a party unable to articulate a coherent vision for the future of Australia. When conservatives abandon policy in favour of whipping up resentment, they're sending out the message that not only have they run out of ideas, but they're far happier to run with immigration as their latest scapegoat. The problem isn't the migrants—it's a lazy conservative movement that would rather stoke division than face the difficult situation that it has nothing genuine left to offer.

THE PLAN TO CUT IMMIGRATION WILL DESTROY THE ECONOMY

The Liberal Party's new proposal to slash immigration isn't a policy—it's political posturing. Despite the party's attempts to position itself as "tough on immigration", both major parties have historically been pragmatic about immigration, adjusting intake levels according to economic need rather than ideology. But the Liberals' new fixation on *slashing the intake* is a familiar script: when facing internal dramas, manufacture a crisis, then sell the "solution" as if it's courageous leadership rather than a reckless sabotage of the national interest.

A figure of a reduction to 100,000 per year keeps resurfacing because former Prime Minister Tony Abbott has been pushing it for years, and it has become a key part of anti-immigration sentiment within the conservative Sky News echo chamber. For those who blame traffic jams, crowded trains, or pressure on services solely on migrant arrivals, that number is the sound of comfort—a promise that life will somehow become a lot better if fewer people arrive here.

But it's an illusion: cutting immigration to this level would shrink the economy by at least 1 per cent, cripple essential industries already suffering from severe worker shortages, and reduce future tax revenues that could be spent on other essential services. Even the housing crisis, which the Liberals falsely attribute to migration, would worsen over time, as fewer workers and less investment would slow construction and choke supply.

The truth is that Australia's economic wellbeing relies on steady levels of migration, and even conservative leaders understand this. John Howard entered office in 1996, offering a tough stance on immigration, cutting numbers in his first two years to project an image of toughness on this issue. But after his political point was made, he quietly raised the intake to record levels—averaging around 186,000 per year for almost a decade—because he understood what the current Liberal Party pretends not to: that a modern economy can't function without migration, whether we like it or not.

The present rhetoric is the same trick in different clothing. When the party megaphones its intention to "cut immigration," it's not offering a coherent policy agenda; it's offering a slogan targeted for audiences over at News Corporation. Just like their fear campaign on net zero—where they claimed the transition will cost $9 trillion or $250,000 per person—numbers that fall apart even after a casual glance at the evidence. Independent estimates put the real cost of decarbonisation at around $300 billion over twenty-five years—roughly 3 per cent of the figure claimed by the Coalition. In other words, 97 per cent of their argument is completely false and exists as an example of retail politics at its worst.

The same applies to their claims that renewables are making energy prices soar or that Australia has "the highest power prices in the world". Both statements are demonstrably untrue—energy prices have risen for many reasons, including market volatility, global fuel shocks and delays in infrastructure builds, but renewable energy is not one those reasons. Also, Australia's prices remain below the OECD average. But, of course, a message of "renewables are cheap and reliable" doesn't fire up the base quite like "the government is stealing your electricity," so the facts are discarded in favour of the lies of retail politics.

This relentless misrepresentation reveals a deeper issue: a party that once prided itself on economic credibility now operates through fear and smear campaigns, misinformation, and their targeted culture wars: this isn't engaging in *debate*; it's just engaging in *distraction*. When a political movement relies on numbers that collapse when the simple facts come out, it's no longer trying to govern—it's just trying to fool people and is unfit for government, if it can ever reach that stage.

The Liberal Party is electorally dying in every state except Queensland—where they survive only through their alliance with the Nationals—and in Tasmania. Their traditional base is shrinking, their credibility is up in smoke, and their once-broad coalition of voters is fragmenting. A party that depends on slogans rather than solutions will eventually run out of slogans to tell, and when that happens, all that's left is the smoke, the mirrors, and the final realisation that the public has stopped buying the act. And, by then, it might end up being too late.

A PARTY THAT FORGOT HOW TO GOVERN

This is a prevalent situation in professional sport: a poorly performing team that ends up constantly losing goes through the process of forgetting how to win games, even the close ones, and once it becomes a bad habit and becomes *all too hard*, they look at other ways to win: cheating, salary cap rorts, illegal payments, blaming the referees, use performance enhancing drugs. And the more they lose, the more they keep losing, because they're just avoiding the hard work that transforms them into a winning machine, and their fortunes only change when new coaches, players and administrations arrive to change this losing culture. It's the same process that applies in politics.

The Coalition's descent into retail denialism and culture-war politics is a different tune compared to when they're in government. As recently as 2021, senior Liberals and Nationals were speaking with confidence and delightful enthusiasm about the fast and furious need for net-zero emissions by 2050.

Sussan Ley, as Environment Minister, declared that "no one wants to get to net zero more quickly than I do," stressing that regional communities were eager to be part of the transition. Senator Bridget McKenzie described net zero as "the right plan for us to back," calling it an opportunity that rural Australia was ready to embrace, and reminding critics that regional communities were environmental stewards way before climate change became ideologically weaponised by the political class.

What has changed since that time? *Absolutely nothing*—except the fact that the Coalition lost government in 2022 and now sits in opposition—and with that loss, it abandoned its own policy positions, its own modelling, and even its supposed belief in net-zero targets.

It's not a shift driven by scientific evidence but by political opportunism. Ley is now leading the party into a *cul-de-sac* of manufactured crises and costings pulled out of thin air, offering no credible modelling and no coherent policy direction. Instead, the Liberals have reverted to the oldest trick in the conservative playbook of trickery and superstition: link all of the ills in society—traffic congestion, energy prices, housing shortages, even the cost of coffee—to immigration, and hope that voters aren't paying close attention. And if that doesn't work, focus on other issues of complaint and link that up to another migrant group: after all, there's always an endless supply of migrants to target in Australia.

This messaging is inane and pure retail politics, built on shallow associations and scapegoating rather than substance. But the 2025 federal election result shows that this tactic no longer works: their scare campaigns fell flat, the cultural wedge issues failed to gain traction, and the party suffered heavy losses once the electorate recognised that the Liberal Party has nothing left to offer beyond the anger, the noise and the mindless sloganeering.

Instead of using its time in opposition to meet stakeholders, consult communities, develop frameworks, test ideas, or refine its philosophy—in simple terms, to become a better political outfit—the party has turned inwards towards the retail zone of emptiness. Policy development requires discipline, intellectual honesty and meaningful engagement. But the fear and smear campaigns are far easier: a collection of smaller tactics rather than an overall strategy, that require no evidence, no complexity, and no courage.

Being in opposition—which now has the potential to reach at least a decade for the Liberal Party—is meant to be a training ground for a future government. It's where parties sharpen their ideas, reconnect with voters, debate within themselves, and define what they want to stand for.

BLAMING THE MIGRANT: THE LIBERAL PARTY'S NEW STRATEGY

But the Liberals have treated opposition as an extended holiday run, almost like a *political sabbatical*, hopping from one episode of Sky News to another, to play out more stunts and act out the culture-war grievance, never doing the hard work of serious policymaking. When it comes a return to government—remembering that all oppositions do return to office, although with this opposition, there's no clear evidence that this will ever happen—this leads to chaos, as we saw during 2013–22; in opposition, it just leads to irrelevance.

As for Sussan Ley's leadership, her future is uncertain in this, the final week of Parliament for 2025. She may last longer than expected—remembering that the previous opposition leader Peter Dutton, against all predictions, limped all the way to election day—but she is trapped in a position defined by two realities: she needs the support of a conservative faction that will never truly back her, and she is leading a party that increasingly believes that the pathway back to power lies through louder populism, harsher rhetoric, and a stronger alignment with One Nation.

What these conservatives fail to understand is that this same strategy is why they keep losing. Chasing One Nation's voter base might work in the short term, but it's corroding the party's moral and intellectual foundations—if indeed it has any—and the long-term cost is very clear. The modern Liberal Party is ideologically hollow, policy-starved, incapable of coherently governing, and reduced to harvesting resentment and a culture of complaint to try and remain relevant.

Retail politics has become the party's entire political identity—and that is the main reason why it's struggling to rebuild itself. As long as the Coalition keeps reaching for the cheap and easy stunts, it will remain trapped in a vicious cycle of the loud noise without any substance and, ultimate, all you'll be leaving behind is a big headache for everyone else. A party that forgets how to govern eventually loses the trust of the public. And then, a party that forgets *why* it wants to govern, loses the public altogether.

***

RUNNING OUT OF PATIENCE WITH LABOR'S CAUTION

1 December 2025

The final week of Parliament for 2025 arrived without the drama of the expected leadership challenge against Opposition leader Sussan Ley, and while the internal machinations of the Liberal Party continue to attract attention, there's an increasingly obvious and painful truth: the Liberals are largely irrelevant in Australian politics right now. Sure, they might be interesting to watch on as political theatre, but they're no longer relevant and not doing much to change that perception. But what mattered in this final sitting week wasn't what the Liberal Party failed to do, but what the Labor government itself continues to delay, stymie or avoid altogether.

Gambling reform, long promised and widely supported by many people in the community, once again failed to appear in any meaningful way. On environmental policy, Labor's ongoing friction with the Australian Greens finally produced a deal on the last day of Parliament, allowing key legislation to pass but only at the last minute, through constipated and long-winded negotiations, and under political pressure after failing to get any traction on this legislation with the aforementioned irrelevant Liberal Party.

But there are familiar patterns of caution everywhere else: Finance Minister Katy Gallagher's call for a 5 per cent "efficiency dividend" across the public service are ringing a few alarm bells. At the same time, the CSIRO is facing the loss of around 350 jobs, on top of the almost 800 positions already lost over the past eighteen months, although the government argues that their overall budget has not been cut. But, for those within the CSIRO who are losing their jobs, it's pretty much a political debating point when its *their* job that going, and the organisation's capacity to do its work is being sucked away.

It's a very obvious contradiction: during the 2025 federal election campaign, Labor campaigned aggressively against the Coalition's proposed slashing of the public service—a plan that would have resulted in around 41,000 job losses—presenting itself as the defender of public institutions and the public service. Yet within seven months of the election, the Liberal Party's language of "efficiency," "restraint" and "streamlining" has returned, although this time it's coming from a Labor government. Whatever it's going to be called—fiscal discipline, managerialism, reality—many voters will see this as a government implementing the practices that it previously condemned.

This, of course, looks at a deeper and increasingly common question: not just what the Labor Party *stands for*, but *why* it exists in its current form. Historically, Labor defined itself through ideology, the politics of social change and reformist ambitions. Today, it's often defined through a comparison with whatever has been achieved by the Liberal Party—essentially managing what's already there, but more stable, less scandal-ridden, more competent—and this is an important factor: yes, competence should trump everything else, especially after the scandals and the incompetence of the Coalition between 2013–2022. But competence alone is a weak foundation for a party whose origins lie in collective struggle and systemic reform.

There is no denying that the Albanese government is vastly preferable to its predecessor, the Morrison government: the 2025 federal election result confirms this point. The chaos, corruption and institutional corrosion of the former government are no longer daily features of national life: Cabinet discipline has replaced the dysfunction of Scott Morrison; policy development, where it occurs, is measured and deliberate. And there are achievements worth acknowledging and any serious critique of this Labor government needs to recognise this.

But comparison to the disastrously low benchmark set by Morrison is not the same as a purpose for being in government. Previous Labor administrations—flawed and far from perfect—left behind clear evidence of positive reform. The Rudd and Gillard years delivered the school halls program, direct household stimulus payments, expansions to Medicare, the creation of the NDIS and major royal commissions that reshaped national conversations in a meaningful way. These were tangible expressions of Labor values, actions that answered the question of *why Labor?* in practical terms.

By contrast, the defining characteristic of the current government increasingly appears to be caution and being in office for as long as possible: there's no recklessness, no ideological zeal, but there is a level of managerialism and restraint. Of course, the lingering shadow of the Whitlam dismissal still shapes Labor's institutional psychology even though that time ended fifty years ago, resulting in a government deeply wary of bold moves. The internal scars of Rudd and Gillard, and the memory of Keating's reform agenda coming against electoral reality—and Labor stopped talking about Keating after his 1996 election loss as if to forget all about his achievements—reinforce the instinct to slow down and to *manage* rather than to *transform*.

And yet the risk runs in the opposite direction. A government that offends neither side ultimately inspires neither, taking in the worst of both worlds. For sure, there is that old adage that if a government is being attacked from both the left and the right, perhaps it's doing something right and there is an element of truth in that. But from a leftist perspective in particular, this analogy wears out when the structural forces of inequality that were created primarily by the Howard government remain largely untouched.

Perhaps it's too much to expect that to fully rework the economic system to benefit the people that the Labor Party would traditionally target, will occur within a single term—or even two—and there have been some piecemeal changes since 2022 that have worked in this direction. But it's not the economic revolution that is so desperately needed in Australia. Tax reform remains the most obvious area: mining super-profits, long-standing concessions to vested interests, and a revenue base mismatched to modern social needs all sit there, all acknowledged by the Treasurer Jim Chalmers, but avoided and left hovering in the background.

As the Parliament rose for 2025, the overwhelming impression of this government isn't one of chaos or crisis, but the exact opposite: *inertia*. Labor governs competently, but *cautiously*: that's not saying anything new, the Prime Minister Anthony Albanese has trademarked his leadership with caution and made this abundantly clear. The question now is whether this caution and competence *without* conviction is sustainable—or whether, in trying to offend no one, Labor risks missing the chance to do something substantial when it had the numbers, the mandate and the moment to create something of *substance*.

WHY DOES LABOR REFUSE TO MAKE THESE POLITICAL CHOICES?

Gambling reform is one glaring example of the areas where this Labor government refuses to act upon, but if there is so much overwhelming public support for reforming gambling advertising—as there is on many other issues—why does the government avoid the issue?

The hostility toward gambling advertising appears to be visceral across all groups within the community. This advertising is constant and widely recognised as harmful—particularly to children and vulnerable people. On the surface, restricting or banning gambling advertising should be political low-hanging fruit: popular, defensible and supported by extensive evidence. Yet the government continues to drag its feet.

Of course, there's an uncomfortable truth with all of this: elections occur every three years; lobbying and stakeholder pressure on government occurs *every single day* of the week. Voters get a fleeting, diluted choice amid the noise of election campaigns and by the time they turn up at the ballot box to have their say, industry groups have already arrived beforehand with their uninterrupted access to ministers, advisers and legislative processes. Gambling companies, like other powerful sectors, don't have to wait three years to push their case. They shape policy during their regular private briefings, and this is a dynamic that applies just as much under Labor as it did under the Coalition.

And this is the reality of contemporary politics: governments don't shy away from reforms because they lack public support; they shy away because the interests opposed to reform are increasingly organised, wealthy and permanently present. In that context, cutting back the public service, imposing "efficiency dividends," or trimming agencies like the CSIRO becomes the path of least resistance. There might be some public backlash, but it's short-lived and all forgotten about when the election arrives at some distant point in the future. Challenging powerful industries, as we've seen so many times in the past, generates sustained resistance from donors, lobbyists and conservative friends in the media.

Which brings the us back to the issue that this Labor government is avoiding: collecting the revenues from the sectors that can most afford to pay. Australia isn't a poor tinpot country that's struggling; it's a wealthy and resource-rich country that's allowing the rich to get *even richer*, a situation that's very evident when we look at the mining sector. During 2022, the combined profits within the mining sector were $295 billion.

Two-hundred and ninety-five billion dollars!

While precise figures since then are less clear, there is no evidence to suggest that profits would have collapsed in the sector. Even a modest super-profits tax—of around 5 per cent—would raise an estimated $10 to $14 billion annually. This shouldn't be a radical proposition—It's a targeted levy on extraordinary profits generated from finite public resources that are owned by the Commonwealth, which in this case means *the public*.

Yes, former Treasurer Wayne Swan's previous attempt at a mining super-profits tax in 2010 was mishandled politically and administratively. That failure, however, has morphed into a Labor dogma for all the things that need to be avoided: not that the policy was flawed in its execution, but that it *must never again be attempted*. And the result from this process is paralysis. *We failed once, and we will never ever try it again, we promise.*

Consider what the revenue from a super-profits tax could achieve: it would immediately remove Gallagher's political rationale for "efficiency drives" in the public service. It would eliminate the supposed need to hollow out institutions like the CSIRO.

Public education systems could be transformed through proper funded, resourcing and staffing levels, instead of a half-baked idea of achieving full Gonski-style reforms by 2034, eight years away. Health systems under severe strain across all the states and territories could be stabilised almost overnight, instead of having the premiers and chief ministers needing to bring out the begging bowls each year in the humiliating process of asking the federal government for more funding to manage their hospitals adequately.

More broadly, shifting the tax burden upward—away from consumption and onto extreme profits—would at least rebalance a system that currently leans hardest on those with the least capacity to pay. No serious argument suggests this would harm mining companies: if 5 per cent of profits could rake in tens of billions of dollars for the government, the industry must be doing *exceptionally well*.

This isn't an argument against success or wealth: it's quite the opposite. Prosperity isn't achieved in isolation—mining companies don't operate without the infrastructure, regulation, and a stable legal system provided by government, or a skilled workforce which comes from the public. It's a collective effort, and pretending that it's otherwise is ideological indulgence from conservative forces. We can all be wealthy, but only if the government wants this to be the case.

LABOR'S CONTINUES TO IGNORE ITS OWN MANDATE

At the end of this year, inflation has edged back up to 3.8 per cent; productivity has stalled—and this is the tailend of all the Howard-era policy changes to capital gains tax and dividend imputation that has caused capital to flow away from productive investment and toward property speculation and financial profiteering—and national government debt is edging towards the trillion-dollar mark.

These are the big fiscal issues that need to be addressed, and competence and managerialism alone are not going to be enough. *Structural problems* require *structural reform*. Australia has been here before: between 1983 and the late 1980s, major economic restructuring was undertaken by the Hawke–Keating government—often painfully—but it built the foundations for three decades of growth after the early-1990s recession. Sure, the electoral benefits of that transformation weren't reaped by the Labor Party but the Howard government that followed in 1996. That experience seems to have left a lasting scar: the belief that reform is electorally painful, and that any rewards to come from this pain could be taken up by your opponents, so it's better to be rewarded for caution and hoard the political capital at every opportunity.

This timidity doesn't only exist in Australia; it appears all across the centre-left in the United States, Britain and other parts of the world, where parties that are supposedly left-of centre, support and create policies that are straight out of the neoliberalist handbook, along with a fear of political capital being "wasted" on causes deemed to be too risky.

Yet, in Australia, this caution is in contrast to the reality of who is actually in power. Senior figures in the Albanese government come from the Labor Left, as does the Prime Minister and key ministers—Gallagher and Senator Penny Wong—with the authority to push creative and progressive policy directions according to true Labor values. What seems to be missing isn't the numbers or the experience, but the *conviction*—and the willingness to spend political capital on the things that really matter rather than on defensive compromises and managing what has been implemented by their conservative opponents.

This government has got the depth, experience and intellectual capacity—or at least, we assume so—comparable to the great reformist governments of the past. But talent only counts if it's used effectively: Malcolm Turnbull openly discussed his progressive agendas *before* and *after* his time as Prime Minister. But he was very quiet about these issues—marriage equality being the exception—during the two years that he held the position. What was the point of Turnbull's prime ministership if all these long-held and firmly held beliefs were discarded the moment he walked into his office? Likewise, for Albanese. What is the point if you're not there to enact the changes that you firmly believe are the correct direction for the country to take?

A government that fades away into being "less bad" than its opponents risks having a patchy legacy: some smaller worthwhile achievements, but many missed opportunities, and a public left unsure why it voted for change in the first place.

Now that the parliamentary year is over, the choice that this Labor government has isn't whether to take on political risk, but *what kind of risk* it wishes to take on. As the singer-songwriter Neil Young once wrote, it's "better to burn out than to fade away". To fade away cautiously is one option but to burn out through reform, leaving an Australia genuinely changed for the better, is another. History suggests that only the latter is truly worth the cost.

***

CONCLUSION

If this year in politics revealed anything, it provided the evidence that the current institutional foundations that Australia has relied upon for many years, are no longer fit for purpose.

The year peeled back all the layers of myth, every assumption about stability, and every comforting belief that the country's institutions were somehow immune to the pressures destabilising many democracies around the world. Although Australia generally tends to avoid the excesses that appear in many other countries, it will never be an exception for ever. As much as we'd like to think otherwise, *it can always happen to us*.

We see vestiges of this throughout much of Australian politics. Failures of leadership repackaged as *pragmatism*. Media disinformation disguised as *balance*. Manufactured outrage used as a *political weapon* from the right. American billionaires interfering in democratic processes with a level of impunity that should disturb anyone with even a passing interest in politics. International partners—especially the United States—are proving to be unreliable and unpredictable, and, quite often, openly hostile to the values they claim to represent.

The ABC's descent into its own brand of caution and capitulation didn't seem to be a one-off mistake: it was the result of almost thirty years of political interference by the

CONCLUSION

Coalition and a refusal to defend its own journalists. And with the horrors inflicted on Gaza by the state of Israel—with the active support and denials from Western governments, including Australia—exposed the moral vacuum at the heart of modern geopolitics.

While this may all seem depressing—*very depressing*—there are some green shoots that are being to appear: there's a growing cynicism about the mainstream media and what they are withholding from the public. There's an emergence of independent voices outside the traditional party system. The increasing recognition that Australia's future lies in the Indo–Pacific region, not in the fading illusions of American exceptionalism or a British imperialism that ended many decades ago. These are small shifts at this stage but they are the signs of a country beginning to confront its own inertia.

If Australia is to avoid the democratic malaise that we are currently seeing in the United States and Europe, we must choose to break from the habits that have defined their politics for too long. That means demanding a great deal more from our political leaders than they are currently providing. It means confronting media monopolies that continue to lie to us. It means rejecting culture-war distractions that offer nothing but division and a paucity of debate. It means rethinking our foreign policy so that it serves *Australian* interests rather than the insecurities of faraway superpowers. It means understanding that Reconciliation with First Nations people will never be achieved through symbolism alone. And that means demanding that leaders *lead*: not react, not retreat, or make the claim that the changes that need to be made today can always wait until the next election campaign, by which time the electorate has forgotten what they were initially demanding and everyone else has moved on.

Democracies usually don't change in the one single moment. History has shown us that they can decline very slowly over time and then, like the final snowflake that ultimately creates the avalanche, it all changes very quickly. Whatever is to happen in 2026 and beyond, will depend on the choices that Australia makes from this point onwards.

But, ultimately, Australia deserves *better* than what given to us politically in 2025. And we deserve a better recognition that the future is not something that just *happens* to us—it's something that we need to shape. And while that is always going to be difficult work, it can happen if we can muster the *courage* to do so, and if we do this before someone else makes that decision for us.

***

INDEX OF PEOPLE

Tony Abbott 7, 22, 24, 127, 128, 139, 148, 156, 231, 233, 261, 282, 339, 360
Randa Abdel-Fattah 253
Adrienne Adams 345
David Adler 91
Anthony Albanese 3, 7, 12, 19, 20, 21, 22, 23, 35, 38, 44, 46, 56, 57, 59, 61, 64, 72, 79, 82, 86, 98, 99, 102, 103, 104, 105, 106, 109, 112, 113, 115, 119, 120, 121, 122, 124, 130, 131, 133, 134, 137, 138, 139, 140, 141, 143, 145, 158, 162, 164, 165, 186, 200, 201, 205, 214, 216, 222, 224, 226, 227, 228, 229, 230, 231, 233, 234, 238, 240, 247, 250, 252, 256, 257, 258, 259, 262, 264, 265, 266, 267, 269, 287, 297, 311, 317, 318, 319, 320, 321, 322, 323, 333, 334, 338, 339, 340, 346, 348, 369, 370, 374, 375
Francesca Albanese 311
Moamen Aliwa 242
Anas al-Sharif 242, 246
Tim Anderson 67, 68
Daniel Andrews 280, 281
Abbas Araqchi 202
Bridget Archer 144
Robert Askin 209
Clement Attlee 348

Adam Bandt 158, 161
Tony Barry 159
Joe Biden 31, 188
Ofir Birenbaum 62, 63, 217
Tony Blair 195, 313
Anthony Blinken 31
Chris Bowen 104, 285
Mike Burgess 264
Tony Burke 211, 258
George W. Bush 58, 82, 195, 252, 312
Ita Buttrose 328
Darcy Byrne 276

Ross Cameron 165
Senator Matt Canavan 158
Captain Blue 331
Tommy Carcetti (fictional) 347
Mike Carlton 52
Bob Carr 282, 356
Jim Chalmers 95, 96, 143, 316, 317, 370
Winston Churchill 348
Helen Clark 282
Elbridge Colby 81
James Cook 33
Roger Cook 82
Jeremy Corbyn 262, 344
Simon Crean 82
Peta Credlin 151
Andrew Cuomo 342, 345
John Curtin 144, 188, 189

Alfred Deakin 151, 179
Matthew Doran 244
Mark Dreyfus 221
Peter Dutton 3, 7, 14, 16, 17, 18, 19, 20, 21, 22, 23, 24, 34, 35, 37, 38, 58, 79, 85, 86, 102, 103, 104, 105, 106, 107, 108, 109, 110, 111, 112, 113, 114, 115, 116, 117, 119, 121, 122, 123, 124, 125, 126, 128, 129, 131, 132, 133, 134, 135, 136, 137, 138, 139, 140, 143, 144, 146, 147, 148, 149, 150, 151, 153, 154, 155, 156, 159, 261, 365

James Elder 302
H.V. Evatt 127, 128, 202, 204

Senator Mehreen Faruqi 162, 235, 236, 237
Archduke Franz Ferdinand 194
Andrew Forrest 138
Jonathan Foster 328
Ali France 106, 143

Zomi Frankcom 269
Josh Frydenberg 106

Senator Katy Gallagher 162, 368
Yoav Gallant 26, 29
King George 36
Julia Gillard 117, 128, 139, 369
Mike Godwin 14, 42
Stan Greenberg 347
Marjorie Taylor Greene 312
António Guterres 256

Pauline Hanson 12, 15, 237
Senator Pauline Hanson 12, 15, 237
Sarah Hanson-Young 334
Gerry Harvey 15
Andrew Hastie 135, 136, 323
Bob Hawke 170, 306, 317, 320, 321, 326, 348, 374
Chris Hedges 301, 302, 303, 304, 305, 306, 325, 326, 327, 329
John Hewson 113, 127
Dyson Heydon 180
Harold Holt 189, 200
John Howard 16, 17, 127, 148, 152, 156, 170, 177, 195, 200, 320, 321, 323, 340, 359, 361, 370, 373, 374
Ed Husic 240, 259

Jay-Z 348
David Jenkins 250

Radovan Karadžić 246
Patricia Karvelas 105
Paul Keating 45, 168, 179, 189, 230, 233, 317, 319, 320, 321, 322, 323, 339, 340, 369, 374
John F. Kennedy 348
Robert Kennedy Jr 294, 298
John Key 282
Mahmoud Khalil 88
Ayatollah Khomeini 267
Jimmy Kimmel 297
Martin Luther King 236
King Charles 10
Rudyard Kipling 338

Charlie Kirk 298
Matthew Knott 251

Peter Lalor 53, 248
Ally Langdon 137
David Lange 60
Mark Latham 126
Antoinette Lattouf 7, 48, 49, 51, 67, 248, 327, 328, 329
Julian Leeser 91
Mark Leibler 51
Malka Leifer 213
Glen le Lievre 52
Sussan Ley 34, 151, 154, 158, 163, 165, 363, 365, 367
David Littleproud 158
Angelo Loras 216
Simon Love 105

Sarah Macdonald 53
Zohran Mamdani 4, 342, 343, 344, 345, 346, 347, 348, 349
Richard Marles 59, 162, 186, 205
Simon Marnie 53
David Marr 326
Groucho Marx 180
James Massola 251
James McGrath 143
Senator Bridget McKenzie 363
Humphrey McQueen 179
Teena McQueen 153
Giorgia Meloni 10
Robert Menzies 96, 144, 148, 149, 188, 321
Stephen Miller 297
Slobodan Milošević 246
Chris Minns 86, 87, 209, 210, 351, 353, 354, 355, 356, 357
Ratko Mladić 246
Man Haron Monis 269
Scott Morrison 7, 17, 58, 61, 80, 97, 98, 105, 125, 126, 127, 139, 140, 156, 181, 182, 202, 203, 204, 229, 231, 233, 261, 283, 298, 304, 338, 339, 369
Rupert Murdoch 11, 15, 34, 63, 128, 151, 179, 220

Paul Murray 151
Elon Musk 3, 6, 9, 10, 11, 12, 13, 14, 15, 34, 42, 187

Benjamin Netanyahu 4, 26, 29, 31, 190, 192, 193, 196, 198, 201, 247, 256, 257, 258, 259, 260, 262, 266, 307, 308, 309, 310, 314, 315, 330
Gavin Newsom 184, 297
Richard Nixon 233
Mohammed Noufal 242

Barack Obama 293, 344, 347, 348
Ted O'Brien 158
Viktor Orbán 10
Michael Organ 161
George Orwell 196, 249

Mohammad Reza Pahlavi 195
Clive Palmer 11, 12
Rita Panahi 153
Kash Patel 298
Senator James Paterson 86
Jeremy Paxman 328
Alex Pearce 331
Dominic Perrottet 356
Mike Pezzullo 203
Governor Phillip 36
Navi Pillay 302
Tanya Plibersek 131
Pope Francis 133, 140
Colin Powell 197
Enoch Powell 347
Senator Jacinta Price 154, 158
Gavrilo Princip 194
Vladimir Putin 74, 281, 282

Mohammed Qreiqeh 242

Ronald Reagan 294
Maurice Reilly 301
Gina Rinehart 14, 15, 138, 160
John Roth 223
Stan Roth 272
Simcha Rothman 257
Kevin Rudd 61, 117, 139, 318, 369

Monique Ryan 105, 106

Khaled Sabsabi 67
Ben Saul 302
SaVĀge K'lub 67
Jeff Schoep 272
Jillian Segal 222, 258, 272, 277, 356
Shahar Segal 220
Hossam Shabat 243
Ali Shamkhani 191
Bill Shorten 105, 124, 129, 139, 140, 171
Chris Sidoti 302
Rod Sims 103
Ellie Smith 106
Jeremy Smith 354
Keir Starmer 31, 81, 225, 262, 297, 329, 330
Justin Stevens 244
Justice Angus Stewart 220
Kerry Stokes 11, 15
Alexa Stuart 121
Zarah Sultana 262
Wayne Swan 372

Angus Taylor 99, 116, 154, 158
Hannah Thomas 205, 208, 213, 214, 215, 353
Whitney Tilson 345
Lauren Tomasi 185
Justin Trudeau 77
Donald Trump 3, 6, 10, 14, 19, 40, 41, 42, 43, 44, 46, 47, 56, 57, 58, 59, 61, 70, 71, 73, 80, 81, 83, 113, 146, 153, 183, 184, 187, 188, 191, 192, 193, 196, 197, 198, 201, 228, 261, 289, 290, 292, 293, 294, 295, 296, 297, 298, 299, 307, 308, 312, 313, 314
Malcolm Turnbull 7, 15, 108, 127, 129, 156, 188, 233, 282, 375

J.D. Vance 71, 82
Otto von Bismarck 347

Senator Larissa Waters 158
Senator Murray Watt 177, 333

Gough Whitlam 79, 82, 232, 233, 317,
    321, 322, 348, 369
Tim Wilson 153
Keith Wolahan 144
Senator Penny Wong 3, 91, 162, 193,
    200, 201, 205, 214, 234, 235, 236,
    237, 239, 240, 258, 265, 269, 348, 374
Neville Wran 356

Xi Jinping 187, 226, 227, 279, 281, 282

Sheik Hassan Yousef 250

Ibrahim Zaher 242
Volodymyr Zelenskyy 71, 73, 81

ALSO BY
EDDY JOKOVICH + DAVID LEWIS

THE SHADOW OVER PALESTINE
AUSTRALIAN PERSPECTIVES OF THE GENOCIDE IN GAZA

THE RED WAVE
THE NEW POLITICS REVIEW OF THE 2025 AUSTRALIAN FEDERAL ELECTION

For decades, the world has turned away from the suffering of the Palestinian people. From 2023 through to 2025, that silence became complicity. *The Shadow Over Palestine* reveals how Australia — a nation that helped found the United Nations and once prided itself on fairness and justice — became an echo chamber for power, lobbyists and media spin while Gaza was reduced to rubble. This is not only a story about Palestine: it's a story about who we have become, and whether our democracy still has the courage to speak for the powerless.

Available in paperback and ebook.

Fixing Australian Politics: How to change the system of government
ISBN (paperback): 978-1-7635701-5-3
ISBN (Amazon): 979-8-2743113-0-4
382 pages

The 2025 federal election didn't just redraw the political map: it exposed the cracks in Australia's democracy and demanded the country confront some hard truths. With Labor's historic victory, the Liberal Party's collapse, and the electorate's disillusionment reaching breaking point, *The Red Wave* captures a seismic moment in modern Australian politics. This is not just a postmortem of an election—it's a compelling narrative about the end of one political era and the uncertain birth of another.

Available in paperback and ebook.

The Red Wave: The New Politics Review of the 2025 Australian Federal Election
ISBN (paperback): 978-1-7-635701-4-6
ISBN (Amazon): 979-8-2-843818-1-6
254 pages

THE AGE OF DISAPPOINTMENT: THE REVIEW OF THE YEAR IN AUSTRALIAN POLITICS

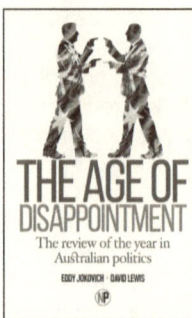

From the timidity of the Labor Party and the crisis facing the Liberals, to the rise of independents and challenges within the Greens, *The Age of Disappointment* explores the shifting sands of Australian politics—the missed opportunities of the Albanese government, the cynicism of Dutton's opposition, and the public's growing disconnection from traditional power structures. Beyond Australia, the book examines the global zeitgeist reshaping Western democracies, the ramifications of Trump's re-election in the U.S. and the controversial support for Israel government, set against the backdrop of an increasingly disillusioned electorate.

Available in paperback and ebook.

The Age of Disappointment: The review of the year in Australian politics
ISBN (paperback):   978-1-7635701-2-2
ISBN (Amazon):   979-8-3025811-6-7
404 pages

FIXING AUSTRALIAN POLITICS

HOW TO CHANGE THE SYSTEM OF GOVERNMENT

Australia's political landscape stands on the precipice of transformation. The need for reform is palpable, driven by evolving societal values, demands for greater transparency, and a push towards inclusivity. *Fixing Australian Politics: How to change the system of government* outlines a multifaceted strategy to reshape Australian politics across various fronts—electoral systems, campaign finance, governance, media, the Constitution, and diversity in representation. These reforms are critical for the rejuvenation of the nation's political framework and the restoration of public faith in the democratic process.

Available in paperback and ebook.

Fixing Australian Politics: How to change the system of government
ISBN (paperback):   978-1-7635701-0-8
ISBN (Amazon):   979-8-3249179-2-0
208 pages

RISING PHOENIX, FALLING SHADOWS

THE YEAR IN AUSTRALIAN POLITICS

This exploration of Australia's political landscape in 2023 uncovers a year that began with high hopes, yet was marred by a series of unmet expectations and enduring challenges: the Voice to Parliament referendum and its subsequent defeat, the persistent housing crisis, cost of living and environmental concerns, AUKUS and Palestine—guiding the reader through the intricate web of political and social dynamics that define contemporary Australia. *Rising Phoenix, Falling Shadows* is a compelling read for anyone interested in understanding the multifaceted nature of governance and public policy in Australia.

Available in paperback and ebook.

Rising Phoenix, Falling Shadows: The year in Australian politics
ISBN (paperback):	978-0-6456392-9-2
ISBN (Amazon):	979-8-8720426-0-0
446 pages

DIARY OF AN ELECTION VICTORY

LABOR'S RISE TO POWER

In early 2020 at the onset of the coronavirus pandemic, Morrison held record high electoral ratings and Albanese was told to not worry about the next election: it was already out of reach and best to focus on the 2025 election and beyond. In 2022, Labor saw an opportunity: Morrison had made promises he ultimately couldn't deliver and it unravelled quickly. *Diary of An Election Victory* explores the key political moments of the 2022 election year, Morrison's demise, and Albanese's ascendancy and victory against the odds. It's a must-read analysis of one of the most dynamic and unusual election results ever in Australia's political history.

Available in paperback and ebook.

Diary of an Election Victory:
ISBN (paperback):	978-0-6456392-1-6
ISBN (hardback):	978-0-6456392-2-3
ISBN (Amazon):	979-8-3681569-7-2
304 pages

POLITICS, PROTEST, PANDEMIC
THE YEAR THAT CHANGED AUSTRALIA

2020 was one of the most dramatic years in human history, shaped by the coronavirus pandemic that influenced society in so many different ways, combining health, politics, economics, business and education into the one sphere—and that proved to be difficult for many governments around the world to manage. *Politics, Protest, Pandemic: The year that changed Australia* is the story of the year in Australian federal politics, told through a collection of extended political essays from the New Politics Australia podcast series.

This is a must-read analysis of one of the most dynamic years ever in Australian political history.

Available in paperback and ebook.

Politics, Protest, Pandemic: The year that changed Australia
ISBN: 978-0-6481644-8-7
ISBN (Amazon): 979-8-7372030-8-5
414 pages

DIVIDED OPINIONS
THE NEW POLITICS ANALYSIS OF THE 2019 YEAR IN AUSTRALIAN POLITICS

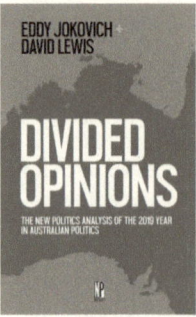

As the mainstream media struggles to retain audiences and survive under new business models and shrinking revenue streams, independents are filling in the gaps left behind by the older mastheads. New Politics is one of the more important voices appearing in this new landscape, and *Divided Opinions* presents some of the best work from the monthly podcast, and a selection of articles published during 2019. Guaranteed to make you think; aggravate, or inform and enlighten—and maybe all at once—this is a must-read analysis of one of the most dynamic years ever in Australian politics.

Available in paperback and ebook.

Divided Opinions: The New Politics analysis of the 2019 year in Australian politics
ISBN: 978-0-6481644-5-6
ISBN (Amazon): 978-1-6611355-7-7
338 pages

www.ingramcontent.com/pod-product-compliance
Lightning Source LLC
Chambersburg PA
CBHW060349080526
44583CB00012B/229